THE DIGITAL STREET

THE DIGITAL STREET

JEFFREY LANE

OXFORD
UNIVERSITY PRESS

OXFORD

UNIVERSITY PRESS

Oxford University Press is a department of the University of Oxford. It furthers
the University's objective of excellence in research, scholarship, and education
by publishing worldwide. Oxford is a registered trade mark of Oxford University
Press in the UK and certain other countries.

Published in the United States of America by Oxford University Press
198 Madison Avenue, New York, NY 10016, United States of America.

 Library of Congress Cataloging-in-Publication Data
Names: Lane, Jeffery, author.
Title: The digital street : adolescence, technology, and community
in the inner city / Jeffery Lane.
Description: New York : Oxford University Press, [2019] |
Includes bibliographical references and index.
Identifiers: LCCN 2018012936| ISBN 9780199381265 (hard cover) |
ISBN 9780199381272 (pbk.) | ISBN 9780199381289 (updf) |
ISBN 9780199381296 (epub)
Subjects: LCSH: Online social networks—New York (State)—New York. |
Social media—New York (State)—New York. | Digital communications—
New York (State)—New York. | African American teenagers—
New York (State)—New York. | Harlem (New York, N.Y.)—Social conditions.
Classification: LCC HM742 .L357 2019 | DDC 302.30285—dc23
LC record available at https://lccn.loc.gov/2018012936

9 8 7 6 5 4 3 2 1

Hardback printed by Bridgeport National Bindery, Inc., United States of America
Paperback printed by Webcom, Inc., Canada

Contents

Preface

The premise of the street code is that respect in the inner city is transmitted through face-to-face encounters. Young people test each other's nerve to fight in front of a peer audience who evaluates each challenger's toughness and heart. Neighborhood reputations hang on this process.

Today such confrontations are increasingly filmed and uploaded to social media or even streamed live. When this happens, youth must contend with a public record of their performance. The meaning of the encounter changes as it moves online, as it did for Rugged, a thirteen-year-old boy I came to know through outreach work in Harlem.

On a Wednesday, in 2010, several of Rugged's friends tweeted about a video uploaded by one of their neighborhood adversaries. I followed a link in one of their tweets to their rival's unlocked Twitter page, which integrated a video-hosting platform that contained several clips seemingly created to antagonize Rugged's group.

The most recent one, titled "GOTTA TOUGHEN UP," was a fifty-one-second video of Rugged taken with a phone. Along with the tagline "UNDER PRESSURE 1 ON 1 SHIT," the video showed Rugged on a popular shopping street where someone off camera held him by his backpack strap with one hand and appeared to film him with the other. The video depicted an intimidation during which Rugged, speaking frantically, swore on his "dead pops" that he did not hang out with his friends on their usual block.

According to urban sociologist Elijah Anderson, the code of the street dictates that kids must be prepared to fight when threatened in public space.[1] But other research by Robert Garot points out that kids, even gang involved, do not always abide.[2] They dodge such fraught encounters or decline to fight, and when they do, they face social pressure to come up with rationales for noncompliance. But Rugged's failure to enact the code of the street was caught on camera.

Before the video, Rugged was known for having brought a gun to school, notoriety he depended on for status and for safety. His reputation was now undermined by a video that was viewed 1,715 times within its first twenty-one hours of publication, with links to the clip and discussion on multiple social media platforms. I observed online comments disparaging to Rugged, and then when I went to his block the next night, he was nowhere to be found. Two girls I chatted with seemed satisfied: Rugged talked "too much," they said. Rugged, a fixture on his corner, did not hang out there for the next eight days.

In court and elsewhere, video is often privileged as a record of the "truth." But the offline story also matters.

In the days following the video, I heard from a girl in the neighborhood that others had been present during the intimidation, but were positioned off camera. As I learned more, I came to believe that Rugged's rival did not act alone but approached with two other boys, both older and bigger than Rugged and previously involved in shootings directed toward Rugged's group.

The online depiction of a one-on-one intimidation was probably three on one, far less shameful by the standards of the street code.

The Rugged incident demonstrated that the street code, traditionally based on the urban inequality that makes poor neighborhoods fraught, shifted also with new media and aspects of digital space. Online fight videos—or nonfight videos—alter the interpretative process through which neighborhood reputations get decided. The secondhand accounts of a fight that those who witnessed it firsthand would tell, in which case the listener accepts as inevitable a level of exaggeration or other distortion, compete now with a video. People can watch for themselves.

For Rugged's encounter, there was no peer audience present. He was held accountable to the code entirely online. The meaning of the event transformed through its visibility and the scale of audience on social media where users can play, replay, and easily share content, and through other aspects of what digital scholars like danah boyd call "networked publics."[3] Played 1,715 times the fifty-one-second video broadened exponentially to about twenty-four hours of total screen time over Harlem and potentially elsewhere beyond the peer context of the neighborhood.

This book is about how the experience of a neighborhood gets filtered through digital technology. It argues that neighborhood-based risks and opportunities associated with urban poverty are socially mediated through the use of popular communication technologies like Twitter and Facebook and the ways teenagers, community adults, and legal authorities handle the designs and features of these platforms. In the course of roughly five years of study, I found that street life had effectively decoupled from its geographic location to split along the physical street and the digital street. In the pages that follow, I examine the parallels, differences, and crossovers between these two layers and forms of sociality.

I show that social processes and outcomes related to "neighborhood effects" and especially the street code are cocreated in the physical and digital spaces of the neighborhood.[4] In particular, the enactment of gender roles, code switching between street- and school-centered identities, informal social control, and formal gang suppression play out on and between the physical and digital streets.

This book focuses on Harlem where the proliferation of social media is changing neighborhood life in a traditionally black community being transformed as well by conventional urban forces. I conducted my study at a time of accelerating gentrification and as the Harlem Children's Zone became the national model of urban education under the Obama administration.

I have written this book with two goals in mind. First, I wanted to examine the connection between physical and digital life in the absence of a dominant account and given that scholars often look at one side without the other. I studied the same people in person and on the Internet to move in real time with naturally evolving situations. By being on the ground and in the feeds and networks online, I was able to see how face-to-face and digital interactions were similar or different, how each affected the other, and, in some cases, why one form of engagement took place over another.

Second, I wanted to center this examination on the street-level experience of African American and Latino teenagers like Rugged to shed light on the digitization of urban violence and promote a constructive response. Early predictions emphasize at least three troubling possibilities: First, violence simply gets worse with increased exposure online; second, the bystander effect carries digitally so that any one person becomes less likely to help the more people look on; and, third, most cynically, online videos of street fights, especially among young black people, are a form of fame and amusement for audiences near and wide.[5]

I saw aspects of amplification, inaction, and entertainment. But I also observed digitization as a tool to anticipate and control violence and to make street life more predictable, utilized by youth and adults, working in tandem, separately, or even opposition. I attribute some of these buffering effects to the specificities of Harlem, but I also see lessons that pertain more widely. I'll spell this out in the coming chapters, which I think will interest both general readers and academics alike, and I end with a research appendix on digital urban ethnography.

Acknowledgments

For the kindness and trust with which I have been received, and for the opportunity to write about their world, I am forever thankful to the young people in this research and to their parents, family members, and elders. I am always indebted to Pastor because he graciously opened a social world for me and then encouraged me to be myself in it. Pastor passed suddenly in 2018, almost two years after the passing of Coach, Pastor's close friend and collaborator, in 2016, leaving a void in Harlem. I hold these men dear to my heart.

I am immensely appreciative of the community leaders, outreach workers, social workers, teachers, attorneys, police, and administrators at numerous community-based organizations, agencies, and schools who shared the workings of their neighborhoods with me.

I thank Richard Lecky and Hearts in the Streets, Inc. (HITS) for sponsoring the college trips I took with young people.

The research for this book originated with my doctoral studies at Princeton University in the Sociology Department. To the faculty, administration, and my fellow graduate students of Princeton Sociology, I am thankful for an intellectual environment that was rigorous, collegial, and flexible—somehow all at the same time. I could not have asked for better training or support.

My dissertation advisor, Mitch Duneier, instilled a love and respect for the hard work that makes any research worth its weight. Mitch showed me the craft of fieldwork and coached me in all aspects of the academic life. He remains a mentor and dear friend I appreciate always.

Devah Pager and Paul DiMaggio, the generous, brilliant mentors on my dissertation committee, challenged and encouraged me from my qualifying exams through my defense. I was honored to have Paul Starr and Bill Kornblum read my dissertation, and I benefited significantly from their feedback.

I thank the National Science Foundation for financial support in the form of a Dissertation Improvement Grant in the early stages of research and the Harry Frank Guggenheim Foundation for financial support during the writing stages of my dissertation as a doctoral fellow.

I'm lifted by wonderful colleagues whom I thank for their support with this book project at different times, in various ways, including, most certainly, Mike Benediktsson, Brandon Berry, Bart Bonikowski, Sarah Brayne, Lynn Chancer, Angèle Christin, Rachael Ferguson, Alice Goffman, Amir Goldberg, Keith Hampton, Patrick Inglis, Vikki Katz, Tami Lee, Jennifer Lena, Alexandra Murphy, Kathleen Nolan, Desmond Patton, Jasmin Sandelson, Mike Schlossman, Hana Shepherd, Christo Sims, Forrest Stuart, Naomi Sugie, Janet Vertesi, Erik Vickstrom, Frederick Wherry, and Terry Williams.

I'd also like to thank Charles Lemert for my introduction to sociology when I was a freshman at Wesleyan University, and for his ongoing support.

I appreciate the editors and reviewers who offered valuable feedback on an article from which parts of this book were previous published as "The Digital Street: An Ethnographic Study of Networked Street Life in Harlem," *American Behavioral Scientist* 60, no. 1 (2016): 43–58.

To my fellow faculty, students, and the deans at Rutgers University School of Communication and Information (SC&I), I am grateful for the vivid thinking, inspiration, and support all around me. Thank you to the Communication Department, Chairs Laurie Lewis and Craig Scott, and SC&I Dean Jonathan Potter, Acting Dean Claire McInerney, and Associate Deans Karen Novick, Dafna Lemish, and Mark Aakhus for the marvelous opportunity to see this book through and develop and teach an agenda around this research. I am very fortunate. I value also the collegiality of the Rutgers University Sociology Department and Chairs Deborah Carr and Paul McLean.

This book was strengthened by the opportunities to present and workshop its contents at numerous universities and institutions: in special gratitude to Elijah Anderson and the Urban Ethnography Project at Yale University; David Grazian and the Urban Ethnography Workshop at University of Pennsylvania; Mats Trondman and the Cultural Sociology and Education Conference at Linnaeus University; and danah boyd and thoughtful commenters Alondra Nelson and Alice Marwick at the Academic Workshop at Data & Society Research Institute.

My experience with Oxford University Press has been inspiring and really fun from the start, especially with the vision and humor of President Niko Pfund. Publishing with Oxford has been an honor. James Cook is an unusually kind editor, and his judicious feedback developed the best of what's written. It's been a pleasure to work with James, and I'm grateful for his encouragement and direction, and each of our conversations.

My sincere thanks to Lynn DeRocco of DeRocco Editorial Services, for thoughtful copyediting on the first submission of the full manuscript and the professionalism and warmth of her service. I thank Victoria Danahy for her excellence in copyediting the final book. I recognize Raj Suthan for his care in the production of the book.

I'm honored that Rodrigo Corral designed the book cover.

I've had exemplary research assistance at various key points, from Andrew Bristow, Joe Cruz, Lauren Davis, Kiara McClendon, and Fanny Ramirez. I thank Rebecca Henretta for her design of the conversation diagram.

I am profoundly grateful to my father, Roger Lane, and my mother, Anna Falco-Lane, for their love and support, and their generosity in all forms. And I thank them for the chats when I was stuck or wavering in my path.

I drew on the inspiration of my godparents, the late Sheila Taylor and Brett Flamm, throughout this project.

To my wife, Emily Henretta, I am forever indebted. I cannot express how much the sacrifices she has made and the love she has provided has meant to me in this writing process.

Author's Note

This book is based on my fieldwork in Harlem, which was conducted in person and online. With the exception of public figures, I have changed the names of the people involved or have referred to them only by title. All digital communication is quoted as it originally appeared, except for the occasional minor change to prevent confusion or mask identifiable details.

THE DIGITAL STREET

1

Introduction to the Digital Street

In 2010, I attended a safety meeting convened by Geoffrey Canada, the founder and CEO of the Harlem Children's Zone (HCZ), at Promise Academy, his flagship high school. As helpers gave out copies of the graphic novel of his memoir, Canada told parents it was "a whole different scene" from what he had experienced growing up. He was not just talking about the proliferation of guns or cops. His point was that kids also experienced their neighborhoods online. Canada called for intervention that was both "old school," meaning measures like curfews, and digital, somehow linked to students' smartphones.

So far Canada's counter to street life was to lengthen the school day and expand what schools gave to the community: early childhood learning programs, youth jobs and internships, parent training, and other wraparound services for enrolled students as well as for their friends and family members. He was struggling now with the changing boundaries of street life as it flowed through digital interaction and with few adults in the community outside of the police monitoring youth on social media. The most serious violence in Harlem, including incidents that had recently claimed the lives of two teenagers and alumni of the HCZ, combined old and new aspects of street life. Gun violence transpired between groups of boys divided by neighborhood turf but connected online through ties to the same girls on social media.

Canada's programming widely served youth in Harlem, and his approach to urban education had become a model that President Obama and other national leaders hoped to replicate. But he sought now another way to address the changing nature of the street life that surrounded his facilities and students. In the neighborhood was another African American man in his early fifties (about seven years younger than Canada) known simply as "Pastor." Pastor understood and ministered to this new social world of the street that operated in the shadow of the HCZ.

This book is about what I learned as an outreach worker in Pastor's peace ministry and through other firsthand research in person and online with teenagers in Harlem and many of the adults worried about or after them. This book examines the experience of street life at a time of quickening gentrification and just as social media became ubiquitous. I ask, how has street life changed with the use of social media and smartphones? The answer, I found, was the emergence and progression of *a digital street*. As those entangled in street life became involved digitally, this domain essentially bifurcated into two concurrent layers of social life that exist on the physical street and the digital street. Each resembles, shapes, and references the other, and yet distinct forms of sociality become possible on and across each location. This book elucidates the digital street in terms of its development and organization, performances and boundaries, mediation and oversight, and surveillance and punishment. I focus on situations and interactions that start either on the physical street or the digital street, carry through in one location, or move between the two in order to understand how these spaces and engagements fit together as street life. In the process, I hope to bring the reader through the multifaceted lives of teenagers and adults at the center of this study, people whose lives have been changed with the spread of sites like Twitter and Facebook.

For youth, digital media have given them new opportunities to construct and live out various social identities, to incite but also de-escalate violence, and to expand their myriad social relationships. For neighborhood adults, it provides a new forum for agonizing over, but also interceding into neighborhood violence. For police and prosecutors, it affords an additional means of investigating, arresting, and incarcerating youth involved in gang violence and those who dare to perform toughness and criminality on the Internet. For scholars of cities, poverty, and violence, it provides an immediate warrant for taking very seriously the role of communication and technology. Outside of the communication tradition, urban scholars typically overlook the use of communication technologies within the geography of the city and its spatial distribution of crime, victimization, and order.[1] Scholars locate the risks and opportunities for young people in the physical boundaries and face-to-face experience of neighborhoods. Urban scholars examine the socialization of youth through interactions with peers, adults, police, and other influencers in their neighborhood. Scholars measure "neighborhood effects" in terms of local friend and dating pools, the availability and engagement of positive and negative role models, and access to public space and local resources.[2] The rise of digitally networked technologies has radically changed the ways people connect and relate, presence and awareness of others, access and exposure to information, and the very structure of everyday life.[3] The use of new technologies shapes the identities, decisions, and behaviors of urban youth within and as a consequence of the neighborhood that surrounds them. The boundaries of urban community are different with digital communication.

Communication scholars who study cities recognize neighborhoods as communication environments that combine face-to-face and technologically mediated forms of involvement. The study of urban neighborhoods and communities revolves around the interconnections of local residents, institutions, and the technology and media they engage with everyday.[4] Communication scholars have embraced neighborhood-effects studies, but most urban research excludes media, information, and communication processes by looking for other mediating variables or mediated effects to explain social order. I hope to bridge and expand both the communication and urban fields by grounding the study of digital media in the people, processes, and craft of urban ethnography.

Urban ethnography developed as a style of immersive research in American sociology out of work in Philadelphia's Seventh Ward neighborhood by W. E. B. DuBois at the turn of the twentieth century and the Chicago School studies starting roughly two decades later.[5] One of the most popular and influential urban ethnographies of more recent years, Elijah Anderson's *Code of the Street*, considers many of the field's long-standing concerns with urban community, inequality, poverty, and racism, and issues of reputation, decency, and respect. Anderson locates the mechanism of neighborhood disadvantage in the interactions that occur on the street, especially those involving youth. In the most economically depressed and racially segregated parts of the city the threat of interpersonal violence creates a form of public order bounded by the home, school, and other domains that challenge or give way to the street code. The code of the street provides an orienting concept for this book for two reasons. First, it allows us to understand digital interaction because the street code depends on the temporal and spatial boundaries of an urban neighborhood and community. Where and how it's enacted and counteracted traditionally varies with the visibility and access of young people to each other and to adults in person on the physical street. Second, the street code joins the teenagers and adults in this study as they dealt together and in their different ways with neighborhood violence. Locally, Geoffrey Canada put in practice ideas he and Anderson share (with one key exception to be discussed).

Canada wrote a memoir of neighborhood violence that motivated his founding of the HCZ with the mission to create "a counterweight to 'the street' and a toxic popular culture."[6] Both Anderson and Canada were responding to an urban environment that for some African American youth was characterized by direct experiences of neighborhood violence and the indirect influence of popular media that, according to Canada's mission statement, "glorified misogyny and anti-social behavior." For Anderson, films like *The Godfather* and *Menace II Society* "along with rap music as well as their everyday experiences, help youths become inured to violence and, perhaps, death itself."[7] Canada and Anderson each imagined that youth related their own experience to the creative expressions of actors and rappers. The relationship between street life and media use has since shifted. Youth face the same people and problems in the neighborhood that they do online. Youth still draw upon popular culture but they live their actual street life in the media they consume and produce. They move between face-to-face and digital interaction to manage their own neighborhood situations.

To lay the foundation for the digital street, I am going to run through what Canada and Anderson as well as urban ethnographers in more recent years have said about the street code. As I go along, I'll update the relevant social changes in urban conditions that coincide with digitization. Here, I preview the findings I flesh out in the coming chapters.

The Digitization of the Street Code

Canada described his own socialization into the street code as a child in the South Bronx in the 1950s and 1960s.[8] Older "sidewalk boys" taught younger boys to fight by matching boys of the same age against each other. The rules were to fight "fair" by using just their fists and not to look afraid or tell the adults afterward. Performance in these fights determined pecking order on the block, but just by refusing to give up boys earned respect. The training served the broader purpose of preparing boys for the more dangerous challenges they faced beyond the periphery of their home street against rival boys who were representing their own streets. Anderson documented a similar set of rules and socialization process in poor parts of Philadelphia.[9]

In the era of the digital street, the street code is also transmitted through social media. The younger boys on the corner of 129th Street and Lenox Avenue—the hub of this study—learned the street code from the older boys, including some of their brothers and cousins, and the digital media they produced. The older boys wrote the initials of their group on the side of the local laundromat and uploaded a photo of that graffiti to their group's Myspace page. That photo doubled as the play button for original music about their beef with boys from the neighboring St. Nicholas Houses and other areas: "I rep Lenox Ave to the fullest; guns I pull it; you ain't gotta play football to catch these bullets." The younger boys learned these lyrics. The younger boys photographed themselves in the same poses and places as the older boys in their photos uploaded to Myspace and Photobucket. As the younger boys assumed their own roles in neighborhood violence, they created their own profiles with content about and sometimes provoking conflict.

Research by Nikki Jones centered the experience of girls. The three Rs of the street code—reputation, respect, and retaliation—structured the social world of boys *and girls*. In recent decades, Jones explained, the survival lessons black girls learned in the face of racism and sexism from the outside whiter world now included physical threats from other black girls. In Philadelphia, Jones found that a subgroup of girls became known as "girl fighters" by courting conflict and backing friends, whereas most girls fought only when strategies to avoid precarious relationships and situations broke down.[10] In large part, girl fighters continued to fight because their reputation effectively became their only protection. Fighting, or being labeled as a fighter, alienated them from school and other protective institutions. Unlike boys, girls also had to consider the costs of fighting in terms of expectations that they appear feminine and attractive to boys. At the same time, girls faced threats of harassment and dating violence from boys, who, by exerting control over girls, especially in the public space of the neighborhood, demonstrated prowess on the street.

I found that the street code affected girls and boys differently. Girls faced more interpersonal challenges whereas boys typically faced conflict based on social geography. As turf lines bound boys to their respective blocks by middle school, girls became uniquely mobile in social space, navigating their own dangers and opportunities, and on behalf of the boys on their home block. On the digital street, girls gained control over their neighborhood encounters. Digital interaction buffered contact in person and attention from boys gathered together on the physical street. But as more girl–boy engagements shifted online, girls' social media accounts increasingly linked otherwise estranged neighborhood networks to create a "staging area" for conflict that undercut some of the safety gains of social media. The digital street really starts with girls and boys and the use of social media to sort out relational boundaries that are woven into neighborhood boundaries. The next chapter explores this starting ground.

Anderson defined the street code more broadly than Canada did, developing the concept in opposition to decency. The street code referred to a *morality* by which conflicts get decided on the basis of "might is right" rather than reason.[11] It was an *orientation* away from schooling, work, family, church, and other conventional values and toward an alternative form of respect through dominance displays in public.[12] Finally, the code operated as a *labeling* process by which neighborhood residents and institutional actors labeled youth (and other community members) based on presumed propensities for violence.[13] The degree to which the morality, orientation, or label associated with the street was stable or internalized among youth was a point of contention in Anderson's work and the many studies it spawned. According to Anderson, not just the fraction of young men in street-corner groups or those doing crime but almost anyone living in ghettoized neighborhoods had to be prepared to fight to protect themselves, their loved ones, or their things. Youth unaffiliated with gangs therefore learned to code switch by acting tough in public spaces. That the street code, at least for most, signaled a disposable way of being posed a major liability for black boys who were viewed far more suspiciously than white boys, who also acted tougher while out with friends. In the Boston area, L. Janelle Dance found that black and Latino boys from violent neighborhoods typically got lumped together by school officials as "street-savvy" even though fewer than 10 percent of the roughly 270 boys in her study committed violent acts. Most posed like they were tough because of peer pressure and because it was fashionable.[14]

By contrast, Robert Garot argued in his study of Los Angeles that the last thing a boy unaffiliated with gangs wanted was to draw attention by posing as tough. Boys outside of gang violence kept their noses down in public. The gang-involved boys were the ones who code switched. They were willing to fight for respect, but they also walked away when given an out or concerned that teachers, employers, or family members would see them or find out. Whereas Anderson stressed that boys in street-corner groups lived by the code, Garot argued that they often skirted its reach. They identified "good reasons" not to fight or retaliate, but they never openly questioned the absolute nature of the code, which explained why its authority remained in the face of counterevidence.[15]

These questions of identity, reputation, and accountability play out digitally. The fundamental challenge of digital street life pertains to the boundaries of its visibility. The social media environment joins settings separated by the scheduling of everyday life that keeps place-based relationships apart. For the boys and girls in this study, to address the street code online generated unique challenges in separating their experiences with neighborhood peers from their attachments to family, school, and work. To code switch digitally, youth learned to harness the publicity of social media to project toughness *on* the street while keeping that image *to* the street. They partitioned audiences by platform, encoded their language, and developed multiple techniques to place street life online without spoiling their reputation in other settings. Or they took another more bold approach by disclosing their experiences of neighborhood violence to solicit the help of their family members and outreach workers.

Meanwhile, Garot's study raised an interesting question: If even gang-involved boys ducked conflict and worried about their standing at school and work, did they still see themselves as alienated as Anderson had thought? The street code, after all, was just one of many influences on the worldview of African American boys in the inner city, a point argued by David Harding on the basis of his own findings in Boston.[16] The digital environment of social media provided a reading of the will and wants of urban youth. Anderson attributed the authority of the street code to a set of structural conditions, including a decimated labor market, racial segregation and discrimination, and the absence of trusted policing, that resulted in "the profound sense of alienation from mainstream society and its institutions felt by many poor inner-city black people, particularly the young."[17] Hope was Anderson's mediating variable between the structural attributes of the neighborhood and the personal agency of violent behavior. If youth looked upon their conditions as utterly hopeless, why protect their reputation in the eyes of the adult world by code switching? By and large, the behavior I observed online and offline suggested that youth in Harlem wanted far more than street respect. They desired education, work, and a steadier adulthood, aspirations that were rarely enabled by material support.

Canada and Anderson both maintained that the street code became more violent when the drug trade expanded into the inner city in the 1970s and 1980s. Along with the contraction of blue-collar labor, Anderson argued that drug trafficking as well as addiction weakened the capacity of parents and "old heads" to regulate neighborhood youth. Men with jobs in the legal economy who once served as role models lost status, whereas drug dealers gained prestige and presented youth with financial opportunities these men could not. Meanwhile, surrogate mothering overburdened female old heads in traditional caretaking roles.

New media create openings for old heads to again become relevant on the digital street. Pastor, who ministered to street-involved youth, followed his charges on multiple social media sites, reaching out digitally, not just in person, in his attempts to provide mentorship and disrupt violence. He monitored the staging areas of social media and created a system of back-channel communication with youth and text-message alerts to neighborhood adults. Pastor developed a mobile infrastructure of communication to join community stakeholders and typically estranged parties. But this infrastructure was not enough without the resources of the HCZ. The financial limitations Anderson underscored also blunted Pastor's interventions. Tech-enabled strategies did not supplant the need for meaningful economic changes.

Canada and Anderson described a transition to gun violence that's relevant in thinking about violence on the digital street. In Canada's day, fights against boys from the other streets got "dirty"—involving knives and makeshift weapons rather than just fists—but guns were very rare. According to Canada, this shifted by the early eighties with the crack cocaine trade. Adult drug dealers, mindful of punitive Rockefeller drug laws, recruited youth to handle drug sales, and these kids armed themselves for protection.[18] Youth around the drug trade also took up arms for purposes of self-defense and social status. The street code's primary measure of toughness became the use of a gun. The turn to gun violence, as Anderson reported also, was tied to financial gain, rather than respect as its own end. Public spaces became market territory, and drug dealers were targets of robbery. Statistical research backed Canada's and Anderson's claims and tied the subsequent decrease in gun violence to the fading out of crack markets.[19]

Since the publication of Canada's memoir and Anderson's study, most US cities became much safer. Fatal and nonfatal gun crime plunged from peak early 1990s levels. Gun homicides declined by about half between 1993 and 2000, from 7.0 homicides to 3.8 homicides per 100,000 people, and that rate has remained relatively stable since then.[20] In New York City, where violent crime dropped even more precipitously than in other large American cities, statistical research by Franklin Zimring found that drug-related violence fell by more than 90 percent between 1990 and 2009.[21] Police played a key part in this near eradication of drug violence by shutting down open-air drug markets, which suppressed drug-turf violence (as rates of drug use remained the same).

During my study, the head of Juvenile Justice for the New York Police Department estimated that 80 percent of neighborhood violence stemmed from status battles between youth crews rather than the drug trade. The Citizens Crime Commission similarly concluded that crews that were not motivated by profit drove the street violence that endured from "the high-crime New York of 25 years ago."[22] The outreach work in this study was based on the same assumption that violence had decoupled from drug dealing. In Boston, Harding found that the most serious violence between boys was usually based on control of neighborhood space as its own justification, not in defense of drug markets.[23]

The neighborhood violence that declined across multiple cities was probably drug related. The violence that remained was the struggle for respect among boys from rival blocks—what Canada experienced in childhood—only now with guns in play because this norm carried forward from the drug era. The return to a social competition without a financial objective converged with the Internet and associated technological changes. Social media use fostered publicity and new opportunities, as sociologist Calvin John Smiley noted, for defiant youth to take credit for violence.[24] Rather than the silence around for-profit violence, the violence that flowed between the physical and the digital streets was expressive, and now much more visible.

Finally, Canada's account of the South Bronx in the late fifties and sixties makes no mention of the police. In Anderson, the code is a form of "street justice" that begins where trust in law enforcement and the judicial process ends. Scholars have since stressed the totality of police presence in poor urban neighborhoods and the ways in which the criminal justice process gets engrained in the everyday lives of black and Latino urban youth, including inside middle schools and high schools.[25] To inherit the street code when or because police had checked out was one thing; it was quite another at the height of crime control and given the visibility of social media.[26] The youth in this study were among the very first to be punished for social media use or what Desmond Patton termed "Internet banging."[27] The digitization of street life, however concealable to neighborhood adults, became the basis of criminal charges as prosecutors utilized the visibility of association on social media to invoke conspiracy law.

The interlocking of the physical and digital streets shaped Harlem during the study period. A series of gang indictments targeted the remaining pockets of gun violence in Manhattan. In June 2014, 103 defendants in West Harlem were indicted in the largest gang takedown in New York City history based on the findings of "[p]rosecutors and investigators [who] analyzed more than 40,000 calls from correctional facilities, screened hundreds of hours of surveillance video, and reviewed more than a million social media pages."[28] The indictments encompassed the streets that were bordering or part of sites of development. The corner of 129th Street and Lenox Avenue became a cliché of gentrification when the indictment of nineteen black teenagers and young adults coincided with the opening of a new coffee shop by two white men and realtors in the former space of a barbershop that was owned by a black man. The last owner had taken the business over from another black man, from whom he had learned to cut hair, and the last owner was passing this training on to some of the shop's young black patrons. The coffee shop formed a new hub of community, attracting a racially mixed clientele who were willing to pay $2.45 for a medium cup of coffee instead of 75 cents from one of the surrounding delis. Lenox Avenue was fast becoming a café and fine-dining destination for new residents and visitors alike.

One block west, meanwhile, on the grounds of the St. Nicholas Houses, a rival area for the boys from 129th Street, construction was moving forward on the HCZ's $100 million facility to house a K–12 charter school and community center.[29] The Department of Education, Goldman Sachs, and other public and private entities financed the five-story LEED-certified building (LEED stands for Leadership in Energy and Environmental Design) with more than fifty classrooms and state-of-the-art technology. The digital street was part of a larger matrix of urban change.

The Study

I came to study the digital street after I met Pastor in the fall of 2009. At the time I was looking for a topic for my doctoral dissertation in sociology in the study areas I cared about: urban ethnography, youth culture, and crime and punishment. I thought I might pick up on matters of race and media that had been central to a book I previously published on assumptions about black and white ball-players in the basketball industry. At age thirty, I was enrolled in the PhD program at Princeton University and had just moved from New Jersey to Central Harlem so that my girlfriend (now wife) could be near Columbia University to complete a master's degree in fine arts. We moved into a one-bedroom unit on the parlor floor of a brownstone building on the tree-lined block of West 130th Street between Lenox and Seventh Avenues, which made us—two white graduate students—part of the gentrification wave.

One evening I went to a community board meeting and learned that a local pastor would be giving a talk on youth crews, which made me wonder about the teenagers I saw hanging around a laundromat and under a police tower on the corner on 129th Street and Lenox Avenue. At a community event space, Pastor projected a map of youth groups he said were engaged in back-and-forth violence generally not tied to drug markets. For this reason, he believed that the community could stop the violence if its adult members came out to prevent kids from fighting. He spoke about young people looking for love and acknowledgment, along with the mechanics needed to stop fighting, which involved holding eye contact with the kids at the front of the action who led their respective groups. He called these kids "the batteries." He also said that he was following 1,500 teens in Harlem and the Bronx on Twitter and that anytime he heard of potential violence, he sent a text message blast to mobilize community members. Pastor told the audience that he needed more people to join him, particularly during after-school hours between 3:30 p.m. and 7 p.m., and on Friday and Saturday nights when teens traveled to and from parties. He gave out his number and asked those present to text him if interested, adding that only people with unlimited text messaging should join his messaging group because he sent texts all day and night. I was curious and paid for unlimited texting, so I sent him my number and started receiving his messages.

About a week later, while I was visiting a friend in Philadelphia, I received the following texts from Pastor. (All digital communication throughout this book is reproduced as written, except the occasional minor change to prevent confusion or mask identity.) "Shootin 135 Lenox—please checkout" (4:22 p.m.); "Just got word. A Women got shot. Caught in shoot out" (4:48 p.m.).

I texted back that I wanted to help when I returned to New York the next day. "Ok," Pastor wrote back. More texts from Pastor followed: "Heard they caught one person and someone ran in building cops have 135th bet lenox and 7th blocked off." (5:08 p.m.) I later learned that a resident in her mid-sixties had been hit in the calf and that a seventeen-year-old boy had been arrested, his identity gleaned from a still of a YouTube video.

The next day, while on a New Jersey Transit connection, I received another group text requesting help. It reported that a teen from 129th Street might be getting jumped after school by teens from St. Nicholas Houses. I texted back that I would meet up. That afternoon we drove to the high school in Pastor's car. He had in the car two seventeen-year-old girls, Rochelle and her best friend since fifth grade, Eyana. We then picked up another adult involved in outreach. I listened as the adults discussed with the girls the latest developments in several rivalries.

We never came upon a fight situation, but I was drawn to Pastor and the two girls. I did not see it at the time, but that first week revealed two keys to the digital street implicit in Pastor's approach. First, to be with the community was to be present in person and online. Second, the girls appeared to have the best information about boys involved in neighborhood violence.

I began to hang out with Pastor and the teens in his ad hoc peace ministry almost every day, mostly out on certain blocks, in the car, or in Pastor's office, the lounge of an elderly housing facility where he worked as a services coordinator. The space doubled as a drop-in for young people, and, months later, when a friend of mine at a Midtown investment firm told me that her office was upgrading computing equipment, I arranged to have their old hardware installed in Pastor's office. I started "The Lab," adding computers, printers, and Internet capacity to Pastor's space and a loosely organized program of assistance with school, work, court, service credit requirements, and other matters. The Lab also served as a place for teens to socialize and spend time online as they pleased. In this setting, I learned about many of the online practices of the more than 100 teenagers and young adults who used the facility, as well as some of the seniors in the building and surrounding area.

Meanwhile, I worked on all parts of the outreach operation: street work during after-school hours and weekend nights, which included "interrupting" confrontations and fights (occasionally by getting between adversaries but more often by taking one side for pizza) and the subsequent facilitation of peace talks after violence happened; and coordinating rallies, vigils, and "Positive Presence 4 Peace" Fridays, which were three-hour street-corner hangouts with local entertainment acts and program referrals.

Much of the day-to-day outreach centered on a rivalry that involved teenagers from the corner of 129th Street and Lenox Avenue against teens from St. Nicholas Houses (just one block west) and Lincoln Houses (four blocks northeast), an alliance called "St. Lincoln." On at least fifty-five separate occasions between 2010 and 2012, one side of this rivalry fired shots at the other, information I tracked during outreach and checked against police data. Police were often prominently visible with a portable tower, vehicles, and officers dispatched to the area. Policing sometimes brought its own forms of antagonism and violence that even official statistics reflected. An analysis of the 2009 "stop, question, and frisk" data published by the *New York Times* showed that police logged 157 stops near the corner of 129th Street and Lenox Avenue and used force in 111 of these stops, with only 5 of the overall stops leading to an arrest.[30]

Over time, I took on new projects and roles in the neighborhood that were both affiliated and unaffiliated with Pastor. I led

17

workshops and wrote curricula at a major municipal summer employment program for three summers, from 2010 through 2012. I consulted on several cases at a public defender's office representing teens and young adults. I was an invited member of a locally and state-funded juvenile gang task force and contributed writing to two of its publications. I led college readiness workshops at an after-school athletics and tutoring program. I spoke at, visited, or conducted observations inside seven schools.

I came to meet hundreds and hundreds of teenagers and young adults, about 500 through the summer job program alone, and many of the parents and other adults in their lives, both affiliated and unaffiliated with institutions. I met a handful of white kids; all others were people of color, predominantly children of African American parents and some whose parents had recently immigrated from the West Indies, West Africa, Puerto Rico, or the Dominican Republic. I observed variations in home and family arrangements (though two-parent households were rare); access to basic provisions, schooling, work experience; and type and extent of court involvements. But the nature of my immersion steered me toward the fraction of young people involved in the social life of the street.

My most concentrated period of fieldwork took place between November 2009 and August 2012, during which I logged 343 entries in my field notes and recorded thirty-seven semistructured interviews with teens, parents, and other adults who lived in or provided services to the neighborhood.[31] Along with scheduled sit-downs, I recorded a number of spontaneous audio interviews and videos in the field, including with a Flip Video camera I occasionally mounted on the dashboard of my car.

I often spent many hours each day on certain blocks, most often on 129th Street and Lenox Avenue, a block and a half from my apartment. When I brought my car around, it became a place to hang out or a shuttle for kids and their family members. I benefited from a routine established, before I arrived, by Pastor and Coach, Pastor's primary collaborator, a retired postal worker who eventually took a paid position with a state-funded antiviolence organization. Gradually, I felt increasingly comfortable being out on the block without either of these two men.

It was important that I had my own identity and relationships apart from Pastor and the outreach work. Playing basketball with many of the boys from the group on the corner of 129th Street helped me achieve that independence. We played in games at a local community center, at a church, and outdoors. Growing up in New York City, I was obsessed with basketball and still played as much as possible. I had leads on multiple games in Manhattan, and I took small groups to half-court games inside two Midtown residential buildings where friends of mine lived and to full-court games at high schools with regular evening runs. One teen nicknamed our impromptu group the "Basketball Crashers," a nod to the comedy with Vince Vaughn and Owen Wilson.

In these routines and evolving relationships, a method of studying the physical street and the digital street emerged. I developed ties with teens, their parents, and other family members rooted in living and doing service in the neighborhood. Our communication naturally encompassed connections by phone and on social media. I joined the social media networks of Twitter, Facebook, and Instagram in that chronological order of local teenagers' adoption. My fieldwork drew on face-to-face and social media ties to about eighty teenagers and focused more closely on a subset of about twenty-five of them—young people who become familiar in the coming pages. Being connected online provided a comparison with what I observed in person. I checked my social media feeds repeatedly throughout each day and incorporated my observations online into my fieldwork rounds and notes by taking screenshots. As much as possible, I resisted the convenience of taking the meaning of these screenshots at face value. Instead, I made a point of asking the author and others involved about the content. Sometimes I messaged the author immediately. Other times, I brought my phone, tablet, laptop, or printouts out to the block to have a short conversation on a stoop, at a restaurant, or in my car. I asked: What does this mean? Why did you say it this way? What happened next? During interviews, I went over a larger number of screenshots that I arranged as a PowerPoint presentation or printed packet. Taking my cue from other scholars who conduct fieldwork online, the more I used screenshots as elicitation tools rather than as final accounts, the richer my understanding became.[32] But I also tried my best not to take personal observation at face value either by looking on social media for information that preceded or proceeded the day's big events in person.

This approach allowed me to study communication in public space, whether on the street or online. I was seeing how things online affect matters in person, and vice versa. But social life, of course, also unfolds through private text messages and social media communication. I asked people with whom I had developed the closest trust to share some of their text and inbox messages, as well as phone contacts and lists of online ties, such as their friends lists on Facebook. We reviewed these data together, drawing linkages between digital and personal events and between one-to-one communication and group-level affairs.

In 2014, I submitted my dissertation and started that fall as an assistant professor at Rutgers University (in New Brunswick, New Jersey). Over the first years of my new professorship, I revisited my fieldwork and wrote the present book. Given the number of years of this project and that I jump between time periods in the text, I want to be clear about the timeline of my research in relation to social media. When I started my study in late 2009, the everyday action unfolded on Twitter. I began my observations on Twitter in real time. I also looked back to teenagers' Myspace accounts, which, in many cases, were inactive but were not first closed before leaving the site. By early 2011, the teens migrated from Twitter to Facebook, which became the dominant platform after a period of overlapping use. The book draws most heavily on the interval from 2009 to 2012 with Twitter and Facebook. After that, my fieldwork continued intermittently through 2015, including onto Instagram, which became prominent without displacing Facebook by early 2014. Along with the primary media of Myspace, Twitter, Facebook, and Instagram, I also discuss secondary, specialized platforms, such as YouTube, that teens used at different points. With exceptions, I studied the same teenagers over this trajectory of adoption as they encountered each site and its designs and possibilities at different points in life, on their way to adulthood.

Finally, this study entailed an acceptance and crossing of social distance. As a white man in his thirties, who was now doing a dissertation at Princeton, I initiated relationships that breached complicated racial and social boundaries in the name of ethnographic research.[33] While I certainly could not resolve eternal dilemmas, more will be said about fieldwork relationships and boundaries in the appendix, especially as they pertain to digital access.

Smartphones and Side-Store Economy

Before I illustrate the digital street, I need to explain how teenagers accessed digital life. Like their more affluent contemporaries, the teens I studied grew up communicating with their closest friends by mobile phone and instant messaging, and connected with these same close friends and their wider peer world through social media (which I use synonymously with social network sites).[34] By the start of my study in 2009, all tech-based communication, including through social media, increasingly converged through smartphones. Smartphones were nearly ubiquitous in Harlem, more so each day it seemed, but were hardly taken for granted given access hurdles. JayVon, a primary research subject, provided a window into what communication scholar Amy Gonzales called "technology maintenance," the constant labor around keeping a phone functional and in service that comes with being poor.[35]

One day in the spring 2012, JayVon asked for my assistance in reinstating his phone service and I agreed to help. When we met up, JayVon showed me a BlackBerry Curve given to him by Tion, one of his friends from 129th Street and Lenox Avenue, with some expectation of later being paid $20. Tion had removed the subscriber identity module (SIM) card to keep for his next phone, so JayVon turned to Isaiah, a second friend from the same corner. Isaiah gifted JayVon a compatible SIM card that JayVon inserted into Tion's old BlackBerry.

For teenagers and their families in Harlem, a local economy supportive of both wider and alternative forms of smartphone ownership and data plans enabled widespread mobile Internet access. Along 125th Street, Harlem's central shopping artery, major service providers like Verizon and Sprint leased stores. If they had favorable credit, parents, grandparents, and other adults who cared for teenage children shopped at these stores. They purchased family plans and other promotions under contract. Meanwhile, youth on their own, such as JayVon, who had not lived with a parent since he was fifteen, and adults without credit shopped instead at the multipurpose "side stores," as locals called them, that dotted the very same street. The side stores offered more flexible arrangements, though often at costs ultimately no cheaper and sometimes more expensive.

JayVon brought us to a side store on 125th Street. Walking past the displays with gold "Gucci" and "Cuban" link chains and videogames, JayVon led us to the store's phone specialist, who explained the charges to JayVon: $10 to activate the BlackBerry plus $60 for the first month of service. JayVon's monthly cost would eventually go down to $45 per month if he was timely with payments for the next eighteen months. JayVon had expected to pay the advertised $45 rate with money given to him by his godfather, his primary adult support, and a $10 connection fee with money I said I would cover. I agreed in the store to pay the additional $15.

JayVon handed over the cash and his phone, and about five minutes later the serviceperson gave the phone back to JayVon with a new number and a data plan that included unlimited talk, text, and web. The serviceperson took no personal information from JayVon, who did not have a driver's license or state identification card or any credit history and was expected to make future payments in cash at the store. "Have a good day," said JayVon, who got on the phone as soon as we exited the store.

JayVon relied on the help of four separate people to obtain a phone and service, with no certainty that a month later he would have the cash to keep it on. But between the side-store and major-provider options, JayVon and his friends managed to own smartphones. Even top-of-the-line devices were within reach through workarounds such as paying for a cheaper phone and service plan with a less expensive carrier and then removing the SIM card for use in a compatible phone of better quality acquired second-hand. They shared, borrowed, traded, resold, and passed down phones and related hardware. On occasion, phones were taken in the course of jumping or getting jumped by rivals. Teens like JayVon scrambled to make monthly phone payments, collecting small cash amounts from the adults in their lives and each other at the last minute. Some experienced lapses in service during which teens buddied up on active phones. But they certainly managed, through mutual support, tips they picked up from YouTube, and therefore they got by.

This book delves into the social life of the street in the digital era for teenagers and adults in Harlem. Over the next four chapters, I dissect, poke, and prod the dynamics of the digital street to explore two interlocking spaces of sociality that exist on the physical street and on the digital street. The digital street really starts with its most basic relations—the interactions and messages between girls and boys—so I begin with this topic to lay out the configuration of street life on the Internet. Next, I examine the fundamental challenge of digital street life—controlling the boundaries of its visibility—by showing how teens managed the street code alongside their pursuit of school, work, and mainstream status and stability, what Elijah Anderson called code switching. Then, I focus on the adults as they engage teenagers on the street. I compare the "bottom-up" social control of Pastor with Canada's HCZ model and then I talk about the "top-down" social control of the police and prosecutors. Pastor reinvented a classic system of street communication that adult authority figures used to serve youth at risk. From Pastor's neighborhood rounds and his BlackBerry phone, I explore the digital street through the eyes of its primary adult broker. After that, I document how youth policing and gang prosecutions quickly evolved to utilize the forensic potential of social media and the production of visible associations. As the gang indictments came down, a cat-and-mouse game ensued from the corner to the inbox. I conclude by piecing together the features of the digital street era as it played out in Harlem and what these first-generation lessons suggest conceptually about urban neighborhoods and practically for violence intervention. After the chapters, in an appendix on digital urban ethnography, I discuss moving through the field by being with people on the ground, in the feeds, and in the networks of their neighborhoods.

2

Girls and Boys

This book is about the decoupling of street life from its physical foundation and the ways in which technology use filters the experience of a neighborhood. Each chapter examines the resemblances, distinctions, and intersections of two kinds of sociality that exist on the physical street and the digital street. To understand the digitization of street life and how a neighborhood gets embedded on the Internet we need to start with relationships between girls and boys and how boy–girl communication in public now transpires. Teens in Harlem connected public urban spaces to online sites in their enactment of gender roles and courtship routines. Their use of regular social media platforms placed them ahead of the introduction of the Tinder dating app in 2012 and anticipated the integration of the Facebook application programming interface (API) and geolocation in mobile dating. Girls and boys in Harlem employed strategies typically used by slightly older persons to screen socially and geographically proximate dating prospects.[1]

Harlem teens also took social media in new directions by using its features to mitigate the anxieties specifically associated with meeting on the street. The digital street allowed youth to alter the pacing of communication, more actively choose their acquaintances and networks, and to establish particular identities without the need to live these out in person. Digital street life introduced new opportunities to closely monitor and potentially sanction the inappropriate behaviors of others. At the same time, new complications and problems arose, especially the pressure to undress for likes and the fabrication of profiles by peers, neighborhood adults, and the police to conduct various surveillance projects.

Interactions between girls and boys also configured neighborhood violence in online space. As girls gained visibility and control digitally, their social media accounts joined neighborhood networks separated by violence on the physical street. This complicated the advantages of online contact because now girls' profiles formed an online staging area for boys bound by turf to perform the street code. The position of girls and their social media at the intersection of neighborhood communication and boy rivalries both elevated and undercut the authority girls held over street life.

In this chapter, I lay out how girls and boys changed the experience of public space in Harlem by using social media to manage their encounters. I show how social media use can buffer physical interaction and the value this holds for girls especially, but boys also. Then I focus on the feedback effects between girl–boy relations and the street code. I want us to come away with an understanding of gender as an organizer of street life and the prospect that we have it wrong when we assume that boys control the street. The overlooked mobility of girls and the tension that follows when boys try to take that freedom away becomes newly apparent on the digital street.

Let's start by looking at how encounters between girls and boys shift as interactions flow online.

Boy–Girl Encounters: From the Physical Street to the Digital Street

Brooklynn Hitchens and Yasser Payne emphasize the resilience of young black women in the context of street life.[2] Elijah Anderson used the terms "contest" and "mating game" to describe the interactions between girls and boys.[3] The heterosexual courtship Anderson and other urban scholars depicted often started right in the middle of the public space. Boys made the first move by calling out to girls. Girls followed with a range of reactions, from ignoring the boys to sharing their phone numbers in the course of a quick conversation.[4] If a boy got ignored, he sometimes turned hostile. Jody Miller found that street interactions among black teenagers in St. Louis vacillated between playful and dangerous.[5] Although the risks of pregnancy, sexually transmitted infections (STIs), and violence were greater for black teens, white teens in privileged locations also jockeyed in much the same way.[6] Joyce Ladner and Nikki Jones, in their respective studies of young black women, underscore the most basic point: Youth in the inner city are more vulnerable than their counterparts in middle-class settings.[7]

Suffice to say that encounters with boys in public can be dangerous, especially because the capacity to regulate attention from boys is limited. The rejection of a boy may lead to heightened aggression. And yet girls and boys meet on these terms. The intensity and risk are a part of courtship. When I observed JayVon's first encounter with Denelle, things on the sidewalk looked fraught.

JayVon and Denelle

On an early spring evening in 2011, I walked along Lenox Avenue, in Central Harlem, with JayVon and his friends from 129th Street, Ren and Pete. The three boys met eyes with an African American teenage girl, who smiled as she passed. The boys turned around, calling out to her. JayVon ran to her. She stopped by a cement planter. JayVon reeled off one question after another, inquiring about her name; destination; if she was going to see "a man." The other two boys approached. She and Pete were already friendly and hugged quickly. Meanwhile, JayVon complimented the girl on her appearance and reprimanded her for not paying attention to Ren, who had begun his own effort to talk to her. Ren insisted they knew each other, claiming that they were friends on Facebook as he waved his phone as if it were proof. The girl moved away from the three of them, but JayVon followed until she stopped in front of a fenced-in lot. JayVon then grabbed her arm. "Stop moving," he said, smiling. She smiled back nervously. After a few moments of tangled conversation in which JayVon told the girl his name on Facebook, she ran off, JayVon still speaking.

I assumed that the young woman was done with JayVon. The interaction seemed to embody the tension of physical street life. But their involvement did not end on the sidewalk, and online the encounter took on a different meaning.

The illustration in Figure 2.1 is a conversation that appeared in JayVon's Facebook inbox. Hours after JayVon aggressively approached Denelle on the sidewalk, even though she never gave him her name, she sent JayVon a friend request, and he accepted.

In contrast to the rapid interaction on the physical street, their inbox exchange proceeded slowly over multiple days, a snippet of which is diagrammed. Denelle initiated the exchange, this time calling him out: "YOU WAS THA BOY I WAS TALKIN TOO OUTSIDE," which JayVon confirmed: "Yupp what's supp." "LAYED UP WATCHIN A MOVIE W/ THA MUNCHIESS— YOOOU," she wrote back.

The following morning JayVon told Denelle that he was not going to school. He was "layed up" because he felt sick.

FIGURE 2.1 Diagram of conversation in JayVon's Facebook inbox.

Denelle offered her sympathy: "Ooo hope uu feel better thuggman." By calling him "thuggman," she seemed to be testing JayVon in private against his performance in front of his friends. "I will nd y doo I gotta be a thug man for thoo whats supp with

31

that lol." "Lol cuz yesterday," she responded. JayVon conceded to an act: "thats me being stupid lol i really dont be like that thoo."

Then he said, "atleast I find u pretty thoo," which began a long effort, following the diagrammed portion, to get them to meet again in person. But Denelle preferred to chat online before allowing their communication to fade out.

The meaning of their encounter changed as it moved to Facebook. Their sidewalk interaction did not sever relations as it appeared. Rather, it enabled them, provided Denelle was able to take back control of their communication. JayVon admitted to his act, retroactively, and Denelle set the terms of future contact. Online, new controls and pacing emerged. Denelle and other girls in her cohort used social media to moderate the attention paid to them in public space and to screen for dating candidates amid the roughness of courtship rituals.

While Denelle reclaimed control in the private channels of the digital street, another girl named Olivia showed me how she managed unfamiliar boys by routing or rerouting their attention to the public space of the digital street.

Olivia

Olivia, a sixteen-year-old Puerto Rican girl, lived with her mother and older sister in an apartment in East Harlem. In December 2010, her "bestie," Keon, introduced her to his friends on 129th Street. Olivia began hanging around that corner after school and on weekends. I met Olivia there and got to know her better over the summer of 2011 when she participated in the summer employment program where I led workshops. In July 2011, I interviewed Olivia at Columbia University, where I had library privileges. On that day, her Facebook profile photo showed Olivia standing in her living room with her palms on the back of her hips. She wore big pink sunglasses that obscured her eyes, a white tank top flipped up to reveal her navel and tattooed hips, and a pair of jean shorts. On her profile, she listed her actual high school, a public school with metal detectors on the Upper West Side, and her fictitious employment as a "Victoria's Secret model." Olivia's mother restricted her use of their home computer to schoolwork because, Olivia said, "She thinks I'm gonna talk to grown men," and her mother feared she might get kidnapped. But she bought Olivia a BlackBerry Curve and paid for her data plan so Olivia accessed social media exclusively from her phone.

With Olivia's permission, we looked together at her BlackBerry to pull up the messages in her inbox. She showed me a message from a boy at 1:30 a.m., the fourth message he had sent her in the last eight days, even though she had replied to none of them. His messages were identical: "Hey, Gorgeous. How you doing, and how's life? Get back at me."[8]

"And who is this guy?" I asked.

"I don't know," she said. She had a message from another young man at 2:33 a.m. that said, "Can I be your man?"

We scrolled to another day (the previous Tuesday), when she had received, in chronological order, the following messages from seven males whom she said she had never met: "WASSUP SEXII"; "WASSUP MUFFIN HOW YUH DOING?"; "Wass good"; "Wassup"; "sup"; "wassup love"; "how u doin sweetie."

Olivia's inbox filled with unreciprocated openings from young men. Some continued writing several messages. Olivia's inbox revealed the digitization of the calling out and harassment that women experienced on the street (and elsewhere in public) and the possibility that such contact had become more frequent because it could now happen remotely at any time. But the digital street also worked as a buffer to the physical street. Girls and boys manipulated their social environment online in ways unimaginable on the sidewalk by first *choosing* the people around them on social media. In Olivia's case, she accepted friend requests from boys whom she had not met in person and then managed their attention from this proximity. The preceding come-ons were all from boys or young men in her Facebook network.

After these inbox messages, Olivia posted to her wall on a Saturday morning: "I swear BOYS Dnt Havv NUFFEN TO Do on FB [Facebook] But inbox me! I Will NEVA RESPOND so Pleasee STOP! Dammm!"

Before this post on Saturday, Olivia had drawn attention to her Facebook wall with a series of posts that received likes:

> "LMS [Like My Status] IF YU MISS ME" at 5:33 p.m. on Friday.
> "GOD BLESS MY HAZEL EYESS :-* I'm THE ONLY CHILD N DA FAM WID DESE EYESS" at 6:10 p.m. on Friday.
> "I'm UGLY ?" at 1:26 a.m. on Saturday.

In response to this last post, two comments expressed reassurance: "NAH SHORTY" (1:26 a.m.) and "NEVA OLIVIA." (1:28 a.m.) When I brought up her post, Olivia said right away, "Oh, I just wanted attention." I asked about the two young men who responded within minutes. She said she had not met either in person. Both were Facebook friends. I asked a lot of questions to understand her perspective on boys' attention:

JEFF : Did you want attention from these guys?
OLIVIA : From this one. This boy is cute [pointing to the one she found attractive]. This one is ugly [pointing to the other].
J : How did you know he was cute?

o : 'Cause I looked at all his pictures [laughing].

J : You went through his pictures, and then you sent him a friend request, or he sent you a friend request?

o : He added me [sent her a friend request that she accepted] .... He lives up the block from me ... but I never seen him [in person].

J : So did he send you one of those [propositioning] inbox messages?

o : Uh-uh [negative response].

J : He just sent you a friend request?

o : And he wrote on my wall, "Wassup?"

J : Okay. So his attention, you didn't mind?

o : Uh-uh.

J : Because he's good-looking?

o : And 'cause he wasn't annoying, inboxing me every single minute.

J : So did you appreciate that he said "Wassup?" on your wall as opposed to an inbox?

o : Mm-hmm [affirmative response].

J : Did it really matter that he put it on your wall instead of your inbox?

o : If it was an inbox, I wouldn't have wrote back, 'cause I don't know him.

J : So it's okay for people you don't know ... to write on your wall, but not in your inbox?

o : Mm-hmm. Because I don't want to have a conversation with you, 'cause I don't know you; there's nothing to hide, so just use my wall.

J : So if someone's sending you an inbox message, it's more intense? It's more like you have to respond?

o : I don't have to. But it's like they want it to be private to try to take it to the next level.

35

Olivia's comments underscored a major difference in how boys called out on the digital street: They usually propositioned girls *in private* rather than publicly, as they would on the sidewalk. Using the inbox feature shielded boys from public failure when advances went unmet. Nineteen-year-old Desiree made just this point: "When you PM me—private message me—you're silently getting ignored. Only you and I know that you was ignored, you know—probably my friends [too], but no one else does." By confining their come-ons to the inbox, boys also filtered for display to one another only propositions that facilitated two-way interaction. On the street, I saw boys pass phones to one another for this purpose. For boys, not just girls, social media eased the pressure of encounters with the opposite sex.

I also heard Olivia's wishes for personal space on Facebook. She wanted strange boys to write her on her wall rather than inbox, which, as she explained at another point in the interview, should be reserved for more personal interactions with friends and family. She appreciated when boys like Kevin followed this protocol, and she publicly disparaged those who did not when she wrote "BOYS Dnt Havv NUFFEN TO Do on FB But inbox me!"

After our interview, I looked up the interaction Olivia mentioned in which Kevin, the "cute" one, approached Olivia on her wall. Some two months before our interview, Kevin posted: "OLIVIA WASS GOODIE." Later that day she replied, "wassup kevinn." As she shared in the interview, Olivia knew Kevin lived six blocks away from her, but they had never met in person. I saw in subsequent wall interactions that Olivia was in no hurry to change this. She repeatedly worked to keep interactions between the two of them confined to the public space of her wall. In one such managed exchange, Olivia first thwarted Kevin's attempts to watch television with her at her apartment and then his request that she inbox him. Keeping interactions on the wall was a pacing strategy with possible safety value.[9] Any tool to pace relations with new boys held special value for girls in inner-city neighborhoods: in Miller's sample of black teens in St. Louis, for instance, 61 percent of girls reported "having experienced some physical violence in a dating relationship."[10] As Nikki Jones observed, adolescent girls in inner-city neighborhoods actively work to develop strategies to control the risks of violence around them each day.[11] By restricting interactions to the wall, girls may receive some degree of protection from others looking on—somewhat akin to safety on the sidewalk through "eyes on the street."[12]

Olivia's efforts to channel the attention of boy strangers included in her network to her wall was also a strategy for peer status on the digital street. When we met for the interview, Olivia's Facebook network approached 3,000 friends. With photos in bedclothes and a video of Olivia and two female friends "twerking" (a dance style and video genre in which female dancers are filmed from behind moving their backsides), Olivia solicited attention *to* her wall. If attention was channeled privately by means of inbox messages, Olivia occasionally used a phone application to redirect private advances onto the public space of her wall. Using an application marketed to young people with BlackBerry phones, Olivia and other girls posted screenshots of repeated and unanswered inbox messages.

Online, Olivia depicted herself in terms of "situational dominance" over males who desired but did not receive her affection.[13] For Olivia, the incorporation of boy strangers into her network and accompanying strategies to manage their interest served to maximize the social benefits and minimize the risks of the attention she received in public: to receive the veneration of being sexy and perhaps to enjoy being sexy with the buffer of distance.

The digitization of public life in the neighborhood introduced valuable new controls over attention from boys. But the underlying objectification of girls remained: The values had not shifted in online space and that undercut some of the safety gains for young women. Olivia experienced gender-related exploitation and violence. Before our interview, a person unknown to Olivia created a bogus Facebook profile featuring Olivia's pictures in an effort to publicly shame Olivia as a "slide," slang for a girl considered promiscuous and what might be termed positively for a boy as a "player." Robin Stevens and her collaborators documented the appearance of such "exposing pages" in the online networks of urban teens.[14] In the months following the interview, two incidents of violence were directed against Olivia, both led by girls. In one incident, a girl—with help from a boy—attempted to jump Olivia at school and take her coat. In a second incident in Olivia's neighborhood, a different girl jumped Olivia. Olivia told me that her reputation as a desired girl made her a target. Although the digital street allowed for the displacement of physical contact, teens were also subject to accountability in person for the identities they projected online, which sometimes reversed the safety value of digital interaction.

Courtship on the Digital Street

The basic values of male hegemony carried over to the digital street. But whereas boys appeared more visible and dominant toward girls on the sidewalk, online girls gained visibility and control with boys. This still-gendered domain worked differently on the digital street. In the case of JayVon, the Internet provided *another* way to call out to girls. The use of social media did not displace his behavior on the physical street. But other boys engaged girls digitally *instead* of on the sidewalk. For Christian, JayVon's eighteen-year-old adoptive cousin, online advances were preferable. "I am not one of them guys that see a girl in the street and then try and talk 'cause I hate rejection," admitted Christian. "It be like in my face: 'Oh, I don't want to talk to you' and girls be making scenes and stuff. . . . On Facebook if you get rejected, it's just, like, whatever."

Nineteen-year-old Smalls gave another reason boys made plays online rather than on the physical street. Compared with face-to-face encounters, "picking up girls" on social media was "more of a calm thing." He elaborated:

> If I'm with a group of guys and there's this one female walking by [and] I'm like "Yo, come here and let me talk to you," she's gonna be nervous 'cause I'm running with a crowd of guys and her first thing could be "I don't know you, so I don't know what your intentions are."

On Facebook, the embodied sense of the surrounding boy group is absent. Girls can keep boys out of their personal space if they choose to, as Smalls explained, "just not respond" to a boy's friend request or inbox message, or "delete" a boy previously incorporated into the network.

Although Christian pointed to boys being embarrassed on the physical street, Smalls sensed that girls found these solicitations uncomfortable, specifically when they involved several boys. On the one hand, Christian and Smalls related to girls in public just as before: Girls were there for advances from boys; to be spoken to roughly (e.g., "Yo, come here and let me talk to you"); or out of line if they rejected a boy (e.g., "girls be making scenes"). On the other hand, significant changes were underway. Social media use was now central to boy–girl encounters, placing temporal and spatial distance between bodies. And boys were learning (or being trained) to channel their initial attention online instead of in person and increasingly to do so online in more subtle ways. Christian, for example, after becoming Facebook friends, elected to like a girl's photographs rather than send an inbox message to express interest. He based this strategy on the grievances Olivia articulated. He said he "talked to a whole bunch of girls" and found that "a girl hates" when a boy writes "a million messages, like, 'What's up, I'm trying to talk to you.' " "A girl would rather a boy" like one of her photos and then "leave it alone" so the next move is hers.

Christian's strategy of liking photos actually resembled street courtship from a much earlier time. Liking photos has as its historical precedence the ritual of "signing on" as reported of Victorian London in working-class areas: "A young man would 'sign on,' that is, show his preference, by 'glad-eyeing' a young woman. Their eyes would meet; both would walk on and look backwards. The young woman might slow down to look in a shop window, while the 'boy' would raise his hat."[15]

In some ways, the transformations I am describing in terms of the digital street looked like changes everywhere in the mechanics of teen dating with the introduction of digital communication to ease interaction, pace intimacy, and read one another.[16] But what was happening in Harlem was also distinct from the norm in more affluent settings. The strategies I differentiate as digital street life were not to create distance in relationships teens already had but to filter their relational prospects in the neighborhood. The teens I studied dated differently from peer worlds based in school, around which the study of digital intimacy has been based. For teenagers in low-income urban areas, the street has long served as a dating site, with documentation dating back at least as far as Victorian and Edwardian London and Chicago in the settlement house era of the late 1800s to early 1900s.[17] Teens in Harlem's street world embraced the networking potential of social media that teens elsewhere *rejected*, and only in recent years have we seen national-level data that indicate teens have become more open to the initiation of peer relationships on social media.[18]

According to danah boyd, early social networking sites like Friendster and Myspace were designed for meeting new people.[19] But teens instead brought their friend groups and existing peer life online. The next iteration of social media companies embraced the for-friends model. In their seminal article to define "social network sites," danah boyd and Nicole Ellison dropped the "ing" from "networking" because communication overwhelmingly flowed between existing ties rather than new ones.[20] A survey of eighteen- and nineteen-year-olds conducted in 2007 found that respondents used social network sites much more for maintaining stronger social ties than for "weaker-tie activities," such as meeting new people.[21] Studies over time of young people in high school and college (based on subjects' self-reports) further supported this norm.[22] "Initiating connections with strangers is clearly not a typical usage of Facebook," stated the authors of one such article based on a sample of college students collected in 2011.[23]

Nationally representative data collected in November 2010 put the median number of Facebook friends for twelve- to seventeen-year-olds at 300 for boys and 350 for girls.[24] By contrast, the teens in my research had friend totals in the high hundreds and thousands. In September 2011, when I looked at Facebook networks of thirty teenagers—fifteen boys, fifteen girls—who hung out on the corner of 129th Street, the average network size was 1,340 friends. Both sets of networks skewed to the opposite sex: For the girls, 2.3 boys to every one girl; for the boys, 2.4 girls to every one boy.[25] In November 2012, mean network size increased to 2,159 friends.[26] Facebook users acquired on average seven new friends per month; this group of thirty teens added on average fifty-nine new friends.[27]

For the teens I studied, their posture online faced outward to the social possibilities around them, and not just to their existing relationships. The digital street opened onto the neighborhood. One young male's Facebook bio announced "ITS YA BOY!!!!!!!!!!!" with the words "Follow Me" and a self-description: "COOL,FUNNY,LAID BACK AND MOSTLY BE ON THAT CHILL TYPE WAVE." Teens invited others to "follow them," carrying the term "follow" from Twitter, which enables one-way ties, first to Facebook (two-way ties) and then to Instagram (one-way ties). Teens also invited followers on behalf of their friends. One teenage girl posted a flattering photograph of a female friend, her lips pursed and head turned to the side, along with footprint graphics to indicate "follow," the words "my baby new insta" linked to her Instagram name, and graphics of a heart and fire. A male teenager did the same for his "bro," posting his picture and the caption: "Everybody Stop What Chu Doing An [footprint graphics] My Bro [Instagram name]."

Nineteen-year-old Eva thought that more meetings took place online than in person. She spoke about Instagram, the photo-based platform where much of the action took place when we talked in March 2014:

> You could throw up one picture and then somebody act like they relate to that picture or they like that picture . . . and then it goes on from there, like "what's your name?" "How old are you?" Then to, like, "Oh, you wanna text?" and some girls be, like, "Yeah, here's my number." That's a little connection right there.

The teenagers I studied had a lot of "little connections" at different degrees of contact, some still evolving while others had been cut or left dormant. Some connections never started or lived solely online; others progressed to text messages or to voice or video; some were experienced face to face. The lines and layers of contact among girls and boys were numerous and shifting. Relations in the neighborhood were unfolding at different proximities and paces on and across the physical and digital streets.

In 1971, in *Relations in Public*, Erving Goffman wrote that "the readiness exhibited by two individuals to transform an incidental social encounter into the beginning of an anchored relationship can depend upon the memory each has of having seen the other before." Whether we recalled the "incidental, fleeting, [and] anonymous" engagement with those around us, it provided "a base for later anchorings."[28] But such contact prior to a proper meeting in person was now less one of chance.

For unacquainted peers, first contact between boy and girl often transpired digitally with the proposal of an online tie—a friend request or request to follow. Acceptances brought unacquainted peers closer online without necessarily implying more. It was a start, but might be as far as things got. These negotiations anticipated or replaced encounters in the neighborhood. When boys on the corner watched girls pass, they sometimes recognized the girls from social media. Among one another they sorted out what name a girl went by on a given platform and whether anyone had her in his network, which was sometimes taken as a cue to conversation.

Sometimes a tie on social media provided the basis for a relationship. Slinky "met" his on- and off-again girlfriend of the last four years on Twitter. Nineteen-year-old Desiree found her very first boyfriend on a now-closed site called Sconex. They became acquainted online and then passed each other on the sidewalk one day. During our interview years later, she recounted their seeing each other on the sidewalk for the first time: "[T]his is how it always [goes]—this happens till this day: 'you look familiar'; 'oh, really, I don't know you'; 'oh, well you have Sconex?'; '*That's* where I saw you from.'" They exchanged numbers, became friends, and transitioned in and out of a dating relationship.

The ways in which teenagers connected the physical street to the digital street approximated how developers of mobile dating sites linked Facebook API and geolocation to segment and localize online dating. "People put their 'hoods on their Facebook," said Rochelle of references to home streets and street-corner groups entered on social media profiles, in named and coded forms. "Slime" as a last name on Facebook, for instance, signaled being from a specific housing project in West Harlem. Other local signifiers included sharing videos by local rappers and posing in photographs wearing certain branded clothing like a down parka made by Marmot (a "biggie" or "Merm") or "Truey and Tavs" (True Religion and Taverniti brands) jeans clothing. Teens used this information to help guide their friending as they scrolled through the networks of existing friends and accepted invitations to "follow me" or suggested ties generated automatically by the platform. Teens joined the geographic space of the neighborhood to its digital extension by inputting the same social markers.

Christian

Sexual assumptions about girls based on public appearance also carried onto the digital street. Christian walked me through the suppositions he drew about young women online and how these checked out in person. An excerpt of Christian's dating career over five months (January–May 2012) reveals some of the range in the romantic and sexual possibilities among teenagers who meet on social media that start with expectations drawn from physical appearance.

In 2012, Christian, who identifies as black and Jamaican, often wore a thin beard and a stud in each ear. Christian was popular with his peers and adults alike. Teachers and administrators at his General Equivalency Diploma (GED) program lit up when they spoke about him.

One day in January I sat with Christian at Columbia University as he logged onto Facebook from my laptop. On the right of his profile, a sidebar of friends available to chat popped up. I counted seventy-four friends at one point—overwhelmingly of the opposite sex. Christian saw a friend request from a female classmate, which he accepted, knowing little about her. "[T]he pictures are the most important thing on Facebook," Christian explained. With the right photographs, "people are gonna wanna know you." Looking at his classmate's pictures, Christian said, "She's more the nasty-girl type . . . . a fast girl." I asked Christian to elaborate. He detailed a set of markers: appearing in underwear, wearing brightly colored wigs, showing piercings or tattoos, and wearing leather jackets made by Pelle Pelle. Christian contrasted a "fast" appearance with that of "a classy girl" who wore sweaters, dresses, and other "nice stuff" in most of her photos.[29]

Christian did not find his classmate attractive, so he moved to another profile of a girl named Khia from the Bronx he found through Facebook (the site's friend suggestion feature). Christian thought she was pretty so he sent her a friend request, which she accepted, and then he liked some of her photos. Christian continued with his strategy, now liking photos of Khia in conservative or comfortable clothing. By paying attention to these photos rather than ones in which she appeared in scanty attire with likes from dozens of young men, Christian hoped to stand out. For now, Christian's contact with Khia was limited to the wall.

Over the five months in question, I learned from Christian of three relationships that progressed from a meeting on Facebook to sexual intercourse. Each of these entailed a period of gradual contact through technology, first online and then by phone (going from text messages to calls) before meeting in person and having sex right away. Two of the three sexual relationships revolved around "booty calls," calling on each other (late at night) for sex without commitment.

The third sexual relationship was more complex. In May, according to Christian, he and Taryn, a teenager from Harlem but residing in the Bronx, had sex at his family's house. This transpired the first time they got together in person, other than a chance meeting on Lenox Avenue. Leading up to sex, they became Facebook friends after Christian saw a reference to Taryn on someone else's wall and sent Taryn a friend request. Over a period of several months, communication progressed from written exchanges (inbox messages and then text messages) to conversations on the phone. They had hardly spent time together in person but Christian expressed a clear sense of what a relationship with Taryn would be like. Over lunch one day at Tom's Diner by Columbia University he said that Taryn would allow him to be out with his friends but would require that he answer her phone calls and come home when told. "I love the way she talks to me. . . . wild [very] bossy," he said.

With the other two sexual partners, sex did not hinge on definition of the relationship. But Taryn, during their intimacy, asked Christian, "Am I your girlfriend?" Christian said he replied affirmatively, without knowing whether he wanted that. On the day they had sex, Taryn took Christian's phone and edited her name in his contacts to appear as "My wife." The morning after they had sex, she wrote on his wall for his network to see, "- good morning babe, see you later;-*." The next day she sent Christian a relationship request, which he accepted. "In a Relationship with Taryn

Corver," his profile read as a public verification of this status. Within about a week, their relationship ended.

The three new girls whom Christian met on Facebook and then had sex with all appeared in online photos displaying what Christian considered the markers of a "fast girl." But none of these relationships transitioned quickly from first interaction to sexual intimacy. Rather their relations passed through stages of contact through multiple media.

In the study time frame Christian also experienced relationships with other girls that began on Facebook and made it to the face-to-face stage but did not lead to sex, even with girls he labeled "fast." In January and February of 2012, Christian went on two dates with Lisa, a young woman he met on Facebook using his strategy of liking photos. The day before their first date, Christian showed me Lisa's Facebook account. The profile picture depicted a young black woman whose lips were puckered into a kiss. She was wearing a silver stud pierced through her left cheek, a tight plaid button-up blouse opened to reveal cleavage, and tiny pink spandex shorts. Christian clicked through other photos—in some she appeared in underwear—and told me that these were "meant to seduce anybody who look at her." Lisa, he said, was "fast." But things proceeded slowly.

Christian took me through his inbox history with Lisa, which dated back about six months before they met in person. The frequency of these interactions alternated between daily communication and gaps of days or even weeks. About five months into their inbox correspondence, Lisa gave Christian her cell phone number, and, a couple of weeks later, they transitioned to text messaging (without subsequently moving to phone calls). They met twice in person, first for a date at the movies. The second and final date took place at Christian's family's place, where they celebrated Valentine's Day, exchanging gifts and "making out" (not

THE DIGITAL STREET

having sex). Christian later reported that he had not talked to Lisa "enough" in the days following Valentine's Day and that "she started talking to someone else." Christian's assumption that Lisa was "fast," based on her appearance, did not hold face to face. Nor did Christian seem that eager to have sex with Lisa.

What can we say about digital interaction and sex in these instances? On the one hand, as was always the case, attire deemed sexy did not match intention to have sex. What was fast—instant—was access to a girl in a state of undress. Boys and girls alike articulated the pressure on young women to objectify their bodies online. "Girls get naked for likes," said eighteen-year-old Lacey. They "gotta front," she said, meaning that girls showed their bodies and wore the "latest stuff," and girls with darker complexions sometimes used a "filter to look lighter." Eva said that "girls be putting pictures up . . . bending over in the mirror," which was taking a big risk since "everybody screenshots everything." The cost of drawing attention digitally was heightened pressure on girls to sexualize their appearance in photographs that stood to circulate and be used against them.

Yet in some cases, the photographs, however revealing, were not of the person behind the profile.

Fake Pages

Across social settings, sexual partners typically find each other through friends of friends.[30] But for the teens I studied, Facebook friend networks included large numbers of unfamiliar people. By friending their friends' friends, the number of strangers in their overlapping networks expanded exponentially. Another flipside of digital courtship was the issue of false identity. Appearance and person decoupled in the case of the "fake page," the local term for a "catfish," a profile depicting someone other than its user. On the digital street, however, fake pages were not simply for interpersonal manipulation. Fake pages, specifically those of girls, served a neighborhood-level surveillance function to monitor and gather intelligence on boys under suspicion. I want to first take a look at how relationships with presumably fake pages even begin.

Christian became Facebook friends with a profile under the name Yelena Linda. Yelena's profile picture showed a young woman in underwear taking a self-photo ("selfie") in the mirror. A hat obscured in shadow the top half of her face. Yelena's bio section, which stated, "Modeling is My Life," contained a challenge:

"EXCUSE ME ! YES YOU I DIDN'T . . . SIGN UP FOR THIS 'SOCIAL NETWORK' JUST TO 'ARGUE' OR TO BE CALLED 'FAKE' If . . . YOUR GONNA BE ONE OF THOSE PEOPLE . . . DON'T BOTHER TO EVEN ADD ME . . .
Ps . . . Hopefully You'll Get Approved."

After becoming Facebook friends, Yelena and Christian shared an ongoing inbox correspondence before transitioning to phone calls. "[F]rom the [profile] picture she's something kinda beautiful," Christian said, and he believed that the voice matched "a cute Spanish girl." According to Christian, he and Yelena spoke roughly every other week—her voice was the same each time, he noted—and he said that on one occasion they had engaged in phone sex.

"Come see me, or I'll come see you; I'll take care of everything—I'll pay for whatever," he said he told her repeatedly. But no meeting ever materialized. "After a while, like, I started even . . . [saying to] her, like, 'Oh, you're a fake page . . . . I don't even want to talk to you.'" Whenever he accused her in an inbox message of being a fake page, she pushed back with a phone call or eventually the concession to announce their relationship publicly on Facebook. But without a meeting, relations faded out.

Christian was never completely sure who controlled Yelena's page because fake pages typically could not be confirmed. But on rare occasion identities were revealed. When eighteen-year-old Sarah, whom I met at the summer employment program, was "going through some things" with her boyfriend and wondered if "he would go talk to other girls," she created a fake page using photos she found on Google of an attractive black woman in her early twenties with "flawless skin." Sarah depicted the young woman as a college student and a photographer who liked to play videogames on Xbox. After building a network of "a good fifty friends," Sarah sent her boyfriend a friend request from the fake page, which he accepted. She later wrote him, inquiring if he had a girlfriend. "[H]is response was, 'Yes, I do have a girl, but I wouldn't mind hanging out some time.' The [fictive] girl wrote back and was, like, 'Well, I'm sorry, I wouldn't want to hang out with you if you had a girlfriend.' . . . [But] they carried a conversation through the night." Sarah later revealed herself when she confronted her boyfriend. Christian's and Sarah's respective experiences suggested intrigue, risk-taking, and gamesmanship factored into this form of relationship initiation with teenagers not only aware of but actually treating the possibility of a fake page as a framework for communication.

In March 2012, I spent some time with the mother of a teenage son murdered in Harlem who used a fake page in her independent investigation into her son's unsolved case. I came to know Monique, a woman in her early forties, after she became an occasional participant in Pastor's outreach ministry. When we met in her home, she showed me Milania Jones, the profile she and her daughter had created in the weeks after her son passed. "I try to be friends with these guys here [pointing out profiles] . . . where I know that my son got murdered at," Monique said. Milania's profile picture, a photo Monique's daughter found online, showed an attractive African American woman of perhaps twenty wearing a bikini in a kitchen. Her bio indicated that she was a fan of a famous rhythm and blues (R&B) singer and a local disc jockey (DJ). Monique told me guys were "just fawning all over" Milania, whose network included more than 1,800 friends. "Sometime we answer them [inbox messages], so they don't think we are a fake page. We confirm friends; I share things to keep the page . . . going." Like Olivia's inbox, Milania's filled with solicitations from the opposite sex. As I scrolled through, I saw an unreciprocated opening—"Washupp"—from a boy in my research.

Through Milania's profile, Monique connected to young men—including the presumed shooter—from the street-corner group near her apartment that she held responsible for her son's killing. She tracked their whereabouts and hobbies and looked for evidence, such as an original rap recording she believed referenced the murder. She shared her findings with an assistant district attorney. She told me she did this because "the police ain't doing their job." She said that the cops "can lock this guy up any time [but instead] this guy walks the street like it's all right." (After our interview, an arrest was made in the case.)

Online spaces allowed new kinds of access and information gathering to community members in the pursuit of justice. Monique's daughter, who was in her early twenties, recognized that the digitization of courtship had created an opening. Police exploited the same opportunity on the digital street. Detectives in all police operations that dealt with teenage boys and young men in Harlem, such as Operation Crew Cut and the Juvenile Robbery Intervention Program (JRIP), used fake pages that depicted local young women of color in sexy dress. The police strategy of fake pages to follow males of interest fed back into courtship to undercut trust between girls and boys. That you might be talking not just to a person other than the one in the photograph but specifically a cop became a warning call among the boys. As the boys wised up, the cops impersonated party promoters instead.

The idea that a girl's profile could serve as a hub of surveillance for peers, family members, and police detectives did not arise arbitrarily. Girls played a special communicative role that extended from the physical street to the digital street, and vice versa.

Network Centrality of Girls

Girls were at the center of the digital street. As I worked alongside Pastor, the first girls I came to know were tangled in violence with other girls and dated boys involved in beefs between neighborhood crews, with boys reputed to be fighters or shooters the most attractive partners. These girls appeared to embrace a dangerous role in the middle of conflict. But over time I saw that girls who wanted nothing to do with drama were also centrally located in social networks that typically included boys from rival areas. Online, cross-neighborhood connections to boys expanded and crystallized.

Otherwise segmented communication streamed through the social media of girls. One Friday night in December 2010, for instance, the 129th Street and St. Lincoln groups fought in front of Jacob Restaurant on Lenox Avenue. Police disbanded the brawl and detained three boys from 129th Street after cops found one of them with an air gun. Two of the three boys were arrested. What happened next was depicted on Twitter, the dominant platform at this time.

Wrote one of the teens from 129th Street who was not taken by police, "Why These Snitch as[s] St. Lincoln [boys]

Neva Get Snapped [arrested] Them Niggaz werkin wit Da Boyz [cops]." "TRUE TALK," tweeted Taye, also from 129th Street. To counter this allegation of police cooperation, Lloyd, a teen from St. Nicholas Houses, wrote that one of the St. Lincoln boys was arrested: "FREE MY SON KEN HE JUS GOT SNAPPED FOR CHASIN DA 29 NEGGAHS LOL." Taye challenged back: "STOPP IT [YOU] NEGGAS GOT SPANKED," he tweeted. Taye and his rival Lloyd continued back and forth.

Taye and Lloyd did not follow each other on Twitter. Neither could see what the other had written on their respective Twitter pages, which were each made private. But the boys followed a number of the same girls. One girl in common responded, "Oh gosh!" to Lloyd's tweet about Ken's arrest. Because Twitter messages are unthreaded, she retweeted Lloyd. Her comment, with Lloyd's original message, traveled to Taye's feed. Taye's response that Lloyd's group "got spanked" flowed back to Lloyd the same way, through a string of retweets. Girls' Twitter (and later Facebook) accounts were the cut-point in neighborhood communication.

It was more than just the digital migration of courtship that explained why girls' social media networks joined those of rival boys. Girls were thrust into a complicated role within a system of neighborhood turf that seemed to both grant and burden young women with a level of authority. I came to appreciate this complexity after Nika explained to me that girls were "knowledge barriers." I met Nika by chance at a sociology conference where I presented a paper that referenced a rivalry involving the block she grew up on. Nika was a rising senior at a top liberal arts college and she said that by majoring in sociology her studies provided an enhanced perspective on her childhood. "This idea of loyalty came up really quickly," Nika told me during one of several interviews. Even as a young adult, returning home on college break, she felt obligated to "the guys on my block." This sense of duty came from a natural caring combined with coercion from the boys, who, she said, "throw it in your face." She imitated the reaction of the boys when she told them she would miss a block party: "What do you mean you can't go? This is your block!"

The expectation of loyalty exacted pressure on dating. She said that when she started a relationship outside of Harlem, the boys on her street questioned her. "Why aren't you dating someone from here?" they would ask. But the biggest violation in their eyes was seeing a boy from an opposing neighborhood in Harlem. "I can't date a guy from Drew Hamilton," she said of boys from a rival area, speaking in the present tense of adolescent dynamics still somewhat relevant.

It went beyond the boys. She also had to be careful about hanging out with girls associated with the enemy boys. "But I know to be cordial," she clarified. "I have to know what's happening," which meant, among other responsibilities, notifying the boys on her block if their rivals were on their way over. On behalf of each of their respective areas, "the girl network" watched over Harlem.

Nika's sociological account of her adolescence illustrated the connection between the street code and dynamics between girls and boys. As girls and boys got older, they looked to date beyond their home block. Only it was much easier for girls to move about than it was for boys. If an unfamiliar boy arrived on a given block, he posed an immediate threat, Nika explained. He was out of place and thus might have a gun. The appearance of a new girl, by contrast, was more easily accepted as a cousin, babysitter, or other tie to a resident on the street. The perception was that girls were less threatening, at least initially.

Boys learned to stay within the boundaries of turf. This was their area of control and safety zone. For boys, their blocks also served as dating sites by calling out to girls who passed by and inviting girls they met online and at school to hang out. When JayVon approached Denelle, they were on Lenox Avenue, his home vicinity, and the boys did not follow her west toward rival territory one avenue over.

Dating depended on the mobility of girls. They were the ones who could move. But as excited as boys were about the arrival of new girls, they quickly became suspicious. Girls became more threatening once they were marked as loyal to boys elsewhere. As Elesha, from St. Nicholas Houses, said, once the boys on 129th Street saw her as "from St. Nick," her presence on 129th Street signaled she was going to set them up. Her response was to downplay her allegiance within the rivalry. "Nobody care about y'all beef like that," she said she countered. But I also observed Elesha, while online, remarking to another girl that she was "going to purposely add" on Facebook a boy from 129th Street so she could watch his feed. In a sense, Elesha controlled the interstitial space between the St. Nicholas Houses and 129th Street and she was one node in the girl network that reached from the physical street to the digital street.

The street code affected girls and boys differently. The girl violence that Nikki Jones described in her study of Philadelphia differed from violence between boys on two points.[31] It did not fit neatly into the system of turf that organized boy violence by neighborhood, nor did it typically escalate to gunfire. In this latter respect, girl violence was limited in the way Canada wrote of his own youth, before guns became commonplace. The violence that boys inherited was more rigid and less communicative. In Harlem, teens, parents, and police all talked about a social divide imposed upon boys before or during middle school. The rivalries that the older boys lived by pressed upon the younger cohort to limit their friendships to peers from the same neighborhood.[32] The seriousness of these microgeographic boundaries was learned under threat of gun violence. During this same phase, the burden to fight for respect also fell on girls. But the socialization into violence differed. Girls communicated threats interpersonally, either in person or digitally. An opening challenge, especially on the digital street, often took the form of a "subliminal" or "sub," a pointed comment usually homing in on a perceived insecurity and written about someone without naming that person. In other words, conflict among girls started as a highly personal challenge rooted in communication even when it turned violent. For the boys, there was nothing to talk about: Conflicts were based on neighborhood lines. It also mattered that girls did not typically fire guns at each other, which kept conflicts from the level of death or maiming.[33]

Girls were in more complicated social positions than boys were, but also ones that gave them power. Girls navigated their own challenges from other girls and dating options in the neighborhood as they managed the neighborhood beefs and loyalty expectancies of the boys. When boys saw that girls had a form of authority over them, boys sometimes lashed out. One day a young man named Shawn from the 129th Street group posted to his Facebook wall "bout to delete these untrustworthy bitches that fuck wit the enemy." I messaged him on Facebook: "What prompted you to write that?" Shawn wrote in dramatic language that he had just deleted about fifteen girls after he saw their wall communication with boys "who want to see my demise." Shawn's friend Taye expressed a similar sentiment after dating relations faded with a girl he believed to be loyal to rival boys from Lincoln Houses. He posted on his wall: "i HATE BiTCHES THAT BE iN EVERY HOOD ON DA EA$T and WE$T SOME OF THEM HEAA ON FB!" The mobility of girls in the physical and digital spaces of the neighborhood was a conditional form of power that girls leveraged or that boys used against them.

Elijah Anderson wrote about staging areas for neighborhood violence. The most volatile setting brought together groups from various rival areas in an especially public gathering, such as at a dance or athletic event.[34] As the jockeying of girls and boys merged with neighborhood rivalries, girls' profiles on social media added another staging area where boys from different neighborhoods eyed one another and sometimes became aggressive. For instance, when one sixteen-year-old girl uploaded a photo of two male friends seated on a bench in the courtyard of the housing development where the boys lived, a rival of the boys and a Facebook friend of the girl posted a comment. A spiteful back-and-forth ensued on her page between boys on both sides of the rivalry. When the boy who commented on the photo was later shot, the victim's crew held the young woman responsible for her alleged communication with the victim's rivals. Boys came after her on a public bus and harassed her by phone and online. Having grown up with and dated boys on either side of this rivalry, including the shooting victim, she was embedded in their conflict, and her profile became a staging area for neighborhood violence.

Among boys boxed in on the physical street, cross-neighborhood communication flowed through girls' digital networks. When Rochelle, a girl from East Harlem I met on my first day out with Pastor, created a new Facebook page in March 2012, I asked to take a close look at her emerging friends list. I picked Rochelle because she gravitated to the middle of neighborhood networks by dating boys with street reputations and rejecting "good boys" and "Poindexters [nerds]" because they were "no fun." We discussed each of the 337 friends she had collected in the first two weeks of having her page. In her network, which was 72 percent male, we identified ties from thirty-four separate neighborhoods in Harlem, inclusive of seventeen housing projects, spanning north, south, east, and west of where she lived. This placed Rochelle at the interstices of no fewer than twenty-four active cross-neighborhood rivalries.[35] Rochelle was literally in the middle of neighborhood drama.

In this precarious position, Rochelle recognized the power she held over boys. She was in an elevated station from the violent gridlock that bounded boys, with the autonomy to move about different areas, with different boys, if she wished. Rochelle could pick her suitors online, from conscribed dating pools, and engage boys at different distances on and across the physical street and the digital street.

Tiana also understood this power. I met Tiana when she was fifteen and saw a glimpse of her dating life over a few years, with boys from and outside of her neighborhood. On multiple social media platforms, Tiana gathered boy followers from throughout Harlem and the Bronx. At one point Tiana's BlackBerry Messenger (BBM) contacts included 968 boys, separated from girl followers under the label "DONT trustNIGGAs." When she was in a relationship, she pared down the number of boys, then brought that total back up when she was single again.

Whereas Nika found the presumed duty to the boys from her neighborhood burdensome, Tiana appeared to lovingly take custody of the boys from 129th Street. I thought about Tiana's dedication when my wife and I took JayVon out to dinner to celebrate his eighteenth birthday. Tiana joined us despite exhaustion and illness. She had gotten up at 6 a.m. to take two trains and a bus to visit two of the boys at Rikers, the same boys she supported by depositing money in their commissaries. At the meal she requested a photo with JayVon that she posted immediately on her wall: "Me & JayVon at dinner:) I love him." She had already changed her profile picture earlier in the day to a photo of the two of them in matching black "biggie" coats. Tiana expressed her commitment at every turn. "I am my brothers keeper," she captioned a photo with a slightly younger boy in the group, their arms around each other.

Girls and Boys From the Physical Street to the Digital Street

This chapter started with a reconsideration of neighborhood courtship given digital options. On the digital street, the calling out to girls by boys in public and in front of their friends shifted to a private act by a lone boy whose presence a girl now had the agency to accept or delete. The digital street eased some of the tension in face-to-face street life and served certain protective and liberating functions for girls while easing pressures on boys as well. In other words, the gender roles remained but the enactment changed to give girls more control.[36]

This chapter then elaborated on gender as an organizer of street life, though not on terms typically emphasized. Elijah Anderson and other scholars of the street code placed boys at the center of street life because of their visibility and displays of dominance toward girls and other boys.[37] As we consider together physical and digital space we see more clearly the centrality of girls in neighborhood networks and the mobility of girls among boys entrenched in turf.

Some of the tension in boy–girl contact can be seen as a social network problem rooted in the gendered nature of the street code. The turf system that infringed upon boys meant that girls were mobile in the social space of the neighborhood. Boys were dependent upon on "the girl network" to broker peer life beyond their block and into rival territory. When boys acted to undercut the freedom of girls, this behavior reflected the desperation of their own immobility and went beyond showing off in front of their friends. Some of the aggression from boys reflects their peripheral position in neighborhood networks. This is not to excuse such action but to understand more fully how it relates to both neighborhood disadvantage and media use.

The street code shaped two categories of girls in the minds of boys. Boys saw the girls on their block as their caretakers and sentinels in neighborhood conflict. By growing up together, girls and boys from the same neighborhood, even if they dated, shared a sense of kinship that could be pressed upon or taken up by girls as the duty to be, as in Tiana's words, their "brother's keeper." By contrast, boys treated girls from other neighborhoods as primary candidates for romantic and sexual relationships. But the same targets of their desire were safety threats based on parallel loyalties to boys elsewhere.[38] This gendered configuration of the street code infused a fundamental tension in platonic and dating relationships among girls and boys and helped to explain why contact in the public space of the neighborhood was as fraught.

On the one hand, the notion of being a girl on the digital street was still defined in relation to boys. The pressure on girls to take care of boys or be sexy for them and the unfair presumption that girls were responsible for violence among boys was now visible and newly enacted on social media. On the other hand, as Nikki Jones explains, "girls are able to challenge and manipulate the constraining social and cultural expectations embedded in gender and the code, depending on the situation."[39] Girls are always powerful actors in their surroundings, and we've seen in this chapter how girls use digital tools to manage complex social identities in order to stay safe and to pursue their own interests.

3

Code Switching

In this chapter, I further examine the placement of street life on the Internet to dive deeply into the ways that teens use online spaces to live out diverse and contradictory identities. I consider the digital migration of the street code alongside other aspects of neighborhood life in the form of family, school, and work. This chapter focuses on code switching and the primary challenge of the digital street: managing the boundaries of its visibility. As teenagers enact the street code on social media, the toughness displayed for one setting of the neighborhood enters an environment where place-based relationships tend to cross and combine in unpredictable ways. Digital scholars call this convergence "context collapse."[1] The teenagers I studied were especially sensitive to context collapse and the efforts needed to meet the expectations of multiple audiences.

Whereas the previous chapter addressed gender, this chapter illustrates another configuration of the digital street in terms of its potential to "collapse" into other contexts and the counteraction of code switching. I discuss the digital strategies teens developed to answer to the street code, but also to neighboring obligations in their lives. They learned, in other words, to harness the publicity of social media. I devote considerable attention to the case of Andre, a chief rival of the boys on 129th Street, to show that respect through violence and conventional means were not mutually exclusive. In fact, street-involved teenagers in Harlem publicly supported each other's scholastic and work-related achievements and expected to survive and move on from street life. This outlook on life suggested a departure from the total alienation of the nineties that Elijah Anderson described among youth in street-corner groups in Philadelphia.

Before delving into the multifaceted lives of youth in Harlem, I want to align code switching and context collapse with the intellectual legacy of Erving Goffman and his concept of "audience segregation."[2] I start with the historical labels of "street" and "decent" in urban studies.

Street and Decent

Most residents of inner-city neighborhoods do not respond to social and economic disenfranchisement with violence. Most get respect through school, work, family, church, and other conventional institutions. In other words, most residents of poor neighborhoods, like everywhere else, are decent.

For many decades, urban scholars drew a distinction between "decent" residents and a smaller "street" faction. The names scholars used varied, but the basic contrast held across various racial and ethnic populations on the margins of urban inequality. In 1945, Drake and Cayton referred to the "respectable" and "shady" people of Chicago's segregated African American section.[3] In 1953, Kuper distinguished between "respectable" and "rough" members of the working class in Coventry, England.[4] In 1962, Herbert Gans saw something similar among the Italian Americans he studied in Boston: "Routine-seekers" were drawn to family life at home whereas "action-seekers" gravitated to the street.[5] In 1985, Williams and Kornblum wrote that adults in poor parts of New York City and Mississippi drew a "basic distinction" among local youth between "street" kids "exposed to the often violent morality of adult and adolescent street culture" and kids who were "not street" because parents and educators had shielded them from neighborhood danger.[6]

Then, in 1999, Elijah Anderson published *Code of the Street*. Rather than referring to people, "street" and "decent" meant different ways of being contingent upon the settings those in poor neighborhoods entered. To get by on the street required specialized behavior and appearance, unlike the reasoning and civility usually practiced at home, school, youth programs, after-school jobs, and other places. For youth especially, it was necessary to put up a tough front as they moved about the neighborhood and even to fight to avoid victimization.

Audience Segregation

Anderson never made the connection explicit, but code switching came down to audience segregation. We all mean different things to different people, which we manage just by going about our day, moving in and out of bounded social encounters. A man, for instance, may exist as a father, surgeon, and drinking buddy because he enacts these roles separately, with different people, at home, work, and the bar. Goffman called this basic premise of social life audience segregation. By following a schedule, we know whom to be when and can cycle through multiple roles without constant dissonance. This natural separation of audiences allows us to present differently and to disclose different information to people in unique areas of our lives.[7]

Goffman based his model of audience segregation on in-person encounters. Boundaries change when we communicate through media. Place-based audiences cannot be as easily defined or bounded, which served as the thesis of a book called *No Sense of Place*, published in 1985 by communication scholar Joshua Meyrowitz.[8] Meyrowitz wrote about this problem of audience in relation to radio and television broadcasts. Writing in the 2000s, digital scholars, starting with danah boyd, called the audience problem on social network sites context collapse.[9] As an environment for communication, social media appear to work counter to the separation and privacy of small, situated encounters. Social network sites foster sharing rather than withholding information.[10] Communication persists after its expression in a broadly visible form. Digital information can easily be duplicated, distributed, and stored in new locations. Networks on social media are unusual because these include people we know from different parts of life, which means that we communicate with a set of people we would never otherwise address simultaneously. But even what we share with this extraordinary audience can easily go beyond our established network to reach others unknown and invisible to us online. Meanwhile, when other people are active online they sometimes reveal information about us that we did not intend to share. Social media are truly transformative of the physical limits of interaction.

For users everywhere, social media have undoubtedly exposed everyday life across its usual boundaries. And yet rarely are people subjected to social rejection or other problems. Goffman of course noted that audience segregation broke down on certain occasions like a chance meeting in public or in a transitional space such as an elevator. What happens then? Not much, typically. People might get embarrassed, but mostly they are just surprised to see each other. When a man, out with his son, runs into his boss, a simple greeting and introduction will do. No one present needs to radically rethink anyone else there.[11] Rather, audience segregation matters most for people with stigmatized identities and involvements. They face the prospect of being discredited. Over time, Goffman clarified that the exacerbation of stigma was the real cost to manage for mixed audiences.[12] Unfortunately, Goffman's takeaway did not carry forward as the point of departure for context collapse research, which typically involves professionals, college students, and others solidly holding mainstream credentials and generally viewed favorably.[13] African American teenagers from poor urban neighborhoods get no such benefit of the doubt and face an entirely different set of risks in the public spaces through which they must travel.

In Chapter 2, I discussed how street life moves online through encounters between girls and boys. Videos of fights uploaded to social media, or more recently streamed live, also link urban spaces to the Internet. Fight videos are a useful starting place to reintroduce Goffman's concerns with the intensification of stigma. Fight videos alter the visibility of the street code. A performance of seconds on the ground extends online through repeated viewing and the wider scale of audience. Before social media, neighborhood reputations hung on the secondhand accounts of a fight that those who witnessed it firsthand would tell to listeners. These accounts are increasingly overshadowed by a video that peers can watch for themselves to come to their own conclusions. The visibility of a fight performance, however, does not necessarily stop with peers. A range of adults from parents and family members to teachers and employers to the authorities may also see fight videos. The challenge for teenagers as their experiences move from the physical street to the digital street is to maintain audience segregation in the porous environment of social media. The goal becomes to perform toughness in front of their peers *on* the street while keeping that image *to* the street. Sarah's fight video shows how this challenge may come about and how it may be met successfully.

Sarah's Fight Video

Sarah was eighteen when we met. She was a student at Medgar Evers College, in Brooklyn, and lived in Harlem in a west-side housing project. I met Sarah through the summer employment program where I led workshops. She attended over two consecutive summers and distinguished herself as an active and thoughtful workshop participant. Seated at the front of the room, she eagerly counseled her peers on the working world, the college application and financial aid processes, and the transition from high school, which she completed a year early, to college.

On Facebook, Sarah generally wrote about her college experience, her boyfriend, her interest in fashion, and other facets of her life removed from the street life around where she lived, units nicknamed "Grimy." In one post, she uploaded a picture of her to-do list with the caption "Have to Get The Work Done Before I Can Party. I Guess Being Successful is My Motivation. #DiaryOfACollegeGirl."

After a job-readiness workshop, Sarah brought up to me something the guest speaker said: "The first thing human resources at a given company does when making hiring decisions is look applicants up online." Sarah told me about a video of a fight she got into with another girl during her senior year of high school that was uploaded to Facebook and YouTube. Sarah said she had been a "star pupil" at her high school, in front of which the fight had occurred. She had feared it might interfere with her standing in school or her pathway to college so she had immediately "reported" the video to Facebook as "inappropriate," and Facebook had taken it down.

A second video of the same fight taken by an eleventh-grade boy still appeared on *his* YouTube profile. When I asked Sarah why this video had not been taken down, she explained that she was under the impression that there was no way to remove a video published by another person, information that was incorrect because anyone logged onto YouTube can report such content.

About six months after chatting at the workshop, Sarah and I watched the precisely one-minute video on YouTube, where it had been viewed 4,842 times in its nearly two years online. Sarah told me the fight was with a classmate named Halima, someone she had previously considered a dear friend. According to Sarah, Halima felt disrespected after a third party told her that Sarah had disclosed embarrassing information about her sex life.

In the video, Halima approached Sarah, who immediately handed her book bag to a friend. The girls punched each other with one hand and used the other to pull clothing or hair. They went to the ground after about seven seconds, with Sarah on top, punching Halima. Then Halima rolled on top, punching Sarah several times in the head. As Sarah rolled back on top, Halima kicked her in the face, which drew "oohs" from the crowd that had gathered.

"Once she kicked me in my face, I knew that all this lovey-dovey stuff that we shared before went out the window. So then . . . I really wanted to hurt her." After the kick, Sarah held Halima down and attempted to push her head against the sidewalk. Other girls intervened, pulling the two apart and back to their feet. Friends then whisked Halima away. "I wanted to fight her again because I felt like she disrespected me . . . . I was embarrassed 'cause you kicked me and it was on video. I was so embarrassed."

We were watching the video almost two years later, but Sarah was able to convey her emotions at the time, as well as what she felt at our interview. When she spoke about the embarrassment of getting kicked in the face on camera, her imagined audience (then and two years later) was her peers, for whom such a hit showed badly. But she also told me that she was proud of her overall performance, particularly in comparison with other instances when she had gotten jumped: "I stood up for myself and I did well."

Sarah also expressed concerns beyond her local peer world. When we first spoke about the video, she told me that she had been afraid that teachers would see it before she graduated from high school. This could have been grounds for expulsion as per Department of Education policy. This possibility seems especially likely for black girls in New York City public schools who, according to an analysis of 2011–2012 data, received school discipline at ten times the rate of their white female counterparts.[14] Now Sarah described the video as an employment liability.

Several aspects of Sarah's fight video were troubling. Sarah had never spoken to the eleventh-grade boy who had uploaded the video and "wasn't a willing participant." One problematic minute of her life stretched to eighty-one hours of viewing time online. As a college student, Sarah had traction beyond her neighborhood that the video might threaten.

At the same time, Sarah had addressed the audience problem. Sarah's impressive showing in the fight video was a resource for status, provided she could keep it in the context of the street. Sarah's name was not attached to the video, nor did her face appear in sharp resolution. Although a detective could presumably locate the YouTube video, which was retrievable by searching the name of her high school and the word "fight," an employer probably could not.

After Sarah told me about another neighborhood fight over the summer between high school and college that also involved videoing and efforts to restrict its exposure to YouTube, I realized Sarah's savvy when it came to code switching. She prioritized the immediate removal of fighting from Facebook because its presence there made her identifiable. But she was ultimately okay with its remaining on YouTube because there—without her name attached—it was not likely to affect her career prospects. After all, she did not take steps to remove the video after I told her she was wrong about YouTube's flagging policy, and she expressed not just embarrassment but also pride that she had handled herself well in a fight, a sentiment shared by peers and even a few adults. In fact, Sarah said she had become known through her fight video. Sarah had figured out how to place her street life online. She had met the challenge of audience segregation on the digital street.

Partitioning Street and Decent

Given Sarah's conscientiousness and high level of scholastic achievement, her precautions online were unsurprising. But did other teens manage street life as carefully? In his account of code switching, Anderson fell back on the idea that some youth, typically those "from homes ravaged by unemployment and family disorganization," really were "street-oriented."[15] Clustered in street-corner groups, they held their peers accountable to the code. The enforcers did not personally code switch, either because they had never learned decent comportment in the first place or they had stopped code switching once it became dangerous to let down their guard. Upon closer inspection, Anderson's model allowed only for "decent" kids to code switch.

The boys I studied hung out in street-corner groups involved in reciprocal violence that had escalated to gunfire. Many of the girls I studied dated these boys and were known as "girl fighters."[16] If their street identities were indeed stable, they would not be worried about what family members, teachers, employers, and other adults thought about them. Or at least they could not afford the public appearance of such worries.

But that was typically not the case. They shared Sarah's concern with being seen as decent, even if they were willing to take greater risks and fight more often. Garot found that gang-affiliated teens often walked away from a fight or retaliation when on the job, in school, or out with family members, or when they believed that such news might get back to these parties.[17] I observed the same concern on the Internet when teens realized their street lives might cross with their relationships to adults in other areas of their lives. Generational separation seemed easy enough, because teens typically adopted sites before the older generation and then moved on before the adults arrived, if they ever did. But Facebook was different: The adults got there first. By late 2009, when I started my research, the teens primarily socialized on Twitter, having created networks that joined peers they knew personally or might come to meet in person, usually, as discussed in the previous chapter, members of the opposite sex presumed to live in Harlem, the Bronx, and other nearby areas. Twitter dominated digital life through 2010, with teens gradually exploring Facebook. During this time, teens related to Twitter in opposition to Facebook and partitioned street life accordingly.[18]

On Twitter, teens rarely used their real names for profiles. Instead, they drew from their nicknames and group names, names of celebrities, consumer brands, the numbers of their streets or building names, and other sources. Faces in profile photos were sometimes obscured and occasionally out of the frame entirely.

The accounts were often protected (visible only to accepted followers). In other words, they kept their profiles visible to each other and nearly invisible to parents and other adults—a strategy common to the teens' worlds that danah boyd observed.[19]

On Facebook, by contrast, first and last names were fairly common. Faces typically appeared in full view. Profiles were rarely categorically closed, as Facebook offered more nuanced privacy settings than Twitter.

In outreach work I noticed that teens generally refrained from aggressive talk and references to rivalries on Facebook; instead, this content appeared on Twitter. During a set of interviews between September and November 2010, using the local term for various forms or phases of conflict, I asked twelve teens from six Harlem neighborhoods, "Is there beef on Facebook?" Eleven of the twelve indicated either that there was no beef on Facebook or that there was far less beef on the site than on Twitter. Said the lone dissenter: "Of course, there's beef everywhere."

When I posed the question to seventeen-year-old Dedra, she cracked up laughing: "Who beef on Facebook? It's uncommon."

"Why?" I asked.

"That's a family network," she replied.

Other teens said as much. They also explained that Facebook was for older, more mature, and more educated ways of communicating. According to Smalls, aged nineteen, people "be talking a whole lot of mess over Twitter," but when I asked about beef on Facebook, he responded:

Nah, not that I know of, and if there is, it shouldn't be on there. I feel that Facebook is more of a thing for mature, adult-type of people. It's more of a thing for college people or people who are just leaving high school. Even if you're in high school and your mind state is mature, you know, you're willing to talk as an adult or handle yourself a certain way, I think that's what Facebook is like. I have not seen anybody beefing over Facebook.[20]

Eighteen-year-old Sierra said, "It's hard to argue on Facebook, 'cause it go on your wall" where "family members see it." She added that "some people hide this [beef] from they family members, like, they outside doing what they do and in the house they a different person. So, like, why argue on Facebook if you know your mother or your uncle or somebody has a Facebook?"

On Twitter, however, teens saw the street code in the workings of the site. "Whoever made Twitter," said Tiana, in September 2010, "designed Twitter for trouble." She explained that she could see her friends' confrontations with people she didn't follow. Tiana was prepared to "jump into" these conflicts and expected her friends to do the same. In the context of the code, Twitter seemed provocative. It placed users before a stream of other people's conversations, with the prompt "What's happening?"[21]

Sierra called Twitter "a big chatroom," likening it to AOL Instant Messenger (AIM), which had been popular for just that feature. On Twitter, teens "put on a show" by arguing publicly, with "everybody watching," as retweets added eyes to any situation and potentially linked instigative remarks to reactive parties. Teens sometimes took these arguments offline to "meet up somewhere and fight," she said. The digital street was on Twitter.

Facebook, at this time point, signaled supervision and calm. Facebook prompted users to provide real names rather than handles and linked profiles by kinship ties. Compared with Twitter, Facebook made it easier for youth and elders to find and connect with one another. Together the two sites enabled a simple structure for audience segregation and code switching. Twitter was a platform for engaging peers, including through conflict, whereas Facebook reached mixed company with adults present.

In late 2010, Facebook represented adulthood and a future without neighborhood drama. As sixteen-year-old Elton put it, "when you mature" and get over "this gangsta stuff . . . then you move to Facebook." Only it was not that simple. The beef did not end just because teens tired of having to always watch their back and because this was "no way to live," as Isaiah said, after having dodged a fight to make it to his civil service exam. Smalls said of his own situation that everyone involved in the beef would have "to let me out of it." Meanwhile, all growing up—aging out of violence included—required extended effort, achieved in fits and starts, offline and online.

By early 2011, the period of overlap between Twitter and Facebook, for all its practical value, ended. The shift looked final one day in February 2011 at the computer lab inside Pastor's office. I noticed that the teens logged onto only Facebook. "Twitter ain't got nothing on it. Everything go down on Facebook," Amina explained. The strategic use of Twitter and Facebook together over the same time period was not planned. As the teens aged up they adopted and abandoned branded platforms. As Elton put it, "all of us just moved from AIM . . . to Myspace. Then Myspace got wack 'cause they made Twitter, so everybody went to Twitter." As they moved to Facebook the transitional phase of overlapping use placed youth with their parents on Facebook, an anomaly.

The centralization of social life on Facebook introduced a new audience structure for teenagers still in the grips of neighborhood violence but transitioning to adulthood. One way teens handled the presence of elders was to again partition street life by creating private group pages with invited memberships. A handful of boys and girls administered these pages, which were usually themed around shaming girls for sexual activity until a "HOUNDOGGS" page to expose boys reversed the usual gendering. Administrators invited rivals, and the pages functioned as private chatrooms for incendiary talk with directives like "YOU FUCKING SKUMBAGS, QUIT PLAYIN' && MAKE IT NASTY!!!" The antagonism online sometimes fed violence in person, and vice versa. Teens also utilized direct messaging to convey threats in the inbox, which brought more one-to-one communication into neighborhood conflict.

But once on Facebook, street life became more visible to the adult world. It flowed onto the regular feeds where new possibilities emerged for cross-generational communication and adult intervention. The teens both preempted and accepted help from their elders. I'm going to first discuss efforts to conceal street life in the mixed company of Facebook audiences by focusing on two young adults, Slinky first and then Desiree.[22]

Tempering Street Life

Slinky

In April 2013, I interviewed Slinky, who was twenty years old. Slinky was part of the social scene on 129th Street. Describing his posts on Facebook over the last couple of years compared with how he presented to friends, he remarked, "I just gotta watch what I say . . . . To my family I gotta be more humble, more concerned about what I say or what I am . . . . I can't put it out there in vulgar terms." If he was mad, he knew not to start cursing repeatedly. "I just gotta be me," he said, only "a bit toned down."

I could easily imagine a twenty-year-old from an affluent suburb taking the same precautions online to regulate how his parents or other adults might see him. But in Slinky's case, he also had to anticipate concerns or inferences regarding gang involvement. In May 2012, an old mug shot of Slinky appeared in a photo roster of gang members shown to community members by police during what police announced as a "gang information meeting." About a year before the meeting, Slinky was shot near his apartment, on the way to a deli with a friend. The bullet shattered his ankle, and surgeons inserted a steel rod running from the bottom of his foot to his knee. Upon his return home from the hospital, Slinky's mother Beatrice put her son on what they agreed was "lock down." He was cut off from seeing his friends from the block and prevented from leaving the house by himself. Beatrice arranged for homeschooling. After repeating both his freshman and sophomore years of high school, Slinky began to excel scholastically with homeschool. He posted photographs of A-range marks and started a photo album titled "100's" on his Facebook page.

Slinky's mother, father, and extended family in New York and Virginia all converged on Slinky's Facebook profile. Said Slinky, "They just had a burst of technology go through them, 'cause they was definitely not messing with no . . . [other] social media." He regularly received their feedback. "During family gatherings they'll talk about what they see me liking or what they see me posting or what I was going through at the time of whatever I posted." Family members instructed him to take down "vulgar" material and gave positive feedback on photos of high grades. Beatrice appealed to Slinky to delete photos depicting "any hand signs" or showing Slinky in large groups for fear these could be used as evidence of gang involvement. Slinky complied.

Slinky's "toned-down" profile was both a response to his family's concerns and a reflection of his maturation. Slinky said he "got respect" on the street for never backing down, but his priority at the time of our interview was preparing for his freshman year at Howard University.

Desiree

In September 2011, I sat down for an interview at Columbia University with Desiree, a cousin of Nika, the sociology major I introduced in the previous chapter. Nika wanted me to meet her cousin because she embodied "the girl network." Desiree was "one of the most connected people you'll ever meet," Nika told me in reference to Desiree's broad knowledge of the street world. During our interview, Desiree paused our conversation to take phone calls from her boyfriend in jail at Rikers Island, whom she said she typically visited twice a week. According to her cousin, Desiree was able to "puppet" young men who "sell drugs or shoot people" and paid the price of this conditional power in fights with other girls interested in the same boys.

Desiree appeared to straddle the street and working worlds. At nineteen, she lived at home in West Harlem and worked at a nearby salad shop while she was also a student at a local community college studying criminal justice. Desiree expressed commitment to her education and planned to transfer to a four-year university. "I live for the Harlem Children's Zone," Desiree said in gratitude for years of internships, summer jobs, college loan payments, $50 stipends for each A in college, and the provision of a mentor.

Like other young people in this study, Desiree exhibited the self-awareness and savvy required to juggle contradictory relationships and expectations that potentially crossed online. Desiree practiced "subliminal" communication on Facebook to manage impressions in the presence of mixed others. On Facebook, Desiree was friends with her mother, her boss, and her mentor at the Harlem Children's Zone, all of whom checked up on her and gave their feedback on her content. Like Slinky, Desiree generally presented a reserved face on the site. When she did provoke conflict, she tempered her posts by couching criticisms intended for specific persons, often other girls, in song lyrics or ostensibly general observations. "Everyone but the person being cheated on knows she being cheated on," Desiree wrote on her wall the day before our interview. By "throwing subs," Desiree sparred in mixed company. As Slinky and Desiree made strides in their education and moved into adulthood they tempered their ties to street life.

Searching for Traction

The code-switching strategies of partitioning and tempering street life showed that even teens deeply involved in neighborhood violence cared about their schooling and employment prospects as they entered adulthood. Status on the street certainly mattered, but it was not the only form of respect they pursued.

On Facebook, traction in school and the working world was a status to own and to broadcast widely, for the adults in their lives but also for each other. Teens marked their routes to high school completion, college enrollment, and participation in the formal economy. They depicted in photographs and screenshots posted online high marks on schoolwork, attendance awards, honor roll and dean's list designations, report cards, diplomas, acceptance letters to high school, college, and other postsecondary institutions, job training certifications, and letters of hire.

Peers did not label this achievement "selling out" or "acting white," as Anderson and others have found of black students in poor urban neighborhoods.[23] I saw playful remarks from friends (when Slinky posted a photograph during homeschooling, for instance, a friend teased that he was doing "5th grade math"), but I never observed any criticism or hostility in response comments. I checked my observation with Pastor and two girls named Eva and Lacey, each with thousands of online ties. They agreed with my observation. The girls brought up criticism of a particular local community college that, as Eva explained, had a reputation for being like "the thirteenth grade" of high school, but neither recalled one peer discouraging another in the comments. "I never heard nobody say don't go to college," Eva confirmed. A math teacher at a GED school where I conducted fieldwork said that students took out their phones when he returned their work and they did well. They photographed and uploaded high marks, even with a wall of his classroom already dedicated to exemplary work.

Teens in street-corner groups also positioned individual success collectively. When Smalls started at a community college 200 miles north of Harlem, he posted on his Facebook account: "THEY THOUGHT ALL THE NIGGAS FROM 129TH &LENOX WASN'T GONNA B SHIT NIGGAS R STARTING 2 PROVE ALL THE NAY SAYERS WRONG SO SHOUT OUTS 2 MY NIGGAS THATS MAKING SOMETHING OF THEM SELF." He tagged in his post those in or presumably bound for college.

These public displays suggested that just as street culture flowed into schools, scholastic culture flowed onto the street. Such two-way exchanges marked a shift from Anderson, who emphasized that the inner-city school had become just another staging area for neighborhood violence. In New York City, from research inside ten "lower-tier" public schools between 1985 and 1994, John Devine wrote, "the schools walls are porous, violence flowing in and out, between community and school."[24] During the 1991–1992 school year, as the teacher's union logged 129 gun incidents, the first set of metal detector systems was installed in forty-one high schools under Mayor David Dinkins.[25] Additional security measures to further police the school boundary followed, including a formalized phone ban by Mayor Michael Bloomberg in 2006. Although street violence entered schools through students' social media accounts and smartphones (at least inside the roughly 93 percent of school buildings without permanent metal detectors), school success also streamed through the same platforms and devices.

On the one hand, this digital picture of progress suggested gains in urban schools and neighborhoods since the 1990s, at least in Harlem. On the other hand, the teenagers I met did not breeze through school. On the contrary, students rarely posted their failures and shared almost exclusively their successes. The same math teacher who spoke of students' photographing high grades told me that daily attendance at his school rarely reached 50 percent. His students who passed the GED were the school's success stories because they were unusual. Even as graduation rates rose citywide, statistics showed that students were less prepared for college.[26] The path to upward mobility was limited or blocked by job opportunities that were typically part-time positions with "open availability" (i.e., no regular work schedule).

Teens posted and validated success online because they understood firsthand how precious it was. Forward progress was not a given, but an ongoing challenge. When I caught up with Sarah at age twenty-one, she was a doting new mother of a two-month-old daughter. She had completed three years at Medgar Evers but was no longer enrolled. Between a debt she owed the college and the fact that her boyfriend, her daughter's father, was in jail, Sarah was not in a position to return immediately.

Slinky was placed on academic probation after his first semester at Howard University, before being asked to leave after his second semester. Slinky said he "fucked around" by partying and skipping classes and exams. But he planned to return, under the terms of "a third chance." He could return to Howard if he demonstrated that he had been productive during his leave. To that end, Slinky worked at a community center in Harlem, interned at a music magazine called *The Fader*, and earned As and Bs at Hostos Community College.

Smalls drifted from community college upstate in his first semester after confrontations with both the instructor of his math class and the basketball coach for whom he expected to play. Back home, Smalls worked intermittently and focused on rapping and releasing singles, albums, and videos online.

Desiree experienced the most immediate career success. She transferred to City College, where she graduated with a four-year degree, and then taught first grade at a charter school that provided teacher training.

The coincidental timing of late adolescence with the emergence of Facebook revealed teens still embedded in neighborhood violence while also in pursuit of change. They were young people vacillating between hope and desperation and new and old routines. In the Facebook era, teens sometimes turned their struggles outward to the adults. Rather than wrestling with the street code on their own and with their peers, they pulled in the adults, many of whom were already concerned. The publicity of Facebook also put the adults more visibly on the hook for the youth in their charge.

Audience Integration

Facebook changed the coming-of-age process for this generation of youth because parents saw more of the risk-taking and identities developing inside peer worlds. Concerned adults witnessed certain test moments and turning points and had the chance to intervene. On Facebook teens sometimes deliberately shared violent situations in order to enlist the cooperation of adults to resolve their problems. These disclosures marked a different manifestation of code switching that turned the typical motive on its head. Rather than sustaining audience segregation, teens were showing both street and decent orientations to an integrated audience of peers and elders alike. We can see this aspect of digital street life in either shorter or longer view. I describe first a single event in Tiana's life and then a pivotal summer for Andre.

Tiana's Retirement

When I met Tiana in 2010, she was fifteen years old and fought as much as several times a week. That year she made herself the president of an all-girls fighting crew and later got a tattoo depicting its name. But in January 2012, at age seventeen, Tiana announced to friends and family in person and on her Facebook wall that she had "officially retired" from fighting. Tiana spoke about leaving Harlem for a fresh start in Delaware and took steps toward enrollment in Job Corps, a federal program that provides no-cost education and job training. She asked me to write a recommendation, which I did.

However, at about 12:30 p.m. on a Tuesday in late January 2012, I saw a post and set of comments on Tiana's Facebook wall alluding to a fight between Tiana and a girl named Gabriella. When I checked again around 1:30 p.m., the material was no longer there, which made me want to find out what happened in that hour. At about 3 p.m., I saw Tiana on the sidewalk hanging out with friends. I bought her a soda, and we chatted in front of the deli.

"My neck hurt," Tiana said, explaining that a hair-extension track was pulled out while she was fighting Gabriella the day before. Tiana said she won that fight. But there was no video to prove it, and Tiana was prepared to fight again after hearing that

Gabriella had told others she was the real winner. Tiana then explained that the conflict was now over.

I found what happened between 12:30 and 1:30 remarkable. The support of friends and family on Facebook helped Tiana walk away from a second fight with Gabriella. At approximately 12:30 p.m., Tiana wrote on her wall, "GABRIELLA BE LYNGGGGG BUT WE GONE SHAKE AGAIN THASS ALL!" To shake meant not to shake hands, but the opposite: to fight.

Within minutes, a set of onlookers discouraged a second fight, reminding Tiana that she had pledged nonviolence. Rochelle, a friend and sometimes rival, wrote, "I THOUGHT U WAS A CHANGED PERSON SMH [shaking my head]." Tiana pushed back: "BITCHES DON'T WANNA SEE ME CHANGE:(but being changed & bein pussy is 2 different things right or right?"

Rochelle responded: "RIGHT BUT U NEED TO LEARN HOW TO BE THE BIGGER PERSON . . . . U GONE KEEP FUCKIN UP UR FACE OVA DUMB SHIT." "But my face not gone get fucked up in this situation I know," insisted Tiana. Tiana's neighborhood friend Mona weighed in: "But your not doing it for ppl [people] your doing it for yourself . . . . Let her [Gabriella] lie."

Tiana, Rochelle, and Mona went back and forth for about six minutes before a friend's mother asked Tiana, "Why do u want to fight Gabriella." Tiana did not respond, but then Tiana's aunt got involved, instructing Tiana to "cut it out." She questioned whether Tiana really knew what Gabriella had said about their first fight, adding that "real" friends would not "feed u hearsay," particularly if they "see u tryin to be a better person." Her aunt then told Tiana she loved her. Tiana stepped down, announcing "IM NOT FIGTHING HERRR . . . . IM JUST GOING TO DELETE THIS POST," which she did.

This semipublic discussion transpired over about forty-five minutes, culminating in Tiana's decision not to confront

Gabriella. Scholars of informal social control maintain that "eyes and ears on the street" keep sidewalks safe.[27] The eyes in this case belonged to community members watching online when Tiana revealed her intention to fight. The event demonstrated the potential for community-level intervention on the digital street. With an audience of concerned and trusted adults and peers, Tiana initiated and took an out from fighting that saved face by showcasing her maturity without negating her toughness.

Andre's Campaign for Respect: Street Life to College Life

With help, Tiana managed to walk away from a fight. But more tests were still ahead. Desistance requires the ongoing vigilance of youth and the surrounding community. I want to get into the complicated and sometimes desperate challenge of getting out of neighborhood violence as it pertains to code switching. Like Tiana, Andre revealed his street life to the adults around him. Only Andre leveraged his disclosures more aggressively, threatening not just rivals but, in a sense, outreach workers to make good on their intervention.

Elijah Anderson wrote about the process by which youth became known for violence and feared as a "campaign for respect."[28] Andre campaigned for respect on these terms but also for the basic dignity of getting an education and having a job. Before I can get into how and why Andre code switched over the summer of 2012, I need to first rewind to earlier circumstances and a decision he made in 2010.

I met Andre in September 2010 when I took him and a friend on an improvised tour of Columbia University's campus, where I used the libraries and conducted interviews. Andre was seventeen and had stopped attending high school. But he insisted he was bound for college and planned to get his GED through Job Corps. Andre lived in Lincoln Houses and said he had been involved in the beef with 129th Street since he was about ten, which he attributed to the disruption of his education. Andre attended eight different middle schools and high schools.

Andre made good on what he told me that day at Columbia. While the St. Lincoln and 129th Street groups were locked in conflict on the heels of two shootings directed at 129th Street, Andre boarded a plane to Buffalo to begin Job Corps in Medina, New York. His departure signaled a radical act of self-discipline and -preservation. Andre, a black and Puerto Rican teenager who had lived his entire life in Lincoln (save for a five-month confinement in a juvenile facility), moved alone to a remote, mostly white area to participate in Job Corps from November 2010 through October 2011. He took GED classes and learned the construction trade, with a focus on roofing. He graduated from the program with a GED diploma, construction-related certifications, and the promise of placement support for college and work when he returned home.

After graduation, Andre moved back into his mother's apartment in Lincoln. The beef between 129th Street and St. Lincoln had subsided following a gang indictment in November 2011 that centered on 129th Street (which will be discussed in chapter 5). Andre searched for work in construction, retail, food services, and other fields. With the help of Job Corps staff, he submitted an application to City University of New York's (CUNY's) community colleges.

Andre did not find work. He grew increasingly impatient as the winter months turned to spring months. In April, he posted on his Facebook wall, "I NEED A FUCKING JOB!" Meanwhile, the violence in the neighborhood picked back up. After four teens in the 129th Street group jumped and robbed

Qadir, his friend from Lincoln, Andre participated in the retaliation, in which a teen from 129th Street was cut badly enough to be hospitalized.

In June, Andre finally had work, seven months after his graduation from Job Corps. His aunt got him a maintenance job with the New York City Housing Authority. But only ten days into the job, Andre encountered some of the boys from 129th Street. They chased him. Andre got away but later ran into one of the boys, accompanied by a girl, who was also from 129th Street. When she placed a call sending for others, Andre punched her in the face.

The young woman pressed charges, and the next day Andre was arrested at home. He spent the night in jail and was arraigned the following day on a misdemeanor assault charge. The judge issued a temporary order of protection against Andre, which prohibited contact with the victim, and released him. Andre told his boss about his contact with the criminal justice system and that he was now on probation. He was subsequently fired.

Andre's plan out of neighborhood violence had come full circle. People in Andre's situation sometimes "go for bad," doubling down on the use or threat of violence.[29] After the assault charge, Andre repeatedly antagonized his rivals, whom he blamed for his troubles. Interestingly, Andre also linked his attacks to his publicly stated goal of making it to college.

At the start of July, Andre called himself "Mr. Unstoppable" on his Facebook wall for the first of several times, taking this nickname from one of his rivals who was incarcerated. A few days later, Andre received the first in a series of acceptance letters from community colleges in the CUNY system. He posted his letter from LaGuardia Community College, which generated thirty-four likes and caring comments from peers and elders alike. The mother of a friend from Lincoln wrote, "Congrats Andre that's wussup proud of u now talk to ur boy [her son] about doin the same thing!!!"

On Monday, July 8, Andre called me to ask if I would drive him to the Bronx to the admissions office at Hostos Community College, his first choice of college, to see if he had been accepted. I agreed to take him in the morning.

When I got up Tuesday morning, I saw that I had missed two text messages from Andre at around midnight. The first text was a photo of Andre laughing in a stairwell holding an Air Jordan sneaker by its laces. The second text read, "Tell your man come get his kicks LMFAO [laughing my fucking ass off]." I recognized the sneaker as belonging to Christian.

I went to Andre's wall, where I saw the same photo posted with the caption: "mr. unstoppable HERE NOW TELL THAT NIGGA I KNOCK OUT TO DAY COME GET HIS KICKS LMFAO AHAHAHA." The post had twenty-six likes, many by other teens from Lincoln. Andre later amplified the aggression by tagging Christian, which linked to Christian's profile picture with the Jordans.

I called Andre. He asked if I had seen "my man's" sneaker. I felt manipulated by Andre, and because I had already agreed to take him to the college, I didn't see why he needed to provoke me. But Andre, who sent the same texts to Pastor, was calling out our commitments to Christian. As part of the social scene on 129th Street, Christian was not just his rival but also his perceived competition for our time as outreach workers. I assumed Andre thought this way because on other occasions he told me in the most matter-of-fact way that he got more attention by creating trouble.

I pushed back on our phone call. "I'm taking you to the college. I'm doing you a favor. You do me a favor and bring me the sneaker." He agreed. But when I went to pick him up, Andre had only his phone and ID. "Where's the sneaker?" I asked. He said a friend had put it on the roof of a building in Lincoln, so I had Andre call his friend to bring it down. The friend did not answer. Andre promised to find the sneaker when we returned, and he kept his word by bringing it over to Pastor's office. Christian had it back by the end of the day.[30]

At Hostos, we walked to the admissions office, where Andre learned that he had been tentatively accepted upon receipt of paperwork from CUNY's centralized admissions. Andre was told about vaccinations, financial aid forms, and other bureaucratic steps to complete his enrollment, all marked on a postcard. We went to the financial aid office on Andre's request. While we waited in line for the clerk, Andre told me that he would be on his "bully" until he found work. "If I'm not working, they not working. If I'm not eating, they not eating," he said.

The clerk called us to her window. She asked about Andre's financial situation, handing Andre forms for him and his mother to sign. She asked if he or his mother had worked in the last year ("no" and "no") and inquired about potential household income streams. Andre explained that his stepfather contributed money and that his family received food stamps.

On the drive back, Andre called his local Job Corps counselor to schedule a consultation to update her on Hostos and to talk about City Year, a federal community service program to which he had also applied. "Miss, Miss, I'm on a rampage right now," he said into the phone, which I presumed was to communicate the immediacy of his case. After he got off the phone, Andre told me he would handle his financial aid forms with his mother right away and asked how soon I could bring him back. He had other outreach workers to schedule for other tasks, such as licensing and placement for work as a security guard. Andre hopped out on 135th Street. "Good looks," he said, meaning he appreciated that I looked out for him that day.

Andre continued with the "Mr. Unstoppable" theme. "I AM OUT HERE AND I CAN'T BE STOPPED BY NO BODY," he wrote in caption with two photos of himself on the street wearing headphones. He also posted a photo of himself holding a Yankees cap he had taken from a teen on Lenox Avenue and another in which he was standing on the corner of 129th Street, with shoulders shrugged, arms bent, and palms turned upward. "THIS IS HOW I WALK HOME EVERYDAY LOL [laughing out loud]," he wrote.

Meanwhile, Andre posted acceptance letters from four other CUNY community colleges. He shared on his wall details from his roughly ten visits to Hostos that he made in July and August to complete placement exams and numerous enrollment-related tasks.

During this period, Andre supported himself by intermittently selling crack cocaine or balled-up bits of toilet paper he represented as crack within the Lincoln Houses. He kept references to this work off Facebook.

On August 31, Andre posted a photo of his Hostos ID card, which bore the sticker "FALL 2012 STUDENT." He included the caption: "COLLEGE LIFE AND IT WAS A LONG WAY COMING!" Along with comments from others, a cousin replied, "Proud of yu fam yu came along frm wen we was in 3rd grade" and "Stick with it cuz [cousin]!! Don't be getting caught up in the street shit leads no where. Good luck."

Rather than separate his street campaign from his campaign for college, Andre stitched these efforts together. He directed "Mr. Unstoppable" not only toward his rivals but also toward the adults he held responsible for helping him. Pastor, to whom he listened by going to Job Corps, was to see to it that Andre had a stable future. Job Corps staff needed to deliver on their pledge to find him a job. As someone in academia who represented "the college life" on our tour of Columbia, Andre expected my help getting into college. Andre made plain the urgency and desperation of his cause by brandishing violence against young persons from 129th Street, his rivals over the last ten years and now the perceived competition for the time and resources of local outreach. I thought Andre already had support without resorting to such measures, but he was not wrong to assume that outreach workers prioritized the most violent cases.

Code Switching on the Digital Street

The management of reputation exhibited by the teenagers in this chapter went far beyond the typical self-consciousness of adolescence. The young people I talked about all juggled multiple forms of accountability to peers and adults in the neighborhood and to themselves and what they wanted at different points in their lives. As teenagers of color who fought for respect on the street, they had to think hard about issues of audience and context collapse on social media because their lives offline were already subject to high levels of concern, monitoring, and suspicion by their friends, rivals, parents, neighbors, employers, teachers, and mentors, as well as, to be discussed, law enforcement.

We see in the code-switching strategies discussed new smarts for the digital street. Sarah learned to control access to fight videos that she did not consent to without destroying evidence of an impressive performance. Tiana was purposefully public with her threat against Gabriella, allowing her peers and aunt to talk her down—a face-saving way not to fight. Andre held the neighborhood captive to his campaign for college.

danah boyd's 2014 book *It's Complicated: The Social Lives of Networked Teens* describes how teenagers on social media "must regularly contend with collapsed contexts and invisible audiences."[31] But for more affluent, better-protected teenagers, the risks are lower when audiences cross. In one of boyd's examples, for instance, a teenager need only get past the awkwardness of joining school friends and camp friends.[32] This chapter suggests a shift for digital scholars to center the discussion of context collapse and online visibility on those with the most at stake when audience segregation breaks down. This turn gets us back on track with Goffman's concern with the intensification of stigma and the countermeasures by those under suspicion. Some of the same code-switching strategies employed by street-involved teens in Harlem overlap with boyd's broad sample of teenagers from across the United States. Similar practices have been described in the business world, in which office workers partition their social ties by platform and temper their communication and content on social media to appear uncontroversial.[33]

But we also see variation. Privileged youth need not call attention to their school success as a badge of decency whereas teens in Harlem cannot take this perception for granted. Credibility was central to Elijah Anderson's earlier work on respect in his book *A Place on the Corner*, about black men who gathered at Jelly's Bar and Liquor in Chicago. These men struggled to be seen as respectable and "must display convincing proof" that they were a "somebody" rather than the default expectation of "a nobody." The evidence therefore was "usually put up front before someone else actually calls for it."[34]

Despite the hostility and challenges they faced both in wider society and within their own community, black and Latino teens in the thick of Harlem's street life did not count themselves out of school or the working world. On the contrary, they recognized and supported the traction of their peers. The action on the street was only one aspect and phase of life for young people reaching at the opportunities around them, through the Harlem Children's Zone, Job Corps, and community college.[35]

The visibility of the digital street poses to the adult world the question of what to do with online access to youth. Goffman outlined a relevant tension. When a person with a stigmatized identity entered mixed company, that person had the chance to find sympathetic allies willing to see the world as they did. Goffman called these allies "the wise."[36] The wise in Harlem would be Tiana's aunt, Pastor, Job Corps staff, and other concerned adults who perceive young people involved in neighborhood violence as needing help. But more often, according to Goffman, when audience segregation breaks down, persons with stigma experience discrediting. They get punished for their marginality. Whereas neighborhood adults and outreach workers apply care, police and prosecutors use incapacitation to reduce violence. Each approach has its strengths and limitations. In the next two chapters, I turn to the social control of the digital street, starting with the "bottom-up" efforts of Pastor and moving to the "top-down" tactics of police and prosecutors.

4

Pastor

We've seen some of how the experience of an inner-city neighborhood digitizes as young people engage each other and the adults in their lives on social media. Over the next two chapters I look at some of the first adults in Harlem to employ digital space in order to influence outcomes in the neighborhood. I examine how the adult world leveraged the digital street in its efforts to control youth on the physical street. This chapter focuses on the mediating force of street pastors who traditionally operate between institutions and people. I look closely at how the subject of this chapter reinvented an established role in the inner city for the present era of street life.

Traditionally street pastors go about their rounds in the neighborhood to move information among youth on the street and the adults and institutions concerned with them. Pastor found ways to, in a sense, be in more than one place at a time with more of the community in different physical and digital locations. Pastor expanded the interactional bandwidth of street-level communication to anticipate and mobilize an embodied response to youth violence. His actions broadened the digital street to enable the flow of information across generations, stakeholders, and technologies. Pastor exemplified how adults could use the digital street to reach youth and again become visible in their lives after Elijah Anderson warned that old heads had dropped off the radar. And yet Pastor's intervention was still not enough to bring about lasting peace.

In this chapter, I discuss the possibilities and limitations of Pastor's role within the larger question of what adults, apart from the police, can do to control teenagers living out the street code. I start with how Geoffrey Canada and Elijah Anderson each approached this question from opposite ends. Canada staffed adults in organizational roles whereas Anderson pointed to the old heads on the street. Pastor, meanwhile, worked the middle space of community between institutions and people. I illustrate Pastor's role in the development of the digital street by examining how he handled an especially violent start to the 2010 school year. This two-week period shows what Pastor could and could not do with his system of communication outside of the Harlem Children's Zone (HCZ). I end by revisiting a missed connection with the HCZ in the fall of 2010 that might have suppressed violence before the top-down press of the police and district attorney that came later. Let's start with how social control works from the bottom up.

Control From the Bottom Up: An Institutional or Old-Heads Approach

Anderson and Canada each believed that control of youth violence came from within the community and not from the police. They emphasized that children turned to violence and street life in the absence of protection and hope from the adult world. For all their similarities however, Canada and Anderson gravitated toward different inclusion mechanisms for youth on the street.

Canada believed that the institutions positioned to counter street life—the school and community center—were underfunded, underutilized, and disconnected. By together building up and expanding what these pillar organizations gave the community, a positive "contamination" would overwhelm the influence of street culture to enable a truly supportive social environment.[1] Canada saw the potential to engineer a neighborhood experience that prepared kids for college, much the way a more affluent neighborhood did. Sidestepping the public-school system and teachers' union, Canada started three new charter schools and opened or rebranded dozens of service-provider sites across Central Harlem in just two decades. Backed by powerful investors, the HCZ packaged education, social and medical services, and other supports and programs into a "cradle-to-college" pipeline, from Baby College for new parents to the College Success Office for new college students. In fiscal year 2013, the HCZ served over 12,300 children (75 percent public-school students) and over 12,400 adults.[2]

The HCZ, however, was not without its critics and pushback, especially that steps to privatize education further gutted the local public-school system that Canada himself experienced as unsafe and failing.[3]

Anderson, like Canada, described the failures and inequities of schools and other institutions that served poor black youth, but he argued that the transition of idle youth to mainstream life actually happened informally in the public space of the neighborhood through the socialization of old heads.[4] Scholars of inner-city neighborhoods have long remarked upon the importance of adult authority figures outside of school in helping teenagers to gain a foothold in established institutions.[5] Self-appointed, community-oriented public characters reached out to local youth to provide counsel and material resources directly. Old heads modeled the stability of having a job and family and prepared their protégés for these responsibilities. They also enforced local order in the short term by stepping in when young people were getting ready to fight and in the long term by backing their interventions with the carrots of opportunity, namely jobs at their workplace or elsewhere.

But Anderson warned that the traditional old head was in decline after sustained economic downturns left fewer black men with steady lives and jobs in hand. Scholars writing after Anderson observed that mass incarceration brought about the more modest mentorship of "redeemed old heads," with lessons of resilience from having survived gangs and drugs and "prisonized old heads," who taught young people to avoid contact with the law in police-saturated neighborhoods.[6]

Canada and Anderson both saw mainstream integration as the best check against youth violence. Both idealized processes, only with different foci at different scales. Canada proposed a tipping-point change model for an entire generation of neighborhood children; Anderson underscored direct mentorship to youth who appeared to need it most. Their reasoning led to distinct ideas about the best placement of adults to sponsor change in street-involved youth. Canada operated from inside institutions out into the neighborhood; Anderson saw that the influence of adults ran in reverse.

Street Pastors as Communication Brokers

Canada and Anderson each overlooked the social role of the street pastor. Street pastors, ordained ministers active outside the church, were vital to the control of street life because they forged and managed ties between institutions and people.[7] They developed an infrastructure of communication that bridged various community cleavages, not only between service providers and community members but also between youth and elders, police and residents, and street-corner groups on opposing sides of conflict.

For decades street pastors literally walked information from one location to the next on their neighborhood rounds.[8] Pastors were among the "roving" public characters Jane Jacobs wrote about.[9] They collected information from storekeepers and other "anchored" public characters and shared news at fixed locations where neighborhood people gathered. Jacobs gave the example of a settlement house director who made his round of the Lower East Side shops to hear from the cleaner about drug activity and "from the grocer that the Dragons [youth gang] are working up to something." On Rivington Street, he intercepted gossip from the teenagers who hung around there. The flow of street-level communication depended upon, as Gerald Suttles said of Chicago, the people themselves as the "communicative devices."[10]

These accounts may sound dated, but this communication system couldn't have changed much until recently because opportunities to socialize and access information were tightly bound to place through the mid-1990s.[11] Mobile and digital communication shifted the availability of information about and among neighborhood residents.[12] The street pastor at the center of this chapter reinvented an established role in urban neighborhoods for the exigencies of the digital street. He collected gossip on his daily rounds as well as through various communication technologies to cover more of the neighborhood at once. Most important, Pastor embraced communication styles that were not part of his own childhood to become visible and relevant to the young people he served.

Pastor

Pastor operated in the shadow of the HCZ, outside of its funding and facilities. The preoccupation of Pastor differed from the longer view on violence taken by Canada and his staff, who were given to the development, administration, and evaluation of schools and programs. Pastor operated in the moment, through talk, gossip, and notification to potentially disrupt the next incident of violence, and willingly placed his body in harm's way.

To illustrate intervention on and between the physical and digital streets, I'm going to delve into my experience running with Pastor over the first two weeks of the 2010 school year, a relatively early phase of fieldwork that turned out to be among the most violent. By zooming in and out over these two weeks, I can show how Pastor employed the full bandwidth of street-level communication to attempt to suppress violence. We see the breadth of the digital street in its employment for intervention. Pastor monitored teenagers on the staging areas of social media while drawing together community members through other technologies and creating backchannels with the teens themselves. As numerous communication technologies converged through the social role of the street pastor, we will see that the results of his intervention were mixed.

Running With Pastor

Around 5:30 p.m. on a Tuesday in September 2010, the day before the new school year started, I joined Pastor in front of the Mormon Church on 128th Street and Lenox Avenue. Pastor had parked his familiar black SUV curbside, and he was greeting passersby. Sixteen-year-old Kaseem, with his red Washington Nationals cap and earbuds, was the first of several teenagers to arrive. A middle-aged woman approached. She asked Pastor if he was the pastor of the church. "I should be," he replied, then quickly added, "Let me stop," feigning embarrassment about his conjecture. But Pastor probably felt that way. For years he lobbied the pastor of the Mormon Church to open his facilities to the neighborhood kids, particularly the basketball gym on the fourth floor, and eventually got his way with the introduction of a Thursday evening basketball program.

Pastor told the woman that his ministry was about engaging young people where they were. "Hang out with us," he said. This was typical Pastor. He showed up on the block each day (and throughout the day), and his consistency and performativity drew people in. When Pastor explained his ministry he contrasted his work with the tendency of local clergy to preach from the pulpit and to fundraise for their church. He told me in an interview: "The streets is where it's at for me—it's where the experiences are, it's where the memories are, it's where the lessons are. That's where the teaching moments are."

By the Mormon Church moments later, fifteen-year-old Tiana, carrying her BlackBerry with its jeweled pink case, walked up with Cheryl, a woman of about twenty. They sang along and danced to "Teach Me How to Dougie" as it played from Tiana's phone.

Pastor chatted with the young women. Cheryl remarked that the boys from the block were in trouble with "all of Harlem" and would "get it" at the upcoming Harlem Day parade (officially, the African American Day parade). On and off for the last three years, Pastor had been dealing with the beef between the boys from 129th Street and their teamed-up rivals from St. Nicholas Houses and Lincoln Houses, "St. Lincoln." On top of this, the

129th Street group had gotten into a separate altercation at a party in East Harlem over the previous Saturday night, which led to a police chase and a number of arrests.

Tiana added to his worries about a violent start to the school year. Tiana was one of the girls whose information Pastor most depended on. Her assistance helped to staunch the same violence she sometimes provoked.

Tiana had just published a series of lists on BlackBerry Messenger (BBM). To the more than 1,000 BlackBerry users, mostly boys, in her following, Tiana broadcasted a list of boy groups of the street world titled "TOP 10 HARLEM TEAMS." Her list placed two age-graded groups from 129th Street first and second. She sent out another list called the "List of Smuts," a term equivalent to "sluts," which included the names of forty-one girls and which of twenty-two blocks, buildings, or neighborhoods across Harlem, Washington Heights, and the Bronx they were from (or assumed to be from).

Rankings and the sexual slander of girls were nasty parts of adolescent competition that played out everywhere.[13] But when the competition unfolded on the street rather than within a school, teens had to defend not only personal reputations but the status of their neighborhood as well, a process that extended to social media.[14]

Pastor understood the digital aspect. He had a BlackBerry and appeared in Tiana's BBM and other social media networks. At one point, Pastor added her iPhone 4S to his service contract with the agreement that she would pay her monthly costs. Even if he could not control Tiana's behavior, he watched over her. Tiana lived at this juncture with her mother in the Bronx, but, according to Tiana, she had been on her own since about age twelve. When I asked Tiana one day if she had a curfew, she replied, "I thought you knew me better than that, Jeff." She explained their check-in system. Her mother would call and ask, "Where you at?" Tiana said. "She don't never say come home."

Pastor was her surrogate parent figure, as he was for many teens. He could relate. Like Tiana, Pastor grew up in foster care and ran the streets in Harlem and the Bronx. Pastor's street credibility was even based exactly where he now ministered. He had been a drug dealer who at one point got his supply on 129th Street and sold it in the St. Nicholas Houses. He had been part of a stickup crew who robbed drug dealers. Pastor had spent nearly a third of his life in jail or prison for drug and violent offenses before he started his youth ministry, in his mid-thirties. In this sense, Pastor was a "redeemed" old head, able to speak from experience about things like revenge or hope or the technical elements of criminal case processing. Pastor's story of drug-trade violence and incarceration differed also from that of Canada. Canada experienced an exceptional trajectory out of poverty in early adulthood by earning a scholarship to Bowdoin College (in Maine) and then graduating with a master's degree from Harvard.

In private, Pastor spoke to Tiana at length about the destructiveness of her lists. In front of the Mormon Church, he chastised Kaseem for "gassing"—encouraging—the lists with his comments online. Then he sent the lists to the adults in the community with a text blast: "Because our youth play points and broadcast it this way. We have violence on our streets. This will be the cause of pre and back to school violence in our communities." He took what he learned from the kids and then blasted it to the adults by text message, the platform most readily on hand to parents, grandparents, and other elders. Later, Pastor texted and tweeted police CompStat (computer statistics) metrics that indicated higher homicide and felony assaults citywide for the year as compared with those of the previous year. "Catch the wave of peace," he added.

Pastor monitored crime patterns published by police but also spoke directly to precinct commanding officers and other police higher-ups. Pastor heard from two neighborhood men, one of whom was elderly, who routinely listened to citizens' band (CB) radio for police and emergency response calls. To stay further in the know, he subscribed to two services that sent automated emails with incident reports related to police, fire, and rescue operations (services that aggregate CB radio, local news media, and other sources).

On the church corner, when a twenty-year-old young man asked Pastor about job leads, Pastor told him to call a partnering city council candidate for short-term campaign work that paid $10 per hour. The young man, who had experienced being shot, expressed worry that he might encounter old rivals if he was placed around St. Nicholas Houses, as he was part of the older cohort before Kaseem's who fought with boys from St. Nicholas. Pastor encouraged him to see this opportunity through, adding that he would need to register online for the Democratic Party. Pastor also said that he'd need to cover up, gesturing to the young man to zip his hoodie and roll down his sleeves to hide the tattoos of his nickname and old crew. "You're there to do a job. You're not there to represent," Pastor said.

Pastor monitored talk among the teens on BBM and Twitter. He was way out in front of the convergence of teens and adults on Facebook that I discussed in the last chapter. In addition to scrolling through his feeds, Pastor used a Twitter application customized by two programmers who reached out after reading about him in the newspaper. Pastor received alerts when specific users tweeted or when slang associated with violence appeared. Each weekend, Pastor tracked tweets about parties in unsupervised apartments or community rooms of housing complexes. "People will just tweet like 'party on such-and-such a block', 'party on this block', 'party on that block'. That's how it go," said Rochelle. Parties became dangerous when youth were "caught slipping," slang for getting jumped away from home turf. Every Friday and Saturday night, Pastor followed party announcements on Twitter with updates from girls as they were out and about. Rather than enter the parties, Pastor usually parked in front, drawing teens to hang out with him and each other, thereby making his presence known.

On the Friday of that first week of school, at about 7:45 p.m., I saw Pastor and his collaborator Coach, a retired postal worker, again by the Mormon Church. I had run to the store only to join the two men when I saw that approximately twenty-five teenagers from the 129th Street group were out. Pastor said he had been walking his wife's dog near their apartment, about three-quarters of a mile away, when he heard that boys from Lincoln were spotted on 125th Street "mobbing up." He drove over immediately.

Along with social media, Pastor's phone network served as a personal notification system. A couple of years into our relationship, Pastor generously shared his BlackBerry with me. I saw that his phonebook included 1,350 contacts, certainly a large number. I selected a random sample of 10 percent (135 contacts) and interviewed Pastor about each one. Aside from a handful of wholly personal contacts, almost everyone fit into a role in his outreach. His network included boys from rival areas and some of their girlfriends, parents, siblings, and cousins, as well as caseworkers from the Office of Child Support Enforcement, a gang intelligence detective, the commanding officer of a housing police sector, an NYPD community affairs liaison, an assistant district attorney, and a federal judge. Also linked were fellow clergy, government- and community-based service providers, professional and graduate student journalists, activists from the National Association for the Advancement of Colored People (NAACP) and the New Black Panther Party, a pastor at Rikers Island who facilitated clergy visits, an NBC anchorman, and a case manager from a senior care center downtown who hired Pastor's referrals. Many of these individuals would not otherwise appear together. Pastor closed the structural holes in his network, in the language of network scholars.

Adult and teen "spotters," as he called them, kept Pastor abreast of happenings in their buildings and on their blocks. Nine of the young persons in the phonebook sample were spotters—boys and girls worried about themselves or their peers and some regularly involved in fights or shootings. When I matched his contacts to his text messages, which I had also downloaded, I could see that some teens texted Pastor about impending fights and unsupervised parties to which Pastor would show up. Pastor also pried and pulled such information out of his young people when he wanted to know something. That young men and women disclosed information about the same violence in which they participated implied a sense of preservation on their part.

On the corner by the Mormon Church, almost as soon as Pastor told me where the boys from Lincoln were spotted, I heard a teen yell Lincoln's name. Twelve or so boys from the rival St. Lincoln group stood on Lenox Avenue, on the same side as we were, between 128th and 127th Streets. Pastor, a Yorkie tucked under his arm, walked toward them, while Coach directed the group from 129th Street toward the other end of the block. Pastor, Coach, and many of the teenagers present had been through a variation of this routine before. There was a script to follow in these tenuous moments that presented a way out of fighting. Pastor announced, "Pastor on Deck," "POD," or simply "Pastor," which meant that violence should not happen at this particular moment. It was a form of deference that legitimized walking away. Sometimes the script worked, and the groups left each other alone. Sometimes the intervention displaced the violence so that it occurred elsewhere or after Pastor left. Sometimes knowledge of Pastor's presence prevented the convergence in the first place. But other times the intervention failed.

Pastor walked into the street on 128th and Lenox Avenue and said loudly, "A-yo, Pastor is here. No violence." I had not yet been involved in this script, but I followed suit. I walked out into traffic to stand parallel to Pastor along 128th Street. The cars waited. Pastor waved the group to the other side of Lenox Avenue like he was directing traffic, and I copied his motions. We ushered the boys to the island that partitions the car flow on Lenox Avenue and then over to the west side of Lenox. If we could keep them walking north past 129th Street, they could then travel west to St. Nicholas or east to Lincoln, out of trouble.

But the intermittent taunts picked up, and the St. Lincoln group stopped in their tracks. I looked over my right shoulder and saw one of the teenagers from 129th Street, broomstick in hand, leading a charge of his group. The two sides squared off in the street on the west side of Lenox Avenue. Arms flailed; bottles were thrown and broke on the pavement. I heard someone yell, "He got brass knuckles!"

The adults' limited control of the situation ended instantly.

"Fall back," Pastor called. We retreated to the east side of Lenox Avenue. Cole, one of the teens from 129th Street, had taken a seat in the back of Pastor's unlocked SUV. Pastor opened the door and handed him the dog. I heard the first gunshot and hurried to the curbside of the vehicle. Pastor yelled, "Get low!" I crouched against his SUV. Others ducked by parked cars. Pastor had come up to a stand, his arms crossed on the top of his car, as he tried to decipher the action. "Get down," I said, as three more gunshots went off.

When I came up from my crouch the teens had all scattered. Some of the teenagers from 129th Street returned from chasing their rivals west along 128th Street. No one was hit. People found each other and chatted in small clusters, reconstructing the scene. An older brother came down to ask Pastor where his younger brother was.

The shooting pushed me to think about what I was doing in my research. I was approximately ten months into fieldwork at the time. I had built new relationships with many of the teens and parents on 129th Street and had also wanted to get to know those on the other side of the conflict. I had jumped right into the outreach work with Pastor's encouragement. He needed all the help he could get. Volunteers came and went, and there was no operating budget. Whereas Canada managed a huge youth-serving apparatus on an operating budget in 2010 of $84 million tied to major private investors, Pastor solicited cash or in-kind contributions from residents, businesses, and organizations for specific events and projects, and received occasional donations in small amounts.[15] Pastor's only consistent financial backing came from his boss, a real estate developer and manager of affordable housing for the elderly. He hired Pastor in 2000 to work as a services coordinator for the elderly tenants in his buildings and later leased him an SUV. Pastor used his modest office as a drop-in space for youth with a mandate from his boss to facilitate engagement between local youth and the seniors.

Meanwhile, I had only started to break up mostly fights between girls that involved Tiana. I had not tried to stop a group fight between boys, let alone a shooting. What did I think I was doing? A public defender told me that she watched Pastor from afar. She said his interventions were "driven by machismo, possibly dangerous, and futile." Maybe she had a point.

Pastor suggested I go home, which I did. He and Coach, meanwhile, put on their bulletproof vests.

I received text messages throughout the night. The first updated residents on the shooting: "About 25mins ago shoots fired 128th Lenox Ave," which he attributed to St. Lincoln. At 1:16 a.m., Pastor indicated that he and Coach had met with one leader from each side following the shooting: "Our attempt at peace with these two is a start of something bigger and lasting—pray with Us!" As Pastor learned about prospective violence or after it was addressed, he shared this information with all or different segments of the community. He organized his contacts into one or more lists to receive his text blasts. His default list comprised the adults, community residents who had specifically opted to join his outreach network (and presumably had unlimited texting plans, which Pastor always asked about). This list received the announcements about the shooting and peace attempt. But there were other lists curated to selectively disseminate information. Whereas one list covered all young people in his ministry, other youth lists were broken down by geography to avoid conflict when he announced job opportunities and programming. Three "media" lists roughly corresponded to news formats (print, television, and radio). There was a "white shirts' list" of commanding officers at local precincts.

At 2:30 a.m., Pastor texted me to ask me how I was doing as I was "in the thick of it now!" The next day, Saturday, I called Pastor. He relayed the ribbing I got in my absence. "This white boy got his cherry popped," said a thirteen-year-old boy, who had also teased me in person after the shooting because I had gotten "too low" when the shots were fired.

Pastor said the razzing meant they liked me and to take it in stride. When I passed the thirteen-year-old that afternoon, I dropped down in mock danger. We laughed and slapped hands. If they liked me, it was mutual. After the shooting, I felt only more committed to the outreach work, in all aspects, including violence interruption, and to the research project I had started.

Meanwhile, the peace attempt did not hold, a point to which I circle back. The older teens from 129th Street wanted revenge. In the afternoon, shots were fired at St. Nicholas Houses and then at Lincoln Houses in the evening. Around midnight, I heard from my apartment the sound of emergency vehicles along Seventh Avenue. Pastor blasted a text forwarded from one of his spotters: "Did you hear me Rev[erend]. 1 shot dead between 132/133st 7th ave. I almost tripped over him. Didn't even know he was there." The victim was seventeen. He died a few days later in the hospital. I immediately assumed the shooting was related to the 129th Street–St. Lincoln rivalry, but the victim was from another part of Harlem—a new conflict for Pastor to address.

More violence followed. On Sunday, a man believed to be in his twenties was shot in the hand on Eighth Avenue, which made at least five shootings in Harlem over the first weekend of the new school year. The parade, a hotbed for conflict in past years, was only a week away. That evening, Pastor texted a recap of the shootings. He gave his count of more than "12 fights from 120th through 139th Madison to St Nic. More violence to come! Community! Community . . . you out here?" He texted again about an hour and a half later. "Many have asked what can we do? Emergency meeting this Thursday at 7:30pm," he announced with the details of the hosting pastor and church location. "Tell three people and call those that want your vote. This violence will only get worse!"

On Monday afternoon, I joined Pastor in his office where youth typically dropped in to hang out. Tiana came by with Cassie, a girl new to the scene on 129th Street. In the middle of a meandering conversation, Pastor asked Tiana where she could buy a gun if she wanted one. Tiana, perhaps caught off guard, offered two names. "Don't snitch on me," she added. By using non sequiturs, provocative statements, and other interactional bait, Pastor practiced what he called "verbal judo" to coax engagement and information. His asks and requests emerged always in the context of an ongoing exchange of help and favors.

Tiana changed the subject to her upcoming sixteenth birthday. She wanted Pastor to arrange the use of the community room across the hall from his office and to "work security" at her party. Pastor left this possibility open and then suggested that she hold her party in the Bronx, away from her friends in Harlem and potential conflict. Other teens dropped by the office: first, a friend of Tiana, who was a junior at a high school downtown, and then JayVon and Cole, who had just gotten tattooed, his arm swathed in ointment and plastic wrap. When it started to rain, Pastor rejoiced and told us it was time to leave so he could finally go home to his wife. Violence rarely transpired in the rain.

I sat up front in Pastor's SUV. The five teens squeezed into the back for drop-offs. We left the boys at a subway station and then drove Cassie to the shelter on Lenox Avenue where she had recently taken temporary residence. Pastor asked Cassie when they were going to have "a talk." "Huh," she said. He said that whenever she was ready he wanted to hear about her parents. In the mirror, I saw Cassie scrunch her eyebrows. Tiana smiled, having brokered the introduction. Like other old heads with magnetic qualities, Pastor relied on passive peer recruitment from teens like Tiana to validate his role and find new protégés.[16] Pastor asked Cassie about her favorite food. When she told him it was candied yams and mac "n" cheese, Pastor promised to take her out for these dishes when they had their chat.

Over the week, I tried to keep the boys from 129th Street away from that block. If I could engage them elsewhere, they would be less likely to be targets or to rally after their rivals. One evening, we drove to a basketball court on Lexington Avenue, a neutral area, to play ball under the lights. On the bench, the boys talked about the seventeen-year-old killed on Seventh Avenue. They said he was a good ballplayer and had just become a father. They speculated about the killing. A young man named Elton said that two girls had been with the victim that night. He and another young man, Isaiah, agreed that the girls were paid to set him up. Online, two friends of the deceased addressed the gossip from the victim's Twitter feed, "Yu All Need 2 Shut All Dha Rumor Shyt Up U Dnt Kno Wah Happen."

Pastor visited the victim's family on several occasions during the week following the shooting. Whenever a teen died violently in Harlem, Pastor attached himself to the family of the deceased. He raised funds for funeral arrangements, spoke to the local press on behalf of the family, and offered bereavement support. In the long term, he encouraged the family members to develop a charity or cause in honor of the deceased. He encouraged or cajoled his contacts privately and publicly to come forth with information about the killer. On Twitter, he wrote: "If a member of KKK killed some one in ur community; would that killer b allowed to walk, enjoy and continue in ur community? WWUD [What would you do]?"

Pastor pursued justice by both calling out community members and investigating matters on his own. One evening in his office, when a teen asked if he worked with the police, Pastor said he would do anything to get a gun off the street but otherwise he dealt "directly with people." Pastor put it to me that he walked "a thin line between community and NYPD." He wanted "a better relationship," in which both sides were "working together for a sustainable community." That meant he supported police for activity he deemed beneficial and criticized what was not, a brokering duty noted of other street pastors.[17] On numerous occasions I heard teens call Pastor a snitch or saw as much written online. At different times, the teens agreed among themselves not to talk about things in front of him. But the teens knew he talked to the police because they called him when they got arrested. His traction with law enforcement and the district attorney's office made him valuable to the teens and their parents, who relied on his assistance to circumvent processing and to advocate for them.

Meanwhile, over the parade weekend, Pastor directed tweets toward the teens that he hoped would give pause to further shooting. He adopted their spelling and language choices and a sense of sarcasm in the hopes of getting his message through: "Last week Dave C was shot in da head! Crazii thing is every week some gettin it bad. And da beat goes on. . . .who next SMH [shaking my head]!" A second tweet read, "So I'm thinkin 2 order my RIP tag early an beat da rush. Forward pic and name 2 gotta get bodiedbagged_dis weekend.com."

The concern about Sunday's parade revolved around a scene that typically formed along Lenox Avenue in the evening, after the procession was over. On the day of the parade, I chatted by a deli with Dorsey from the 129th Street group. "It's gonna be Grand Theft Auto out here," he said, a reference to the top-selling videogame in which players earn points for violence. That morning on Twitter, teens retweeted: "Is It Gonna Be A Parade Or A War?" Dorsey said there was a postparade tradition of settling scores. But then he said that much of the anticipation was just "talk on the Internet."

At about 6:10 p.m., I went out to Lenox Avenue, one avenue east of the completed parade route, to find a teenage scene under a level of police scrutiny I had never seen before. I saw police patrol cars, auxiliary police cars, mobile command units, Interceptors, motorcycles, police on horseback, a retrofitted school bus painted police blue, and a range of unmarked vehicles from Chevrolet Impalas to Jeep Cherokees. Police vehicles with flashing sirens drove in caravans up and down the avenue.

Spotlights were set up on street corners while police personnel in uniform and plainclothes patrolled. I noticed some neighborhood adults present, mostly men.

Groups of young people hung out on corners and in front of stores until instructed by police to move along. Boys called out to girls; some girls stopped, but most kept walking. The teens traveled in bunches. Some called out the name of their group or neighborhood as they walked up and down the avenue. The names I heard most often referred to two rival cross-borough gangs under which some of the smaller block-based groups were aligned. At one point in the night, six police officers on horseback were behind a group that spanned an entire block, pushing the teens north. I recognized Cassie at the front of the group. She had cultivated 2,074 followers on Twitter, roughly 95 percent of whom were male from my estimation.

The police presence offered a controlled environment for rival groups to posture back and forth, for hours. There was no significant violence that night, no major group fights or gunplay or anything beyond the level of what Pastor called "a skirmish" in one of his text blasts. Instead, teenagers dramatized the action on the digital street with tweets about the dangers they survived. Meanwhile, Pastor, Coach, and other old heads doing outreach repeatedly urged the teens to go home before they got arrested.

On Monday afternoon, Pastor and I watched 129th Street from his parked car. Things were quiet, which Tiana confirmed when she joined us to charge her phone in the cigarette lighter.

Mary Pattillo writes that pastors play a "middleman" role in the black community, which means this figure "speaks at least two languages in order to translate [between 'the man' and 'the littleman'], has two sets of credentials for legitimacy, and juggles a double-booked calendar."[18] On Tuesday morning, I accompanied Pastor to a Religious Leaders Breakfast hosted by the district attorney, with about twenty black clergy members. Over eggs and coffee, the DA, Cyrus Vance Jr., thanked those present for their community work and fellowship, twice acknowledging Pastor by name. After the event, Pastor talked to the DA about a teenager doing time for a shooting he did not do. The DA directed one of his assistant district attorneys to take down the details. The teen was later released.

Pastor was an informational juggernaut. Over two weeks of back-to-school chaos, Pastor leveraged numerous forms of public and backchannel communication along the street, pooling eyes and ears of the neighborhood. He had advance warning of potential conflict and up-to-the-minute shooting and fight updates. He redistributed the information he received, often in aggregated, filtered, or translated form. He spoke to the teens on Twitter, affecting his language accordingly. "Crazy" became "crazii." "This" became "dis." He used text blasts to report the status of neighborhood violence to the adults, with a forecast of what was to come in the absence of action. Yet the community did not come out in force. Pastor was unable to stop the shooting on the first Friday of the school year, and the treaty he established after the fact broke down the next day. Communication, knowledge, and connectivity were not enough.

The Possibilities and Limitations of the Street Pastor

For a long time, I did not know what kind of pastor Pastor was. "Some would call me a Baptist-Pentecostal. Some would call me nondenominational," he said, when I finally asked. "But a child of God—that's all that I really am." It was not that Pastor bucked the cloth. Quite the contrary, he was licensed in 1999 and ordained in 2000. He held a Master of Divinity from the theological school at Drew University. He presided over funerals, officiated marriages, taught Bible study, and did all the other stuff I assumed pastors did.

Yet, Pastor did not have a church. When I asked why, he said, "Getting other people to understand what it is that I do outside of the pulpit is difficult. People have a traditional idea of what a minister is, and they'll read in the Bible about Jesus and how Jesus went from place to place teaching hope and spreading the good news, but they don't see that that is the role of preacher or minister."

There is a tradition of unusual men like Pastor in African American communities.[19] His social role has a long historical precedence, is recognized by residents, and reappears over time in different cities. The street pastor serves gang-involved youth and other community members typically estranged from church. They operate in the middle of the community to mediate its disputes.[20] Pastor embodied what Max Weber theorized as charismatic authority, which was distinct from rational–legal and bureaucratic forms but legitimate nonetheless.[21]

Street pastors have no formal power. Unlike the cops or other agents of the state, they cannot make anyone do anything. Whatever influence they may hold is voluntary. Researchers who have studied such men attribute their authority to their unique expertise in street life, the community's faith in their good intentions as clergy, and the strength of the street pastor's social ties and resources within his network.[22]

Being outside of institutions, facilities, and formalized operations distinguished Pastor's intervention but also handicapped his efforts. Street credibility often works against institutional legitimacy, and vice versa. For a well-known street pastor in Chicago, for instance, allegations of protecting youth gangs created a funding barrier.[23] When Pastor and I sat down together to write for a grant for his work in 2012, we tried to quantify his impact. We counted the number of guns handed over to him (nine) and areas in which the number of shootings had decreased contemporaneously with Pastor's outreach (four). We could not, however, disentangle Pastor's part in the reductions. We discussed teens who had desisted from violence and went on to college, job positions, or both. But then there were numerous teens in confinement or maimed or even killed by the violence. With some of Pastor's charges, he intervened in their fights over and over again, repeated the same conversations, and effected no clear behavioral change. But then again Pastor's care was always unqualified and sometimes even unsolicited. He got angry with some of the teens or they got angry with him and they stopped talking. But it was generally only a timeout in their relationship. It might have been that Pastor's biggest success was the provision of unwavering support and its general acceptance by the teens. The case has been made that old heads offer an unconditional, open-ended relationship to youth, and that that is enough.[24]

But Pastor was on the beat of youth violence like no other community adult; his issue was stopping it. Even when kids themselves wanted out of violence (which I found was frequent), Pastor needed an alternative to place before them. It had to be significant enough to suggest new respect, routines, and relationships, which pointed back to Anderson and the notion that old heads were only half-relevant without jobs or other opportunities for their protégés.[25] Pastor needed to route youth away from the street and reward nonviolence if he was to prevent fighting and enforce his treaties.

Meanwhile, Canada held a local monopoly on jobs, paid internships, and programming of all variety for youth. With a steady line on such resources, Pastor would have been able to back his

intervention with opportunities and incentives to offer and re-
scind. Street-corner groups were friend groups that evolved together and in parallel with opponent groups. Had Pastor and
Canada partnered, they might have reorganized these groups into
peacekeeping teams that worked in collaboration on the resolution of their own conflict, with a graduated reward system for
its sustainability. Pastor's text blasts failed in many instances to
mobilize parents and other elders. Canada's HCZ served both
youth and adults and offered students and their family members interlocking programs. What if these program opportunities
and corresponding rewards and incentives were applied to youth
and their family members as they all worked on peacekeeping
together?

Missed Connection

It was mostly in retrospect that I wondered about this partnership
and what it might accomplish. Unfortunately, the missed connection passed right in front of me. Following the first two weeks of
the 2010 school year and the murder of another teenage boy that
month, the HCZ initiated a street safety patrol in October. The
Safety Corridors program placed teachers, administrators, after-
school workers, and other staff along portions of 125th Street
and portions of Fifth Avenue and in the vicinities of all HCZ sites
when youth returned home in the afternoon. On the first day of
the program, while walking along Fifth, I happened upon a program manager in an orange HCZ t-shirt with the words "Safety
Knights." We spoke about how we might be useful to each other
and exchanged contact details. Minutes after our conversation,
we saw each other again in the scramble to break up a fight between the 129th Street and St. Lincoln groups in the park on the

corner of 130th Street. I gave the program manager and other staff who had joined background on the conflict. A supervisor said she wanted us to come to their meeting on the upcoming Monday because we seemed to know "the pulse" of the neighborhood.

The next day I received a form-letter email from the program manager that noted the commitment of the HCZ to positively changing the culture of the community and included an invitation to a meeting to discuss their new safety initiative, "Saving our own in the Zone."

On the Friday before the meeting I attended a panel on youth and gun violence at the Schomburg Library that Pastor was on. The subtext of the event, according to another panelist who spoke to me outside the auditorium, was to showcase the community figures and organizations outside of the HCZ who were also doing important antiviolence work that merited funding. Leading up to the HCZ initiative, a local cleavage had already formed between the perceived "haves" of the HCZ and the "have-nots" outside its umbrella of resources and money. Monday's meeting in the cafeteria of HCZ's Promise Academy did nothing to bridge that distance. Rather than a discussion, the meeting was an event with presentations by Canada and others, and during which Canada's staff distributed the graphic-novel version of his memoir.

Pastor and Canada knew each other, but apart from a few conversations they never seriously discussed a partnership. That was too bad: Their methods were complementary. Pastor owned the communication infrastructure and Canada, the institutional infrastructure. What if Canada invested in Pastor the way that Stanley Druckenmiller, a billionaire hedge-fund manager, once invested in Canada? Canada had become one of the most formidable figures in all of urban education.[26] What if he now invested in someone else's model and gave power to Pastor's street-side intervention? But as far as I could tell, the HCZ did not fund other charismatic leaders; they developed their own best practices. Only a foot patrol was far too conventional for this digital era of street life.

A coordinated effort by Pastor and Canada would have given the community its best shot at intervention without the use of formal gang suppression.[27] Before I examine the criminal justice response in the next chapter, I want to close with an insight about outreach on the digital street that my time with Pastor brought forward.

Digital Street Outreach

We saw in this chapter how Pastor reinvented a recurring social role in urban neighborhoods for the contingencies of digital life. He adapted to forms of communication that did not apply to when he ran the streets as a teenager in order to make himself relevant to youth and to work within public spaces that were networked digitally. Old heads on the digital street see the physical street online—they recognize that teenagers digitally telegraph at least some of their movements and intentions and that the street is thus partially legible on social media. When outreach workers use this vision advantage, even violence that appears to get worse through the use of technology becomes knowable. One Friday, for instance, Stan, a leader of the Lincoln group, posted on his Twitter account an invitation to "crash 29 [129th Street]" with St. Lincoln and another group. Stan instructed anyone interested to "RT [retweet]" his message, which extended the invitation exponentially. Although such tweets scaled up the number of potential participants in violence, the choice to publicize preparations also reduced the uncertainty of where youth would be that night. Even communication considered cavalier or destructive on the one hand offers on the other a measure of predictability. Adults doing outreach (and police and youth themselves) recognized the practical value of the visibility of the neighborhood online. On the night of Stan's rallying tweets, like countless others, Pastor moved about by keeping one eye on the digital street and the other on the physical street.

The old heads that don't reinvent themselves for the digitization of the street ultimately depend on those who do. Pastor started his youth ministry with Coach in the 1990s. Coach grew up in Harlem and worked for the post office and coached youth baseball and basketball. After his retirement, he dedicated himself entirely to youth work and was every bit as committed as Pastor. But his style was traditional face-to-face mentorship. He shied away from social media and in 2010 still used a flip phone for calls and texts. The teens loved Coach, and they shared a close bond that was much less complicated than their relationship to Pastor, given Pastor's interstitial role. But Coach did not operate in the same communication environment as the youth he served. He depended on Pastor for much of his information, especially beyond 129th Street. Coach went out to the block each day, but he did not link his rounds in the neighborhood to communication online, which made him less proactive than Pastor. Coach located himself more traditionally on the street rather than within a "networked locality" that, as Eric Gordon and Adriana de Souza e Silva write, "contains annotations and connections, information and orientations from a network of people and devices that extend well beyond what is in front of him."[28] It's both a relational and perceptual shift that comes about when an outreach worker connects to the social media feeds and networks of their charges. And yet knowing and being able to respond to conflict situated online and offline does not make for successful intervention—resources and opportunities are still key.

5

Going to Jail Because of the Internet

Pastor was not the only adult reinventing roles and practices for the digital street. This chapter examines how police and prosecutors use young people's online behaviors to criminalize them. In so doing, they go deeper into personal histories, relationships, and activities to hold youth accountable for what they say and do on the Internet. The chapter title comes from something a young man named Akil said in the months after his brother and several friends from 129th Street were indicted on gang conspiracy charges. Akil's claim warrants examination to show how the law works in the twenty-first century and what its consequences are for those who get wrapped up in it.

This chapter shows how gangs get produced on the digital street. As youth stage their street lives online, police and prosecutors collect, interpret, and edit their content into criminal charges. The digital street offers these judicial actors the means to capture and control the information of suspects without the public tension of stopping a young black man on the physical street. I found that the penetration of social media by law enforcement shifted the onus of guilt back onto youth themselves to criminalize each other through their own use of networked platforms.

In the pages that follow, I examine how the authorities used the digital street to define, prosecute, and suppress gang activity.

I describe how police identified a new universe of digital street crews that were then prosecuted as gangs under conspiracy law. I look closely at how prosecutors unearthed the forensic potential of social media as criminal evidence and the leverage and control that bought on the physical street. This chapter considers also the pushback of youth under surveillance whose code-switching strategies shifted from managing the impressions of their elders to the "cooling" of content likely to further rouse police within the gang hot spots. I end by considering the collateral costs of the gang indictments and taking inventory of the workings of the law on the digital street. In this chapter I make greater use of document analysis than I do in the previous chapters. I refer to police documents distributed to the public and law-enforcement community and publicly available legal documents in addition to my fieldwork.

Gang Control From the Physical Street to the Digital Street

Anderson conceptualized the street code as filling in for judicial authority.[1] Residents recognized the street code as an alternative form of public order given a sense of police indifference and legal injustice. The code was thus enforced among community members, and teenagers code switched to manage peer impressions and those of their parents, neighbors, and other concerned adults. In the chapter on code switching, I discussed how this process extended to social media and the ways that teenagers both eluded and were held accountable to the street code by the surrounding community.

As the police have become much more enmeshed in urban communities, urban scholar Victor Rios has focused on the role of criminal justice actors in the reinforcement of gang identities among black and Latino youth. According to Rios, police aggressively seek out potential violent actors as social control has reached a level of "labeling hype."[2] Authority figures draw the deviance out of young people of color they place under relentless surveillance and effectively double down on potential gang labels. The labeling hype undercuts the dynamism of young people who code switch and their good-faith efforts to change and improve their circumstances.[3]

On the physical street, gangs are constructed based on their visibility in public space. By gathering in public and being accessible to law enforcement, police suspect youth for the commission of crimes in the area and begin to routinely question and pick them up. According to classic research by William Chambliss, these interactions develop over time into mutual dislike and forms of antagonism that lend support and evidence to the original presumption of wrongdoing.[4] More recently, Rios found that gang-suppression officers spent most of their shift carrying out youth checks and stops on the street. Rios saw how easy it was to generate negative interactions, whether police initiated by being cordial or hostile. Each side's perspective was bound to collide with the other. Law enforcement operated from a threat and crime-prevention perspective whereas youth perceived law enforcement as disingenuous and hassling. As one young person told Rios, "No need to fake it officer. You don't like me, I don't like you .... Just search me and get it over with. Save the hellos for the gueros [white people]."[5]

The digital street presents a much easier path to surveillance and data collection, the primary goal of the officers in Rios's study. On social media, teenagers intentionally and unintentionally disclose information that police collect without the interactional tension that mounts in person. To youth, digital checks are typically invisible events.[6] On social media, police look for evidence of a crime or gang affiliation, which means they select on the street side of the code-switching dynamic. The surrounding circumstances and facework behind teenagers' content—all that came into focus in the code-switching chapter—gets stripped of what digital scholar Helen Nissenbaum calls its "contextual integrity."[7]

As the suspects' information moves to the district attorney's (DA's) office, prosecutors edit their content into a narrative of criminal conspiracy charges. Like journalists and editors in the newsroom, prosecutors exercise their "editorial control" to include and exclude information in support of their framing.[8] This is not to say that gangs are made up of nothing. On the contrary, just as journalists respond to events coming at them and create stories from information at their disposal, prosecutors make gangs from the materials youth produce as they stage their street lives digitally.[9] Let's look at the gradual process by which the first gangs were made in Harlem from their social media content.

Making the Digital Street Crews

Police originally called the groups in question, "crews." The NYPD's Juvenile Justice Division started on social media in 2006, which placed its personnel among the first movers not just in the department but also anywhere in American law enforcement.[10] I became acquainted with the division's social media specialist, a white man with more than twenty years of NYPD experience, when we served together on a government-sponsored youth gangs task force in East Harlem.

Just by being online, police in Juvenile Justice, a tiny office in a precinct on the Upper West Side, saw neighborhood youth in an entirely new way that moved beyond the tactics and technologies already in play. The police were not doing sophisticated technical work; they were just repositioning themselves on the digital street, which opened a frontier to collect information regardless of cooperation, legitimacy, or other limits on the physical street.

The specialist told me his first breakthrough came on the social network site Sconex, where he matched a series of cell phone robberies clustered around the St. Nicholas Houses to posts about the thefts by teenagers who appeared to be bragging in the name of their group. The group name took the familiar street-corner form of three words abbreviated by their initials. The specialist used three-letter tags to link to the digital street. He photographed three-letter tags around crime locations—not bubble letters associated with artists but thin, rough lines—to use as Google search terms. If the three-letter acronym led to a YouTube account, he watched the videos of fights, rapping, and mobbing (youth out in large numbers, calling out their names and neighborhoods, and occasionally going after groups), and read the comments, looking for affiliations and rivalries typically written as three-letter initials followed by the caret symbol ("^") to affirm one's group or the letter "k" to put down or "kill" another group. These were keyboard versions of classic gang graffiti and other expressions of what Desmond Patton named "Internet banging."[11]

When Myspace supplanted Sconex, Juvenile Justice accessed a medium that boy groups used to promote their "street teams," the term circa 2007. To be a street team, from what I gathered from the teens, entailed the creation of a team page on Myspace linked to the profiles of its members and as many girls as possible. These profiles were often left on the default setting of public, and many were still up years after their last updates when I started my study in 2009. The pages brought visitors to the hangouts of the groups and dramatized the excitement there. One such page featured a photograph of a big stoop party as the profile background with the words "140TH & LENOX!!BANG!!" Text entered in one of the biographical fields read, "WE DONT TALK SHIT WE SHOW IT,MONEY,GUNZ, HOS,CLOTHES,HOW YOU LIVIN?"

Part of the appeal of Myspace for users everywhere was the freedom to customize profiles through a technical glitch that rendered code within boxes designed for text entries, an error Myspace embraced rather than patched.[12] This design decision proved consequential for Harlem teens who dragged and dropped photographs (or photo Uniform Resource Locators, or URLs) from another low-security platform, Photobucket, where teens saved images from their phones and digital cameras. The photos that appeared in the "About me" and other boxes on Myspace created a backdoor into Photobucket albums, which I learned by visiting the Myspace pages to find that photographs could be clicked upon.

Each Photobucket album I found contained dozens if not hundreds or more than a thousand photographs. Some of the pictures showed friend groups posed on the stoops, courtyards, and corners of their neighborhood, sometimes modified to name and illustrate its subjects. But they also contained images from sleepovers, birthday parties, school dances, family functions, and other scenes from adolescence. While I assisted at the public defender's office, the entire contents of such albums sometimes came from the prosecutor's office as an evidence dump prior to trial.

Police downloaded photographs from Myspace and Photobucket and focused on group photographs on the street, "RIP photos," as they were commonly called, that memorialized the deceased, and the fraction that depicted youth holding a firearm ("gun photos"). Starting with recent homicides in a given area, police linked the Myspace and Photobucket photos, as well as other digital content, to the people, rivalries, and weapons they thought were involved. Then they did the same for shootings. In 2007, Juvenile Justice first codified a new universe of suspicious groups called the "Manhattan North Youth Crews," starting with a list of ten groups identified by name, street or building location, and local precinct, with a total of 150 presumed members. The youth crews were classified separately from the gang databases maintained by the NYPD gang unit and Department of Correction's Intelligence Unit that were directed toward adult suspects.

By 2009, Juvenile Justice listed twenty-nine youth crews with 1,000 total members deemed responsible for 29 percent (7 of 24) of all gun-related homicides and 30 percent (31 of 102) of all nonfatal shootings in upper Manhattan. The specialist continued to grow the list and link the crews to a greater percentage of the shootings reported in police data, which was key to the internal legitimacy of work that was uprooting the gang division, according to officers I spoke to. At a task force meeting in 2011, the specialist brought an updated list of forty-eight crews that noted alliances with groups in the Bronx. In August 2011, Juvenile Justice expanded into a social media unit with special jurisdiction citywide.

These first moves online set the foundation for a new and fast-evolving approach to gang policing centered on social media and its access possibilities. In an attempted murder case in 2012 for which I obtained court transcripts, one Harlem-based gang detective testified that he maintained a Facebook account to monitor and interact with presumed gang members. An operations order on social media procedures codified in September 2012 specified the necessity of "using an online alias" to access closed networks. In addition to fabricated accounts that depicted local girls and, later, party promoters, public defenders complained that detectives pressed youth they arrested for their login details. Private social media data became accessible formally as well, through a subpoena, court order, or search warrant that typically included a nondisclosure order to prevent the company's notification of the user.

The crew list set in motion hundreds of arrests under Operation Crew Cut, the strategy by the DA's office to prosecute the crews under conspiracy law. Under Operation Crew Cut, the crews became gangs and suspects' social media use became criminal.

Prosecuting the Digital Street Gangs

In 2010, Cyrus Vance Jr. replaced Robert Morgenthau as the DA, becoming Manhattan's first new DA since 1975, when Manhattan saw 648 murders. In Morgenthau's last year, 2009, that figure was down to 59.[13] Vance would focus on the remaining pockets of gun violence, primarily attributed to the Manhattan North Youth Crews.

In September 2010, when I attended as Pastor's guest a Religious Leaders Breakfast hosted by the DA, Vance presented to about twenty black clergy these year-to-date violent crime figures for Manhattan North, shown in Table 5.1.

TABLE 5.1 Year-to-date (YTD) violent crime figures for Manhattan North.

	2010 (YTD)	2009 (YTD)
Murder	34	29
Shooting Victims	146	112
Shooting Incidents	128	87
Robbery	1,649	1,599

Then he broke down these numbers by hot spots. He projected a map with the locations of shootings with victims and shooting incidents (without victims). These crime events, he said, coincided with youth gang activity. His office would be on the offensive against these groups, which he referred to interchangeably as crews or gangs.

Inside the office, the Violent Criminal Enterprises Unit (VCEU) oversaw gang detectives, assistant district attorneys (ADAs), and investigative analysts working toward the Operation Crew Cut prosecutions. The VCEU combined several intelligence and evidentiary sources, especially social media, jail phone calls that were automatically recorded (for which the DA developed a specialized transcription and analysis program called InPho), and debriefings.[14]

In the targeted areas, all arrests of young people were funneled through the larger purpose of gang intelligence vis-à-vis the debriefings. From what I learned from prosecutors, once a suspect was arrested and brought to the precinct, that suspect was first debriefed at the precinct level by the field intelligence officer and often a gang detective and then again debriefed downtown by a prosecutor in the complaint room at the DA's office. Before meeting their attorneys at arraignment, suspects were interviewed by prosecutors under the assumption that they were involved or otherwise knew about the gangs in their area. The debriefings provided face-to-face intelligence to corroborate information gathered online and elsewhere. Prosecutors presented photo sheets to confirm names, aliases, and social media details of presumed gang members and asked about their status to update an internal list of top-ten priority targets in each group. They asked about shootings, for which dossiers of presumptively relevant social media content were eventually prepared. Prosecutors sometimes exchanged leniency in the arrest charge, but more often received information without concession. Between social media, jail calls, and debriefings, prosecutors had much of what they needed in the gang cases, though they also used other traditional sources in more limited fashion, such as confidential informants and court-authorized wiretaps. The combined channels established a nexus of surveillance and evidence collection within and between the neighborhood and jail system. Legal scholar Elizabeth Joh notes that whereas the determination of suspects in the criminal justice system once rested on questioning witnesses and victims of crime and other direct communication with community members, the use of new technologies drastically lowered the bar to surveillance, which was simply ongoing in designated areas.[15]

This informational apparatus fed the end goal of large-scale gang prosecutions and, in the process, unearthed the potential for self-incrimination on social media. The social media that prosecutors brought forth as evidence incriminated their targets and linked them together in advancing and taking credit for violence for which they had physical evidence. They utilized the visibility of association among social media users and between users and content.[16] Prosecutors leveraged the possibility that any content anywhere on the site—even private communication—could be called publication and thus action. Social media use dovetailed perfectly with the conspiracy statutes prosecutors already employed to target gang membership, which New York state law tends not to explicitly criminalize.[17]

Conspiracy refers to an agreement between two or more people to commit a crime that either appears in writing or can be inferred from other facts. All who entered into the agreement can be charged with conspiracy, provided one person has committed an "overt act" that somehow furthers and provides open evidence of the intended crime.[18] Legal scholars Markus Dubber and Tatjana Hörnle note that although conspiracy means an agreement by the letter of the law, in reality it is often applied to a group and its membership.[19] Prosecutors apply conspiracy law to various types of criminal activity, and it can be used to charge a large number of individuals at once, even those not at a crime scene.[20]

129th Street Indictment

The gang indictments started in Harlem in 2011, first on 137th Street near Abyssinian Church in February, and then on the corner of 129th Street and Lenox Avenue in November. Youth on 129th Street grew up with a mobile police tower that first appeared on the corner in November 2006. Police activity was entangled in their social world. But up until late 2011, they had not yet felt the full force of the criminal justice system, nor realized the extent of its surveillance. In November 2011, the DA's office secured an indictment that accused nineteen males between the ages of seventeen and twenty-five of a conspiracy that roughly began in January 2007. The indictment named three allied street gangs that "sought to assert control over the vicinity of West 129th Street, between Lenox and Fifth Avenues, by means of violence." The defendants allegedly conspired "to an agreement to possess firearms . . . for the purpose of protecting their territory" from surrounding "rival street gangs." The two oldest defendants provided "counsel to younger members . . . on the importance and necessity of obtaining firearms" and, under these two men, the seventeen other coconspirators served "to acquire, possess, transport, keep readily available, display, and discharge loaded firearms."

By the charging language, nineteen people were parties to an agreement to criminally possess a weapon. All were charged with conspiracy, a felony. Most defendants were additionally charged with other felonies that included attempted murder, attempted assault, and criminal weapon possession. In furtherance of the conspiracy charge, the prosecution enumerated seventy-one overt acts. Thirty-three referred to activity in person, thirty related to behavior with guns or ammunition—the possession, display, retrieval, sale, transport, handling, or discharge of a firearm. The other three referred to a confrontation with a police officer, a visit to Rikers Island, and a conversation about firearms.

Thirty-eight acts referred to communication or other activity through technology. Twenty-two acts were on social media: one video published on Myspace and twenty-one photographs that appeared on either Myspace or Photobucket. Sixteen acts were recorded phone calls, typically on lines from the Rikers Island jail facilities.

Under New York state law, the DA must present its case to a grand jury before felony charges can be brought. The grand jury must find reasonable cause to believe that the defendants committed the crimes alleged by the prosecution. As allegations, the burden of proof falls below the trial threshold of proof beyond a reasonable doubt. By New York statute, grand jury proceedings are closed to the public and conducted by the prosecutors. After prosecutors have presented evidence and advised the grand jury on the law, the grand jury votes. If a majority of the twenty-three grand jurors votes to indict on felony charges, an indictment is filed and the DA's office prosecutes on those charges. In the 129th Street case, a grand jury indeed returned an indictment, and arrest and search warrants were issued and executed.

The roundup started in the early morning hours on a Thursday. Some of the nineteen defendants were pulled out of bed or taken from school. Others turned themselves in or were already serving time for another case. Online and offline, the teens from 129th

Street sorted out what was happening, who had been arrested, and who might be next. On Facebook, Tiana, after her boyfriend was arrested, wrote "FREE MY Husband & My Bros" and then "can't stop crying." Some wrote cautiously. When one teen asked, "Who got snapped [arrested]," the response was "I GOT 2 TLK TO U IN PERSON."

The next day the DA called a press conference. Guns obtained during the investigation were displayed, and it was announced that the FBI had been involved. "We believe we have dismantled one of Central Harlem's most violent and destructive criminal street gangs," the DA said. The press release repeated the information and included the names, birthdates, and charges of each defendant. The news media covered the arraignments and some defendants were photographed in court. In the afternoon, I found JayVon and three others a few blocks away from the four news vans parked on 129th Street. JayVon stood with me for a minute as I pulled up the press release on my phone. I told him that I was concerned I might see his name. Then I wondered aloud why he was not in the indictment. "I don't know," he replied. "I'm scared."

Questions about the indictment quickly emerged among the teens and the adults in their lives. The acts repeatedly referenced "unindicted coconspirators." Why were some but not others indicted? The conspiracy charge itself raised eyebrows. How could the prosecution prove that nineteen people—not to mention unnamed others—had all agreed to possess a weapon? Was it the same gun or several? What would such an agreement even look like? Was it legal to charge defendants as adults in reference to "overt acts" committed while they were minors? Some of the overt acts were crimes already adjudicated. How could these come back? By November 2011, the teens had long stopped using Myspace and Photobucket. One photograph dated back almost five years. Was the evidence still relevant?

133

But there was also a sense that the indictment had to be coming. The police tower was only the most obvious sign. The violence had gone on for years. There was a major public safety problem. Conflict between the 129th Street group and its rivals accounted for sixteen shootings in 2011 alone, according to police. Despite our best efforts, Pastor and the other outreach workers, myself included, had been unable to bring about a lasting ceasefire. The violence was intractable even to the teens and young adults who were focused on college and other parts of their lives. After fourteen young persons from 137th Street were indicted, the DA publicly called this measure "an important step in our office's deliberate, focused strategy to work with the NYPD to attack gang violence neighborhood by neighborhood." He said, "We anticipate other gang takedowns in the future." Between the first and second indictments, Pastor had taken to warning youth of a wave of indictments and arrest warrants in the hopes of discouraging violence. The DA and law enforcement responded to the violence on 129th Street by incapacitating persons in three cohorts that they believed controlled the guns and the shooting. Only one person's name came as a total shock to Pastor, Coach, and others closely following the violence.

On the Wednesday after the indictment, NYPD's Community Affairs Bureau, under which the Juvenile Justice Division was nested, hosted a community forum on the basketball court inside the Mormon Church to address the indictment. About 130 people attended. The commanding officer of the local precinct began the evening by giving out his cell phone number. "I'm a very big fan of texting," he said, and encouraged community members to tell him what was "going on." He asked residents to put on their "thinking caps" in relation to youth on the streets. Then he turned the meeting over to the social media specialist.

Referencing the maps and lists of Manhattan North Youth Crews by the entrance, the specialist described a world of street-corner groups in conflict across Harlem. "You will not hear Bloods, you will not hear Crips or Latin Kings." He instead described the two- and three-letter acronyms for "territorial groups" that fight on the basis of "you live there, I live here." Holding printouts of "RIP photos" of recent homicide victims, the specialist said, "We have lost too many kids to this nonsense. Anybody have any idea where I got these from? You can get them, too—right on the Internet." He paused, then added, "We need to get in the game. I've laid it all out for you: I've given you a simple list." He told the room that a new shooting in connection with the rivalry centered on 129th Street had taken place the day before: A fifteen-year-old had shot a sixteen-year-old. "Does anybody know what the original beefs are with these groups? Anybody? No, they [the kids involved] don't. They absolutely don't."

An older woman in the audience asked how many kids were involved in such neighborhood beefs: "Fifty thousand? One hundred thousand?" The specialist responded, "Miss, we're not talking anywhere near that. When you talk about kids who run around in these crews, somewhere around 1,500 in the borough of Manhattan."

Fifteen hundred was a small number of kids in Manhattan. This represented a focused target population for law enforcement that contrasted with stop-and-frisk tactics and other facets of criminal justice understood to cast a wide net. The estimate stood for about 1 percent of the roughly 150,000 persons entered over time into the California database CalGang.[21]

At the forum, and outside this meeting, community members expressed diverse perspectives on the indictment. Some felt that the surveillance could have been used to help the kids rather than lock them up. These were kids publicly "struggling," according to one resident. But others believed the authorities had gotten the bad apples and expected the neighborhood to become safer.

The digital turn in youth operations placed police further at the forefront of intervention, which was not the right role for police. The social media specialist asked for partners at this event and at countless others. He offered the attendees at the forum a map and list of crews with the instruction to follow their kids online, as he did at task force meetings, youth and community development summits, community boards, and schools. He wanted to see more parents, mentors, service providers, and other concerned adults online, and elsewhere, with at-risk youth. Police could then fall back to what the specialist called the "last line of defense," for which they were better suited.

During the bail hearings I observed the next day in the courthouse, I thought about what the police and prosecutors had seen in the photographs referred to in the indictment. Cases were heard throughout the day before the judge. Dozens of friends and family members came and went. Because all of the defendants were in custody, each approached from "the bullpen" behind the judge. Court officers brought out one eighteen-year-old being held in custody as the ADA read his charges: two counts of criminal possession of a weapon and one count of conspiracy.

When the teen's mother got upset, two girls, close friends of the defendant, walked over and sat on either side of her. They rubbed her back. "Are you okay?" one asked. The reactions and movement of the young people in attendance appeared to agitate the judge: "This isn't a school day?" he asked sarcastically.

The ADA recommended bail at $75,000 cash, an amount the prosecutor argued was consistent with the facts of the case and the risk the defendant posed to the community. The prosecutor summarized the defendant and his case. The teen was apprehended, along with two others, with a loaded handgun, he said, in reference to an arrest about eleven months earlier. According to the prosecutor, he belonged to a gang and he was like other gang members "in Harlem who feel the need to post photographs of themselves holding weapons." When the judge asked if the photographed object was a "real weapon," the prosecutor argued that, although it might not be, the guns recovered in connection with the conspiracy were "real." He added that even with a fake gun, "there are real consequences of pulling it on people." I heard from a codefendant that the object in the photo was a BB gun, and from the prosecutor's response, this sounded possible. But the prosecutor did not bring up the photograph to corroborate the gun charge. Instead, he used it to establish that the eighteen-year-old defendant was at present a threat for committing additional offenses.

The defense attorney countered that the photograph was almost three years old and that his client had a "bright future" and was "arrested while in school." In contrast to the prosecutor, the defender called on the other side of the code-switching dynamic. He recommended that his client be released on his own recognizance. The two sides went back and forth with the judge, who ultimately took issue with the fact that the defendant had previously been shot but had not cooperated. The judge remanded the accused and set bail at $50,000 bond or $21,000 cash, an amount the defendant's family was unprepared to pay. The defendant was remanded until his next court date.

For other defendants called, the photos proved less persuasive to the judge as he took other facts of the case into consideration. The indictment charged Dorsey, aged twenty, with two counts of conspiracy and named him in five overt acts. One alleged that he possessed a loaded and inoperable semiautomatic gun on a date in 2008. During Dorsey's bail hearing, the ADA recommended

$50,000 bail and told the judge about the gun possession, noting that it was a "YO," which meant Dorsey had received a youthful offender adjudication. The ADA also called Dorsey "a gang leader." Countering, Dorsey's defense attorney explained that the YO adjudication included an offer to earn probation because the defendant had left college in New Jersey to work construction and other jobs in New York. He had completed probation a month earlier and had returned to school, only to be called back to turn himself in on the conspiracy charge. In addition to the previously closed gun case, which had been sealed by the terms of the YO, Dorsey was named in four other overt acts, all for images posted before he was arrested with the gun at age seventeen. Three of the four images were of Dorsey with other defendants. Each of the three photos included text with their nicknames and a reference to their group name. In one photograph, the text also contained slang about guns. In another, the text included threatening language directed toward a rival group. The last of the four images contained no people. It was a graphic of the group's initials in big letters surrounded by nicknames of eight defendants and others unindicted.

Dorsey's case underscored the associative aspect of social media use and the fact that social media users relinquish some control of their self-image to the people in their networks. Dorsey was alleged to have posted only one of the four photographs; the three others were attributed to another defendant, whose own media use exposed Dorsey.[22]

Once the defense attorney made clear that the photos predated the gun conviction, the ADA's case was weakened. The prosecutor countered that his office had information implicating Dorsey in "planning meetings" related to gang activity. The judge asked if these meetings took place while the defendant was in college, to which the prosecutor responded, "I don't know." The judge decided, "based on the record here," to release Dorsey until his next court date in February. "Praise God," I heard his mother say. Outside the courtroom, the three of us discussed his intention to return to college, which he did. At his next court date, however, Dorsey lost his traction in the case. The ADA said that Dorsey had been arrested in New Jersey in January on another matter related to a fight. The judge remanded Dorsey. Now the digital traces that tied Dorsey to the conspiracy were sticking.

For youth in Harlem, the focus on the crews centered police and prosecutors on an entrenched public safety threat. But it also put the pressure of the criminal justice system on all youth within this vicinity, especially those with associations to the crews that were visible and recoverable on social media. Photographs of behavior or relationships that were outdated but easily located online potentially prompted authorities to overreach. Many in the neighborhood were stunned to learn that a seventeen-year-old named Drop was indicted—his was the name that stood out first to community members. Whereas others in the indictment attended school or worked, they had not taken as many steps as Drop to distance themselves from the social life of the street.

Between November 2009 and November 2011, not once did I see or hear of Drop involved in any violence. But he was charged in the indictment with the baseline conspiracy charge through two acts. One referred to possession of a loaded handgun in July 2009, for which Drop was arrested at age fourteen, after he had run from police and dropped a plastic bag containing a gun. "As soon as I got into the precinct I told on myself," said Drop when he recalled the event years later. Drop pled guilty and received a YO and five years' probation. After his gun case, Drop increasingly oriented his schedule toward basketball, school, his job as a counselor at a HCZ program, and staying home. Outside of basketball games on Thursday nights, I almost never saw Drop.

When I did, he reminded me that he was "in training" for his basketball career. He still loved his friends dearly, but he had created distance.

Along with the adjudicated gun case, the second act referred to a photograph posted by a codefendant on Myspace in March 2010. It depicted Drop with three other indicted "conspirators" and "other individuals." Drop told me that he made a "west-side" hand gesture in that photograph, although that detail was unspecified in the indictment document. No text was added to the image. This was a simple group photo.

On the basis of his appearance with the others in a photograph, Drop, at seventeen, was arrested and charged with conspiracy. The court-appointed lawyer whom he met at his arraignment failed to prevent the press from taking his photograph, which subsequently appeared in news coverage already shaped by a press release from the DA's office.

In February 2012, with a new lawyer, Drop entered a guilty plea with the understanding that the court was giving him a chance to supersede his felony with a disorderly conduct violation. In April 2013, after four court dates that established that Drop was in college and had not been arrested again, Drop was allowed to withdraw his original guilty plea to plead guilty to disorderly conduct.

For Drop, an old photograph with his peers that he did not post was the sole evidence used to generate a new felony charge from a previously adjourned juvenile case. Drop's case raised questions about the leverage these photographs afforded prosecutors and the admissibility of online content. With Drop's cohort as their training data, prosecutors were learning to build gang cases through social media. I want to look more closely at what prosecutors did with these twenty-one photographs from Myspace and Photobucket, low-security sites being used by teenagers who were originally naïve to the scope of the authorities. To understand how gangs get produced on the digital street, we need to examine the prosecution's use of social media as criminal evidence and the gradual uncovering of its forensic potential.

Social Media Evidence

Photographs

The prosecution used three types of photographs in the 129th Street indictment: photos that depicted a defendant holding a weapon (four such "gun photos"); photos of defendants with text added (fourteen, including one graphic of names but not people); and plain group photos, without a weapon shown or the addition of any text (three).

Prosecutors employed the photos in at least five ways. First, the photos served as overt acts because they were *posted*. Posting was an action attributable to a defendant, who, in the language of the indictment, "caused or permitted" the photograph "to be posted." Each upload was an act said to further the alleged conspiracy. The productive aspect of social media was a resource to prosecutors.

Second, the action of the photo post allowed the prosecution to introduce new charges against defendants with previously adjudicated cases, including "sealed" juvenile cases. By causing or permitting a photograph to be posted, defendants had allegedly acted to further a conspiracy of which their earlier crimes were now a part. Thus past crimes for which the defendants had been punished were retroactively redefined as aspects of a conspiracy—a new crime—on the basis of photographs they or an alleged coconspirator posted.

Third, the photos tied the defendants together. Through appearances in the photos or added text, the photos provided connections between the codefendants and across age-graded groups defined in the document as "three allied Central Harlem street gangs." The transmission of the street code could be traced back through photographs that preserved cross-cohort association.

Fourth, the group names added to the photos implied that the defendants had self-identified as gang members. According to the prosecution, the three group names written on the photographs articulated the conspiracy or criminal enterprise with which the defendants identified.

Fifth, the photos tied the defendants to particular presentations of self. In other words, out of all the defendants' photos, thousands combined across each of their albums, the prosecution selected only twenty-one images seen as consistent with the case.

Starting with these images, prosecutors were learning to criminalize social media use. In photographs, they found the connective tissue to link defendants to each other and to new and old crimes. But they had only begun to unearth the forensic potential of the digital street. There were significant questions surrounding the photographic evidence that the defense attorneys either challenged or could have if given greater opportunities in the criminal process, a point to which I return. What did co-appearance in a photograph really mean? How did these photos show that nineteen defendants conspired to criminally possess a weapon? The timing of the photo uploads and specific shooting incidents generally lacked coincidence. If the defendants weren't apprehended with the guns depicted in the photos, what connection was being drawn? The DA's office appeared to recognize the limitations of photographic evidence and developed new and more compelling forms of digital evidence in the next indictments.

Getting to the Inbox

The nineteen-defendant indictment on 129th Street was the second in a series of gang indictments in Harlem that focused on gun violence and drew on social media and conspiracy law. The first such indictment charged fourteen persons in February 2011. Five subsequent indictments together charged another 165 defendants. From February 2011 to June 2014, the DA charged a total of 198 defendants in seven different indictments.

The prosecution alleged a total of 1,281 overt acts in the seven indictments combined. Of these acts, 616—48 percent—referred to social media use. The first indictment featured eight Myspace or Photobucket photographs. In five of these photos the defendants simply appeared together; no weapon was depicted or text added. As 8 out of the 129 overt acts of conspiracy, social media activities played a small part: 6 percent of the evidence. By contrast, social media activity comprised about 60 percent of the evidence in each of the last two indictments: photos and videos, status updates, and, most of all, messages and conversations on Facebook. Social media moved to the center of the gang indictment at the same time as the number of defendants increased and the surveillance penetrated the inbox. Over the course of the indictments, prosecutors started with voluntary disclosures within the defendants' network (e.g., a posted photograph) and progressed toward private communication between two people, which meant the use of warrants or other court authorization or else access to a login from a suspect in custody or a confidential informant.

The evidence evolved significantly between 2007 and 2014, the time frame for the overt acts cited across the seven indictments. Along with the tactics of the prosecution, the popular brands and features of social media changed. Photographs were constant across all years. In 2010, tweets and Facebook status updates first appeared, along with inbox communication; that is, direct messages. From 2011 to 2014, surveillance centered overwhelmingly on Facebook: photos, videos, status updates, and inbox messages or conversations. Inbox communication quickly ascended to the most commonly cited evidence. Of the 616 social media acts, 421 referred to a Facebook message or conversation.[23]

Prosecutors advanced toward written communication, moving beyond associations through photographs to typed admissions of guilt. In tweets and status updates, the prosecution had time-stamped statements they could link to specific shootings and other gun crimes. Inbox communication on Twitter and Facebook provided particularly detailed statements from one-to-one interactions presumed to be private and evidence that codefendants interacted over time about presumptive crimes, contact more pointed than posing together for a photograph. Prosecutors connected the dots between what seemed like the backstage preparation of crime and its actual commission, moving between both digital and physical locations, and private and public (or semipublic) spaces on social media. For instance, regarding three overt acts in one of the indictments filed in April 2013, the prosecution alleged that a defendant (a) participated in a shooting, (b) discussed "the price of a firearm, whether the seller had ammunition for the firearm" and other details in Twitter messages four days before the shooting, and (c) posted a tweet the day of the shooting with the words 'SHOTS FIRED LML [laughing mad loud] TH[a]T THEM [the name of his crew] BOYS JU [you] HE[a]RD.' The prosecution coupled events on the physical and digital streets more closely.

The exclusive selection of social media content that reinforced street-based behavior and identities made strategic sense for two reasons. First, in the legal community, explained a supervising attorney at the public defender's office, "We have a rule, basically, if you say something essentially inculpatory about yourself—you know, 'I killed somebody,' 'I beat somebody up,'—that's admitted as an admission [of guilt]. If you say, 'I didn't kill anybody,' that's considered self-serving and not gonna be admitted." Street talk was incriminating. Second, talk on social media served the prosecution as self-incrimination rather than admissions coerced by law enforcement. Direct quotations came not from police paperwork but from the accounts of the defendants, which allowed the prosecutors to distance themselves from the evidence, as if to let it speak for itself.

The prosecutors learned to more fully harness social media to define and prosecute youth gangs. I was told by a prosecutor that they shifted away from viewing photos as overt acts to instead using them for backstage intelligence tools, for instance, to identify suspects present at a party or a coat worn in a grainy surveillance video. Or they gleaned the metadata from photographs to identify when and where they were taken and the serial numbers of cell phones to place suspects at crimes.

Language played a larger role in the later indictments. Prosecutors argued that the defendants communicated as a gang with a distinctive system of code words and phrases that concealed references to firearms, rival gang members, and gang activities. The prosecution compiled and presented a list of slang in the conspiracy narrative as a specialized gang vernacular. By presenting quotes in which defendants communicated in this vernacular, the prosecution was able to present the youth as gang members. That the quotes selected also showed unconventional spellings and grammar also might have drawn the grand jurors' attention to the language rather than the crime itself—language that might cast the defendants as less credible.

Editorial Control

As the indictments expanded across Harlem, community members and defense attorneys expressed real concerns. The supervising public defender felt social media communication was being treated as self-evident. In other words, writing something down made it objective. In the courtroom, social media was "over-weighted":

> Teenagers talk shit . . . . If you eavesdropped on any corner in 1970 . . . [you'd hear] the same stuff: you know, "I get my own. I'm the baddest this. I do that." But nobody had it recorded. Now, they type it down, it stays up forever, and some DA gets to say . . . "You're not violent? Well, why are you saying [online] you can beat everybody's ass?" [Because they can't say] I'm sixteen and I don't have anything, I don't work anywhere, I'm flunking out of school, and this is the way I feel better."

The defender echoed Nissenbaum's argument that information lifted from its original location lost its local meaning in its reassignment for a new context. Had tough talk and other posture been redefined as intent and admission when transferred from the neighborhood to the courtroom?

According to surveillance scholar Samuel Nunn, law enforcement interprets communication on social media in terms of probable cause for an arrest or as evidence that a crime was committed.[24] If, as Nunn notes, the goal of surveillance is the production of "incriminating transcripts," this interpretative framework holds potential for overcriminalization. Patton emphasizes that black teens in urban areas use culturally nuanced language and modes of expression on social media that can be difficult to understand for outsiders. Even gang-involved black and Latino young men (insiders) may find it hard to determine the degree to which a tweet is threatening.[25] These points challenge the capacity of police and prosecutors to reliably interpret peer-directed communication from a population they may have almost no contact with offline, apart from the context of criminal justice. Such disconnect raises questions about the defendants and evidence in the indictments.

At the same time, the transition to the inbox enabled detectives and prosecutors to access communication presumably about the transactions and logistics of gun crime, content directed and probably more specific than posts to an entire following. Social media was also one key input in a much larger intelligence-gathering operation carried forth over years. Police and prosecutors believed that more sources of intelligence allowed them to do a better job: The more extensive and intrusive the investigation and surveillance, the more just the outcomes, a both reasonable and disturbing possibility.

Ultimately, the prosecutors controlled the legal interpretation of the communication they cited. They exercised editorial control. The prosecution decided which content to include and exclude; where to start and end quotes; and when and how to summarize the defendants' communication. Editorial control extended to the choice of defendants. Social media provided not only an input but also an output of prosecutorial discretion. As I learned in my conversations with prosecutors, the meaning ADAs attributed to the defendants' communication reflected more than just criminal intent; it reflected organizational choices. In each indictment area, prosecutors were monitoring more suspects than those they ultimately named. The indictments were constructed by taking into account a wide range of related cases. The indictments included defendants who were considered top-ten priorities— those seen to be the drivers of violence—and individuals they had for a specific role in a specific crime. But they also included lower-level suspects to potentially "flip" on priority suspects in the absence of other cooperation leverage, meaning certain excluded suspects had already cooperated. Some such individuals were referenced in the overt acts as "unindicted coconspirators." The choice to include or exclude communication served broader prosecutorial aims and tactics in each hot spot.

Leverage

Social media provided extraordinary leverage for the prosecution. The seven indictments generated convictions for 190 of the 198 defendants in total. This is an astounding figure, even as it refers to a conviction on any charge. Part of this leverage came down to a system that privileged the discretion of prosecutors and grand jurors. Only 12 of the 198 defendants took their cases to trial. The court actors involved treated plea-bargaining as a caseload necessity. At the Religious Leaders Breakfast, the district attorney estimated that his office processed 110,000 cases each year, among 535 assistant prosecutors. Trials were simply not possible very often. In the 129th Street indictment, the judge felt the same way, repeatedly discouraging the need for a trial. At bail continuation hearings, at the end of February 2012, the judge finalized a trial date he clearly did not want to see happen: "If anybody really thinks a trial is in their real interest then that's really the date if we're going to do it."

Meanwhile, the defense attorneys complained that, four months in, they still had not received the prosecution's "discovery," the evidence opposing lawyers were expected to share with one another before trial. Still, most of the defense attorneys, also with stacked caseloads, motivated their clients to plead guilty to lesser charges. Of the nineteen defendants in the 129th Street case, three sat trial in May 2012.

The three defendants from 129th Street fared relatively well at trial. One was acquitted of all charges. The other two were cleared of more serious charges and convicted on only the lowest charge against each of them, the baseline conspiracy charge against all defendants (a class E felony). Another nine defendants charged in three other indictments also took their cases to trial. They fared worse than the 129th Street group: Each was convicted on multiple charges, including at least one felony above class E. This might have meant that the evidence was stronger than what the prosecution had in the case against the 129th Street group. The prosecution certainly improved upon its evidence over the course of the indictments. But there were far too many variables to draw such a conclusion. The bigger point, however, is that only twelve defendants went to trial, period. One hundred and eighty-six defendants pled out, including all sixty-two defendants in three indictments for East Harlem in April 2013. Barely any cases were affected by the examination of the evidence at trial. The meaning of the content was barely explored.

The critical stage for all defendants proved to be the grand jury: the accusation phase. Each grand jury heard the prosecution's evidence in the absence of a judge or defense attorney. For grand jury proceedings, prosecutors may include only the evidence they think they need to return an indictment under the lower proof threshold of reasonable cause and with the knowledge of low vetting of evidence compared at trial (although grand jurors can ask questions and request witnesses). Once the defendants were arraigned, some defenders complained that the prosecution held its evidence close to the chest. Unlike in other counties with policies of "open file" discovery or "discovery by stipulation," in

Manhattan (New York County), discovery is effectively pinned to trial. Yet trials are rare. In the indictment cases, the evidence from social media had such force because, like all evidence, it was hard for defense attorneys to poke holes in what they never had. In this system, prosecutors avoided potential challenges to the strength or admissibility of their evidence.[26]

Controlling the Digital Street

Suppression

By controlling their suspects' digital communication and its legal interpretation, police and prosecutors controlled the physical streets to a large degree. The focus on the digital street crews and the use of indictments produced clear gains in public safety, at least in the short term. This suppression effect implied the social media data the prosecution collected, edited, and leveraged incapacitated the primary players, deterred activity, or both. The district attorney pointed to major declines in gun violence in East Harlem and West Harlem in the first year following each of the two indictments.

In an April 2014 press release, about a year after the indictments in East Harlem, the DA noted: "Before the takedown of these three gangs, during the period from October 2009 to April, 3, 2013, there were 7 homicides, 46-non-fatal shootings, and 17 shots fired in the 23rd Police Precinct in East Harlem. Since the takedown of these three gangs, there have been two homicides, three non-fatal shootings, and zero shots fired in this same area."[27]

The office took credit for a precipitous decline in violence in West Harlem also: "According to statistics compiled by my Office's Crime Strategies Unit, in the three-and-a-half years preceding the

June 2014 gang indictments, there were 10 homicide victims, 46 non-fatal shooting victims, and 27 confirmed incidents of shots being fired. Fast-forward a year later, and there were 2 non-fatal shooting victims, 8 incidents of shots being fired, and one homicide victim."[28]

Murders in Manhattan dropped under DA Vance. There were seventy in 2010, his first year, and seventy-one in 2011, the year the gang indictments began, just above the last figure under Morgenthau (fifty-nine murders). In 2012, there were sixty-three; the total fell to thirty-nine in 2013 and thirty-seven in 2014. During a talk at the Association for a Better New York in 2014, Vance concluded that his approach to the youth crews had worked, so much so that it was time to move on to other crime. "With murder rates at historic lows, our agencies are now walking in lock-step to apply proactive strategies to target persistent crimes—now no longer violence but . . . identity theft, grand larceny, narcotics, and domestic violence. So we're going to take the strategies we've used to effectively reduce violence in Manhattan and we're now going to apply them, in collaboration with the NYPD, on other areas."[29]

The effect of law enforcement was felt around 129th Street. The authorities had suppressed activity online and offline in the first months following the indictment. "Everybody's still shaky," Tiana said, in December. "It's quiet, real quiet, real slow outside. It's boring." I observed as much. Some of the teens from 129th Street went offline, at least temporarily. Some deactivated or even deleted Facebook pages, as Tiana did for her boyfriend. I asked Taye in December 2011, "Do you feel like the cops are watching your Facebook?" He said, "Yeah, they are, everybody Facebook." I asked if everybody understood that. "That's why people deactivate they pages," he responded. Old photos came down in some cases. For fear they might become "conspiracy pictures," Slinky, at his mother's request, deleted photos that depicted "any hand signs" or showed Slinky in large groups. Law enforcement had pushed the teens off Facebook, or at least forced certain changes in online communication.

Whereas the teens first learned to code switch to hide street life from their family members, they were now increasingly concerned with police. The teens and young adults on 129th Street and elsewhere in Harlem learned to censor themselves for fear of self-incrimination or the incrimination of their friends. I observed this shift when I drove Akil, JayVon, and Isaiah, three friends from the corner of 129th Street, to Tom's Diner for lunch on a sunny afternoon in March 2012. In the car, Akil, sitting up front, turned to JayVon and Isaiah in the backseat.

> "Yo," Akil said, getting their attention. "A lot of y'all niggas be hot on Facebook. I seen Talib talking about he got the chase from the boys [cops] and he tagged, like, everybody else that was there."
>
> "Nah, he ain't tag me, 'cause I wasn't there," JayVon replied.
>
> "Y'all niggas is wild."
>
> "I don't care," JayVon said, defensively.
>
> "I'm just saying in general."
>
> "I know that. I know what you talking about. The stuff I be writing, I be saying it from [song] verses."
>
> "If y'all niggas ain't realize, most of these niggas that's from the block is in jail it's because of the Internet."
>
> "Yeah, I know that."

Akil listed his brother and four others included in the indictment who by that point had "copped out"—pled guilty.

> Akil finished his point: "You gotta relax on that Internet."

By telling JayVon and Isaiah to "relax" because they were "hot on Facebook," Akil adapted a lesson from the physical street. In Skid Row, Los Angeles, urban scholar Forrest Stuart examined strategies of "cooling off the block" by people under surveillance to deflect police suspicion.[30] "You hot" served a similar function on the digital street. Youth warned or chastised each other for being "hot" in the moment before talk online veered toward incrimination. In response to Akil, JayVon said that he knew to use lyrics to encode his posts, a practice teens sometimes used when making threats or after incidents of actual violence as a way to take credit without specifics. But the indictments that followed 129th Street included rap lyrics posted by defendants, raising doubt about that strategy. Eventually, even attempts to cool the digital street were criminalized within the conspiracy as an overt act "to discourage members and associates from cooperating with law enforcement." A defendant in one of the West Harlem indictments was said to have posted a Facebook message that instructed another defendant "to take down a Facebook post because it was 'HOT'" and would be used to label the group as a gang.

The teenagers were restricting their content in response to each new form of criminal evidence. By the time teens transitioned to Facebook in early 2011, gun photos were exceedingly rare. When they appeared, it was a dare to police, especially after news coverage of the February 2011 indictment called attention to such images uploaded by one teenage defendant in 2009. In case of any lingering doubt, Tiana posted in January 2012: "Message to y'all dickheads: STOP POSTING PICS WITH GUNS & YAPPING ABOUT GUN PLAY or in a year or so you would be in jail. Atleast 3 of your [Facebook] friends that you don't know are the FEDS."

The cat-and-mouse game with police pushed youth into their inboxes, where detectives and prosecutors eventually swooped. In July 2012, during a workshop at the municipal summer job program, the social media specialist told roughly 300 young people from 129th Street and neighborhoods throughout Harlem, "You better make sure your Facebook pages are clean." Bringing up Myspace, he asked, "How many of you have cleaned it up before you forgot the password?" Old content might "bite you" when applying for a job or taking the civil service exam, he said. The specialist was forthcoming: "Guess what? The police are monitoring Facebook . . . with a whole unit dedicated to [this work]," a reference to the social media unit.

Apart from the shooting the day before the community forum, 129th Street was without any gun violence until February 2012. The antagonism then flared up again around Andre, the teen from Lincoln Houses whose "campaign for respect" I discussed in the code-switching chapter. Conflict came to a head over the summer with a shooting in St. Nicholas that left one dead and wounded three others. Police responded with a barricade of 129th Street and eventually created within the enclosure a "play street" that was closed to cars during the day for sports and recreation (and occasionally for kids and cops to play together). In August, Coach said, "Things have been quiet," referring to relations between 129th Street and the St. Lincoln group. He added that it had "nothing to do with us," meaning the outreach workers. He pointed to "the older guys" who sold drugs around 129th Street and the Lincoln Houses, respectively, having facilitated a peace treaty. In addition to the indictment on 129th Street, an indictment centered on the sale of narcotics inside the Lincoln Houses came down in May 2012. Between the peace treaty, the indictments, and the outreach efforts Coach questioned, this was the broadest set of intervening actions yet. Over the next months and then years, the violence subsided. Shootings between the rival groups was down to a single-digit number in 2013 and 2014, combined. Said Shawn, of the thirteen- and fourteen-year-old boys from 129th Street, they are afraid of "being locked up for what they do on the streets or what they say on Facebook."

The indictments had a disciplining effect on youth inside the hot-spot areas as they perceived themselves the subjects of surveillance that extended from their neighborhood to social media accounts.

Collateral Costs

The 129th Street indictment in conjunction with other important factors appeared to break or at least stall a cycle of reciprocal violence. In the years after the indictment, the young men appreciated that travel in public space became easier and the greater probability that their younger relatives would not go through the traumatic violence they had.

But the indictments came with serious costs for those locked up in an exceedingly violent jail and prison system. On the streets, the teens experienced awful violence at the hands of each other as well as of law enforcement. The teens described numerous police brutalities, from being punched in the face while handcuffed in the back of a police vehicle to getting picked up only to be dropped off where their rivals were. Now the incarcerated faced the violence of fellow inmates and correction officers, especially inside Rikers Island, where Department of Health and Mental Hygiene logs showed nearly 5,900 incidents of traumatic injuries sustained by inmates between July 2010 and June 2012.[31] After the dangerous conditions of incarceration, young persons convicted of a felony would return home with a record that spelled

155

almost certain discrimination in employment, housing, and other parts of their lives.[32]

The digital turn to the crews meant those indicted were the sacrificial lambs in what the DA called "neighborhood transformation." Worse, the DA's office identified and prosecuted higher-priority offenders most responsible for gun violence but went ahead and also indicted lower-priority targets with the intention to "flip" them. Some community members expressed their belief that prosecutors overreached, which, as in Drop's case, worked against the forward momentum of young men aging out of violence. Family members of multiple defendants in the West Harlem indictments told a local journalist that evidence from social media was used to rehash adjudicated cases for crimes committed as minors.[33]

Prosecutors retained near-total editorial control of the meaning of the content they captured. That discretion proved horrifying when used against the wrong person. About five months after the 129th Street indictment, Akil, Dorsey's nineteen-year-old younger brother, was arrested at his girlfriend's house. In April 2012, he was charged with two counts of attempted murder in connection with the shooting of two teens in front of the St. Nicholas Houses, based largely on a single eyewitness. At his arraignment, the prosecutor used his likes on Facebook to characterize him as a gang member from 129th Street. The judge denied bail. Adamant about his innocence, Akil expected to be exonerated shortly. But the case dragged on. Offering twenty years, the prosecutor urged him to take a plea, pointing to his co-appearances in Facebook photos and contacts on his iPhone as indicative of gang involvement. For various reasons the case was repeatedly adjourned and Akil spent roughly nineteen months in Rikers Island. In November

2013, the judge—the second to preside over the case after the first judge retired—granted bail. Four months later, the judge dismissed his case on the lack of a speedy trial or a "30.30." Akil was jailed for almost two years.

How the Law Works on the Digital Street

The use of the digital street to define and prosecute youth crews as gang conspiracies emerged as a signature practice on the physical street lost legitimacy. In New York City, after stop-and-frisk policing peaked in 2011 with reported stops at an all-time high of 685,724 citywide, soon-to-be Mayor Bill de Blasio and fellow mayoral candidates in the 2013 election, city councilmen Brad Lander and Jumaane D. Williams, and other politicians, as well as national civil rights leaders, rallied against its overuse in mostly black and Latino neighborhoods. Stops dropped precipitously to 45,787 in 2014 after the deployment of stop-and-frisk was found unconstitutional in 2013.[34] The same politicians critical of stop-and-frisk supported the refocusing of antiviolence efforts on youth crews that were identifiable or identifying themselves online.[35]

The digital street presented an opportunity to police the same youth in the same neighborhoods, and specifically in neighborhood hot spots, without the publicity and interactional tension of stops on the physical street. From the perspective of violence reduction, Operation Crew Cut worked, if only in the short term. Shooting totals declined in the targeted areas. In the process, social media were turned into forensic spaces utilized by law enforcement. Gangs were made through the editorial control of suspects' content with their authorship used against them as prosecutors' ascribed meanings under conspiracy law. This was a new location and exercise of police and prosecutorial authority and discretion. Those indicted were accountable to any information from anytime, anywhere, on their social media accounts or the accounts of others. For this reason code-switching strategies shifted from impression management within the community to cooling police presence. Contrary to their more successful efforts with adults in informal roles, the teens were largely unable to keep police at bay and saw even efforts to thwart their own surveillance criminalized in the indictments.

The shift onto the digital street brought up other socio-legal issues. We saw in Drop's case the decoupling of the digital and physical streets. In the two years leading up to the 129th indictment, one wouldn't find Drop involved in street life, unless he was searched online where his footprints were recoverable. This decoupling effect potentially worked against aging of violence and gang involvement, which research finds to be a common trajectory.[36]

Forms of association in the neighborhood, including what David Harding called "cross-cohort socialization," that were traceable online were subject to criminalization.[37] Social media data that tied together young persons in three age-graded groups on 129th Street enabled felony conspiracy charges.

Whereas some teens are involved in street violence, most teens are around this activity only because they share neighborhood space with conflict-involved peers. Assuming social media users become "hot" as they discuss neighborhood violence, their communication exposes themselves and their peers to the authorities. This creates a situation in which peers facilitate the criminalization of each other. Such an arrangement cuts through the interpersonal life of a community and stands to undermine trust, especially between girls and boys, given the central position of girls in neighborhood networks. The use of social media by police, including by means of posing as neighborhood girls and getting to the inbox, also stands to further strain community trust in law enforcement. At the same time, police and prosecutors work and achieve public safety gains where they are not seen as legitimate and in the absence of help from community members. Police penetration and control of communication among community members appear to serve as a substitute for direct relationships.

In the case of the first digital street gangs, police and prosecutors used their surveillance of social media to address crime places established on the ground. Given multiple sources of intelligence and all the time they took to build their cases, they were able to decipher reasonably well the drivers and the coordination of violence. However, greater police use of automated and continuous surveillance online, especially through third-party applications marketed to law enforcement, may reverse the sequence so that the digital street determines hot spots on the physical street.[38] As suspicious places and people emerge remotely, we may expect to find less careful criminalization with a weaker rationale and structure for investigation. Perhaps in recognition of the limitations of digital policing, the NYPD, in 2015, introduced neighborhood coordination officers deployed for face-to-face communication and relationship building. In New York and other urban areas, the workings of the law will be configured across the physical and digital streets and the possibilities and constraints of each.

6

Street Lessons

Over the summer of 2014, I sat with Drop on a bench at the park on 130th Street and Fifth Avenue. Drop was twenty years old and working for the summer as a counselor at A Cut Above (ACA), the HCZ's year-round youth development program for middle school students, before his sophomore year of college. Drop had graduated from ACA and had worked there on and off since tenth grade. A career in social work was his back-up plan, but what he really wanted was to be a professional rapper, which was why he had called me to the park: to play an undercover cop in a video for his song "Loyalty." As we waited on the videographer, a friend from the neighborhood, we talked about his lyrics that he wrote on the notes application of his phone. The first verse began:

> *Bitch a scream r.I.p*
> *for a nigga*
> *Then the same bitch*
> *a go and chill*
> *With his killa*

Drop had seen a status update on Facebook by a girl he had added. He told me, "As soon as I saw that line I'm like I'm gonna make a song about it." Drop riffed on the theme of loyalty and the song became personal:

> *I got locked for the hammer*
> *Ain't mention a name*
> *Told on myself*
> *I'm in the jail of fame*

"That's from when I was fourteen," he said of his statement to police after his gun arrest:

> *Some may call it stupid*
> *Call it loyalty*
> *And if I had it*
> *Ill pay the lawyer fee's*

After paperwork had resurfaced in relation to the indictment, a friend and codefendant said his admission was "stupid." Drop's lyrics pushed back as a reminder that he had taken the blame rather than diffuse it onto others present at the time. He also expressed that he wished he could have hired private attorneys for all of his co-indicted friends: "Maybe some people could have gotten less time."

It was fitting that Drop addressed the past in his music. His youth had been embedded in media. His loyalties extended from the neighborhood to social media, and he continued to work through the meaning of these relationships online and offline. Drop's youth was part of the transformation of street life in Harlem between about 2006 and 2014.

During this time, the adolescent experience of Harlem was reconfigured through the use of social media and smartphones. The digital street emerged as a layer and mode of street life.

I have conceptualized of the digital street as an extension to the physical street and an online staging area in the neighborhood where residents perform street life for each other to preview or displace what might happen in person, creating new forms of sociality in the process. Along with youth, street pastors, outreach workers, police, prosecutors, and other adults charged with neighborhood control draw upon and participate in this digital street life. I've described a single set of neighborhood actors locked together in each other's lives in person and on the Internet. By examining the similarities, differences, and crossover between the physical and digital streets, we can understand more of what a neighborhood is like. Roles and practices that play out in public urban space have parallel versions in online space that shift with the possibilities of digital interaction. Neighborhood social life is cocreated physically and digitally as the opportunities and risks that young people face based on where they live are shaped by the technologies they and those around them use.

I've shown that the digital street affords easier interaction (e.g., for boys to call out to girls or police to search suspects) that may carry through to intended outcomes on the physical street. But I've also demonstrated that digital action does not always influence behavior on the ground. For instance, Pastor mobilized a community response that fell short in the absence of broader institutional support from Geoffrey Canada. I presented numerous examples of digital content that did not match offline from various posturing to the extreme case of fake pages. Youth in Harlem, despite the variation in their behavior and strategic nature of their online communication, were held accountable to their digital traces by peers, neighborhood adults, and especially police and prosecutors. The digital street offered a space to criminalize online activity under the broad reach of conspiracy law.

Social media use linked the enactment of the street code to its punishment.

The digital street provides a way to conceptualize how a neighborhood changes with the digital use of its residents and the judicial actors charged with the control and public safety of the area. Contrary to recent arguments by Lee Rainie and Barry Wellman, neighborhoods and neighborhood-based groups do not mean less with new media, not here at least. I did not discover a "new neighborhood" online but the extension and reworking of the same neighborhood space inside which these young and marginalized tech users reside.[1] This is not to dismiss the global reach of online platforms but to emphasize that tech use may first address the most local and immediate life circumstances. In the context of Harlem, the Internet and social media did not make the risks of dating or gang violence worse. Digital space often buffered physical contact and provided an outlet for action or an off-ramp for individuals headed toward conflict.[2] The digital street offered a tool for intervention.

Digitization poses a challenge to the conceptualization and measurement of neighborhood effects. Quantifying time spent with peers in specific geographic locations captures a thinner slice of this place-based presence and interaction than before social media and smartphones. The more we can match sociality set in person to its digitally mediated extensions, the better we account for peer influence and neighborhood exposure. Studying the communication environment holistically better reveals how peers navigate violence and other concentrated risks and access opportunities. To position our research accordingly means that standing on the corner is not enough for fieldwork and that ethnographers as well as interview and survey researchers need to collect social media and smartphone data. By joining and comparing physical and digital modes of neighborhood life we get a much deeper sense of urban community. This integrated approach to urban sociology and communication and technology was a staple of the classic Chicago School neighborhood studies.[3]

I hope this first book on the digital street gives readers ideas for positive responses to the digitization of violence and poverty. The cases discussed reveal protective aspects of social media use, rather than simply the worsening of violence. That situations on the street are visible online can be taken as a resource for intervention. I want to end by outlining a few intervention ideas.

The first lesson is to empower girls. If we want opportunities and messages to span neighborhoods and reach the widest audience, girls and their social media accounts are uniquely positioned to share resources and model positive experiences. Girls of color in urban settings merit investments in their own educational and financial prospects, and they are already brokers of opportunity within and beyond the neighborhood for themselves and their peers. "The girl network" seeks and disseminates information for and across their home streets. The challenge would be to upgrade this role to a position of community leadership so it moves far past a position of tension or simply taking care of boys. To the end, we'd invest in an identity framework of leadership that acknowledges the power of girls and that endows this role with resources.

The second lesson is to sponsor positive turning points when youth themselves call out for support. I studied a cohort of street-involved teenagers open to help and who helped themselves and each other. They used the Harlem Children's Zone, the alternative high schools and programs of District 79, Job Corps, the community college system, and other recent and older antipoverty initiatives. These efforts fell short in many cases, but they made them in the first place and publicized their progress. The adult world can empower *their* choices with timely infusions of social, informational, and financial support.

Victor Rios writes that authority figures select on the wrong side of the code-switching dynamic. They respond to street identities and reinforce them. Rios asks: "What might be the implications for programs and policies if we were to recognize that young people indeed have the ability to shift seamlessly between conventional and deviant displays with minimal intervention and within a few hours' time?"[4] Rios asked readers to imagine "a helmet camera" on youth that shows portions of their life as they move through different settings with a zoom-out lens and a second camera, at a cross angle, to show youth interactions with institutional actors inside these settings.[5] This scenario plays out to an extent on social media where youth share versions of themselves and their experiences with institutions. In Harlem, police were the first movers on social media. Their invisible or covert presence generated punishment in response to code switching. This could change with an infusion of parents, outreach workers, old heads, educators, service providers, and other caring adults prepared to sponsor youth as they announced their commitments and traction in school, work, programming, and other sources of fulfillment.

Scholars point to variations in how new communication technologies are embedded in communities and the degree to which this communication infrastructure can facilitate individuals' access to resources.[6] Over the years of my study, much more could have been done with the online visibility of youth at risk than constructing gang rosters and collecting conspiracy evidence. The police and prosecutors I spoke with did not disagree. More nonpolice adults were needed in youth communication networks to provide nonpolice action. In the case of the public-school system, a seemingly rational policy formalized in 2012 to prohibit teachers in New York City from following their students on social media meant that police were *instead* following their students.

Another way to change the audience structure would be to invite a new state agency to address the hot spots of violence. This agency does not yet exist. If it did it would be allowed to help only by addressing problems of mental health, addiction, family crisis, and poverty. This hypothetical unit that only served, assisted, referred, supported, built, and gave could have set up shop in the same locations and online and offline networks targeted for multiyear investigations and criminal indictments. If there was such an agency—one funded and empowered by the state—it might offer a way past the inherent contradictions of what Forrest Stuart calls "therapeutic policing," in which cops are the ones diagnosing and implementing ideas about residents and their problems, and relying ultimately on the threat or use of criminal sanctions.[7]

A third lesson is that street life is a media "career" based upon a desire to be seen and heard. The street lives I discussed were all about campaigning and competing for attention and presence in the neighborhood—making a name for oneself and one's friends. From childhood to early adulthood, the friends from 129th Street cycled through expressive roles in public space, starting as dancers and then basketball players, becoming fighters and finally rappers. These roles and phases played out in parallel with their peers in the same constellation of neighborhood groups. Not just Drop, but also Smalls, Shawn, Tiana, and other friends from 129th Street transitioned to rapping. The violence and policing of their youth provided source material that was sometimes still emotionally raw and being worked through. They were serious about their music as a fresh form of identity and way to get money, they hoped.[8] Over the 2015 Memorial Day weekend, I saw the group perform downtown at Webster Hall. They shared a long bill with rap crews from all over the city. About thirty-five friends and family members attended, many joining the performers on stage for their set. When Smalls took the microphone, he performed right into the camera of one of the group's two designated videographers, generating footage for their social media feeds and related future projects. They had created new roles for themselves in the media arts, not just as performers, but also as videographers, video editors, producers, managers, and clothing designers. Fifteen years earlier, *New York Times* journalist Amy Waldman documented this progression out of violence and into music production for young black men on the very same street.[9]

As their interests evolved with age, the violence was never that far off. The same weekend of the Webster Hall show, back in the neighborhood, a young woman home from college was shot in the side, and the bullet grazed one of the young men from 129th Street. Boys from Lincoln were believed to be responsible, which posed the dilemma of whether to hit back. In moments like this young people need reasons to not just say, "fuck it!" starting with financial stability and positive social support.[10] The adult world can help by finding ways to channel the expression and collaboration of street life into work and profit opportunities in the cultural industries of music, film, fashion, marketing, and advertising. Otherwise only the branding professionals get to remarket the styles of black youth in places like Harlem to broader demographics.[11] The digital street is nothing short of the creativity and innovation of young people whose talents go untapped.

Appendix

Digital Urban Ethnography

I want to use this appendix to talk about the style of research that developed over the course of this study, what I'm calling *digital urban ethnography*. It's an approach that weaves together fieldwork on the ground and in the feeds and networks of a single set of subjects to extend the "shoe leather" of neighborhood-based ethnography to social media and mobile communication. By integrating these multiple perspectives on the same field site, we can collect data with greater validity than the typical yield of either urban or digital strategies alone.

In urban ethnography, the shoe-leather term stands for a commitment to being in the field day in and day out over the long term.[1] It also means that for all the graciousness of those who allow us to study their lives we pursue more than their word. We observe to see if people do as they say. We seek documentation to corroborate what we're told. We find those on the other end of interaction to get their account. Shoe leather is the data-quality standard in urban ethnography.

Social media and mobile phones are shoe-leather technologies of the highest order. They render and preserve what subjects say and do. They are facework stages and archives of interaction. Comparing these trace records with our neighborhood fieldwork makes our data more robust by capitalizing on communication previously bracketed off as somehow outside the field site of urban ethnography.

Digital ethnographers have not made the same omission. In contrast to urban ethnography, digital studies typically start with subjects' technology use. These ethnographies examine the affordances of new media and the ways in which the digital introduces new social settings and reconfigures traditional ones. Digital ethnographers capture forms of presence, inter-activity, and practice through and with social media—vital aspects of the social world urban ethnographers just leave out.[2] But digital scholars rarely invest in the sorts of offline roles and routines of urban ethnographers. Digital ethnographers often presume going online matters locally and in-terpersonally but still conduct their fieldwork as if they can rely on online relationships to their subjects.[3] This is another form of ethnographic negli-gence. How can the claims upon any social context not improve or shift by getting to know even one subject in person?

Just as urban ethnography needs a digital commitment, digital eth-nography needs shoe leather. Digital ethnography checks the tendency of urban ethnography to thin social life down to face-to-face communication. The urban tradition checks the acceptance of fieldwork at a remove that thins digital work. Done together, researchers can draw inferences that are more reliable than either study enables on its own. This methodolog-ical upgrade boosts data quality at a time of public and scholarly calls for greater accuracy in various forms of research and reporting.

How Do We Know What We Know?

All researchers face the same epistemological dilemma: How do we know what we know? As ethnographers, we argue that it isn't enough to ask people about their lives because what people say often fails to align with what they do. Colin Jerolmack and Shamus Khan recently took up this ethnographic warrant in their article "Talk Is Cheap."[4] Only by observing situated social activity can we compare attitudes with action and come to know people's lives beyond abstracted self-reports—what interview and survey research typically rely upon. But I'd like to push further this core strength that sets ethnography apart. It's no longer enough for ethnog-raphers to observe people only in person and to be present with them as they go about their day. Assertions and behaviors cannot be evaluated exclusively within face-to-face situations because the social environment has evolved. Saying and doing are situated online and offline, which requires our attention to the overlap and tension between the two. We can generate real gains in the quality of our data by examining a wider range of interaction.

In the appendix section, urban ethnographers ruminate on what it means to gather data in the ways we did for the claims we made. We usually tell roughly the same narrative of how our analysis derives from the closest forms of access or what we call "getting in." I'm likewise going to talk about how I became embedded in a community through groundwork that remains essential. But I also came to know my subjects through digital modes of knowledge that expanded the shoe leather of urban ethnography. By some combination of good fortune and intent, I found a way to improve upon our answers to how we know what we know that harnesses the fact that young people take everywhere in their pockets social technologies seamlessly integrated into their daily lives. After I recap my fieldwork on the ground, I'm going to address my fieldwork in the feeds and networks of social media. These examinations proved indispensable to my knowledge in person, and vice versa. Bringing the digital into urban fieldwork increases opportunities to directly observe and corroborate situated interaction and behavior. It enables more being there, there, and there as Ulf Hannerz has said of multisited ethnography.[5]

Starting with a familiar story of neighborhood fieldwork, I'm going to pull apart three integral ways of seeing and being in the field that interlocked to go beyond the usual limits of knowing our subjects for both urban and digital researchers.

On the Ground

The way I started this project was very conventional for urban ethnographers.[6] I lived in the neighborhood I studied. I met a sponsor in Pastor and adapted a role alongside him by becoming an outreach worker in his antiviolence ministry. My early experiences being on the street with Pastor in the first months of 2010 amounted to what, as a professor, I now caution (or reassure) graduate students: Fieldwork requires a lot of standing around like an idiot. I felt that way the first day I suddenly stood unaccompanied on Lenox Avenue after Pastor and Coach went separately to "sit on" two different groups of boys they were monitoring after shootings the previous night.

"Mister, what are you doing here?" a girl asked.

"I'm helping Pastor today," I replied dutifully, before introducing myself as Jeff from 130th Street, which sounded unnatural. I played up that I lived around the corner to echo how I heard Pastor vouch for me: "This is Jeff, he's good. He lives here," which indicated that although I was white I was not a cop.

Although even "hard-to-reach" populations are visible on the Internet, the model proposed is not a reduction in neighborhood fieldwork. On the contrary, it's a continued commitment to building relationships in person over time—all the more important given the crossing of multiple social boundaries in my case and others. Elliot Liebow, a white ethnographer who studied black men on the street in the sixties, said "the degree to which one becomes a participant is as much a matter of perceiving oneself as a participant as it is of being accepted as a participant by others."[7] I came to feel like an increasingly legitimate part of the lives I studied by being out each day—being consistent in my presence—and by gradually assuming more responsibility.

I participated in Pastor's and Coach's rounds of checking on the crews and the social scenes on multiple blocks, first riding with either Pastor or Coach before eventually using my own car. I joined their efforts to track and disrupt a cat-and-mouse game among rival groups of boys that played out during after-school hours and on weekend nights. By becoming an outreach worker, I could see what youth violence looked like and experience the challenge of trying to stop it.

In July 2010, I volunteered to write curricula and lead workshops on topics like health and financial literacy at a major municipal summer employment program for the first of three consecutive summers. I met hundreds of young people assigned to worksites in Harlem who gathered for weekly workshops. For the fraction of teens whose participation overlapped with street life, I got to know them across both settings.

That summer I also helped Pastor to organize a series of Friday-evening programs called "Positive Presence 4 Peace" with local entertainment acts and program referrals in a different location each week. I learned more about areas other than 129th Street and Lenox Avenue, the primary hub of my fieldwork that was only a block and a half from my apartment.

In September 2010, my fieldwork advanced along multiple tracks. I started doing audio-recorded interviews with some of the teenagers in the outreach work, often using nearby Columbia University. I paid $20 cash for each interview. Three girls also helped me to arrange these interviews, and I paid them a small referral fee. I started playing basketball with several of the boys from 129th Street. We played first in Harlem and then elsewhere in New York City in pickup games with some of my friends. Basketball let me share aspects of my life apart from Pastor and the outreach work. I also began spending time with Andre and some of his friends on the St. Lincoln side of the conflict with 129th Street, using my car as much as possible to keep these meetings separate. Finally, I began to get a better sense of the criminal justice response to the same violence the outreach focused upon by serving on a government-funded youth gang task force that convened in East Harlem.

Later that fall I started a computer lab in Pastor's office with equipment donated from an investment firm where a friend worked. I called this space "The Lab" and gave out card-sized flyers with the hours. The Lab contributed resources and programming while it gave me the research opportunity to observe and ask questions of teenagers as they used social media. Back on the street I had by now become comfortable going out to the block entirely on my own and using my car as a place for teenagers to sit and to give rides to youth and their family members. In November, I led a weekend college trip to my alma mater, Wesleyan University, with nine teenagers and three other chaperones.

These fieldwork activities carried through the winter and spring, including a trip to Howard University in April 2011 (funded by a Howard alum who helped finance the trip to Wesleyan through a youth nonprofit he founded). I added a new role, consulting at a public defender's office as a "gang expert" in cases that involved social media, which offered a further perspective on criminal justice. I did not consult on any of the cases that involved 129th Street, but after the indictment came down in November 2011 (see Chapter 6) I shifted my fieldwork to attend court dates and to examine how communication was affected by the criminalization of social media use.

In 2012, and in a limited capacity after that, I focused more on criminal case processing and on shadowing across social settings a subset of young people who by this time were my primary subjects, including JayVon and Christian, whom I observed in their respective schools.

I could go on, but urban ethnographers have already described steps similar to these to study the multifaceted, multisited lives of a set of young people involved in street life and adults concerned about them.[8] Instead I'll discuss the digital fieldwork I completed on top of and to shape my fieldwork in the neighborhood. Because community members came to know each other through technology, not just in person, tech-based connections became part of my process of familiarity too. I exchanged mobile phone numbers and social media handles with teenagers I met in the neighborhood. We connected first on Twitter, then Facebook, and later Instagram, in following with the teens' uptake pattern. Along with in-person conversations about my research with teenagers and their parents and family members, I messaged teens immediately after I sent or received a friend or follower request on social media to the effect of "I'm interested in writing about your online and offline lives for my dissertation and I want you to know that you may delete me at any time without any explanation."

For the teenagers, the online connection wasn't any more unusual than the fact of my presence offline, but in terms of urban ethnography my fieldwork evolved very differently from previous studies. Being connected to about eighty teenagers on social media (Figure A.1) brought me into the feeds of my field site. I entered another mode of knowing.

In the Feeds

Young people especially use their social media feeds to share aspects of their life and curate their identity.[9] They communicate their expressive and instrumental goals, expecting their peers to take notice and engage with

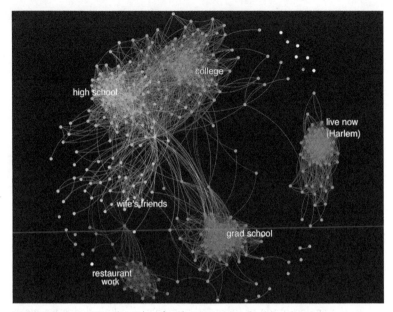

FIGURE A.1 Visualization of author's Facebook network at one point in the fieldwork.

their content. Ethnographers need to be in the feeds also to know whom their subjects claim to be and how they enact these dispositions. If we want to see whether intentions match actions, that line often starts on social media or extends there.

I was there on Facebook for the announcement that "on August 11th at 3:11 Smalls passed away" and that we should "now welcome" him by his real name. The real-named version of Smalls made better choices than the "gangsta" associated with his nickname. This declaration prompted my questions about whom he wanted to be and what he needed to get there. His post invited comparison with his actions. Ethnographers follow their participants over years to see how their lives evolve. The feeds stream their stated intentions.

In the feeds, I reacted immediately to what seemed the most pressing, contingent, or fleeting. When I saw Tiana write at midday what suggested that she had fought a girl named Gabriella and planned to fight her again,

I took screenshots of the post and comment thread. I wanted to know if Tiana had reversed course on her efforts to squash her various beefs and "retire," an expression she used with me in person. When I checked Tiana's Facebook wall again about an hour later, the material was deleted, which made me even more curious. I set out to find her that afternoon, and we spoke by a deli. Tiana confirmed that she had indeed fought Gabriella the day before and complained about pain from having her hair pulled. She also confirmed that she allowed herself to be talked down on Facebook from another fight by her aunt, who told Tiana "to cut it out."

What people say and do digitally and in person each matters in terms of the other. Tiana moved the conflict with Gabriella online by posting her intention to fight again, which opened a pathway for her aunt's intervention and the digital equivalent on Tiana's part of walking away. I concluded that Tiana wanted to remain retired despite the initial fight because I did not see her go after Gabriella while I was present with her that afternoon and over the next days and learned of no such incident online or from others.

In the analog mode of urban ethnography, the knowledge we glean tends to begin when we meet our subjects and end when we part ways. Digital urban ethnography incorporates ongoing, feed-level observation. I knew of Smalls's announcement and Tiana's situation because I checked my feed repeatedly throughout the day whether I was in Harlem next to my subjects or apart. I checked while I was elsewhere, alone or with people. Checking my feed kept a foot in the field regardless of my geographic location. I took screenshots of content that related to existing concerns and new curiosities. These stored to my photos synched between my phone and laptop. I used this content to ask the authors and those referenced about what it meant and if they were doing anything in relation.[10] While I saved Smalls's screenshot to discuss in an upcoming interview, I jumped at Tiana's post and went to investigate. Once I caught up with her in the neighborhood, we discussed the content itself and what happened before its publication. Then I watched for what would happen or not happen next. I kept a digital notebook also synched across devices into which I inserted the screenshots I took and annotated this content with what I learned by asking and observing my subjects.

Digital urban ethnographers carry a partial visualization of the field at each moment. On my feed I had a sense of where my subjects potentially were in their respective and sometimes converging days. On the first Tuesday of summer jobs through the municipal employment program, for example, my feed filled with morning updates.

"Up Getting ready for Work i was really bout to go back to sleep but . . . Stack or Starve, Good Morning everyone;" wrote Christian.

"Heading To Work I Love My Job Being A Personal Assistant!" Sarah posted.

Another young worker was "up early *".

"Good Morning ; Off To Work I Go ♥" updated a fourth person.

Compared with the analog tradition, I was stepping into my subjects' days with a sense of events in progress and deciding my rounds accordingly. Being in the feeds brought the news and gossip to me. I learned Christian passed his GED when he wrote "FUCKING RIGHTTTT MY TEACHER JUST TEXT ME & I DID IT . . . I FINALLY FINISHED SCHOOL IM TOO HYPE RIGHT NOW!!!!"

I messaged him immediately: "yo, you passed!"

"Yessss Jeff i just got the News."

I read the feeds as a stream of notices and impressions put forward by authors being deliberately public with aspects of themselves. These were openings to investigate the motivations and circumstances surrounding the content, the responses of others, and what, if any, changes were to follow.

By bringing knowledge in the feeds into alignment on the ground I eventually came to understand a gap between portrayals of school and attainment. Depictions of school success on social media gave me an initially positive perspective of the school experiences outside of my meet-ups with teenagers in the afternoon. Online I saw photographs and screenshots of attendance awards and high marks in school and almost no negative expressions of scholastic involvement. My dissertation advisors

encouraged me to examine school more closely, given this prelimi-
nary digital finding. I asked my subjects more detailed questions about
school, interviewed educators, and ultimately shadowed first Christian
at his GED school and then JayVon at his alternative high school. Going
further offline revealed that the social media feeds overrepresented successes. I learned about the frequent disruptions and school changes in
many of my subjects' educational histories and just how much school
they could miss while still maintaining enrollment. Being in school with
Christian and JayVon showed me both successful and chaotic classrooms
and gave me the chance to talk to their teachers and administrators.
I learned that by getting his GED Christian stood out as daily attendance
barely reached 50 percent and passing scores were unusual. By bringing
the digital side into alignment on the ground, I could reflect on each
fieldwork location more meaningfully. The high regard for scholastic
achievement was tied to knowing firsthand just how difficult and slip-
pery this often was. They were trying to hold whatever traction they had,
and by expressing their aspirations publicly they challenged the negative
assumptions they often faced.

The school example shows how the integration of digital and traditional fieldwork enables new forms of verification. We can cross-reference
feed-level and face-to-face data. The flipside is that we stand to draw the
wrong conclusions when one form of data collection outpaces the other.

I want to continue to discuss the examination of saying and doing
across physical and digital space and the degree of triangulation that can
come about by situating our studies accordingly. I'm going to illustrate my
process of verification by revisiting how I determined that it was indeed
normal for girls and boys to meet on social media, a simple but pivotal
finding for the conceptualization of the digital street. My finding went
against everything I read about school-based peer worlds where young
people overwhelmingly bring their existing relationships online rather
than use social media to form new ties. But I saw the phenomenon of digital meeting in dozens of different ways that, when combined, provided the
confidence to write about this as a local norm.

I sensed that meeting was digitizing by being physically present. On
the sidewalk, I observed JayVon stop and entangle Denelle while JayVon's

friend Ren gestured with his phone and told Denelle they were already Facebook friends. The encounter suggested neighborhood peers met both in person and online. I observed boys talk on the sidewalk about girls who passed that they recognized by having "added" on social media. On other occasions, I saw boys hand their phones to show each other reciprocated, two-way communication after they had successfully initiated contact with a girl. In the computer lab, I witnessed girls and boys sending, considering, and accepting friend requests from seemingly new people.

On my feed, I noticed girls post screenshots of repeated and unanswered inbox messages from boys that implied that these boys had friended them and were now being rebuked. I saw Tiana post, "10 likes & I'll name the top 20 flyest boys in my friends list from what I seen in person not on FB!" I read the words "follow me" in profile bios, and I noted posts in which teens invited followers of the opposite sex on behalf of their friends. Girl–boy acquaintanceship seemed as much the point of social media as engaging existing ties.

Even in interviews I was able to *see* the phenomenon. When Olivia told me about attention from unfamiliar boys, she showed me the unreciprocated messages in her Facebook inbox. I did not have to take her at her word alone. When Olivia described a strategy she used of accepting friend requests from new boys and engaging them on her wall, we looked together at examples of such wall interactions. By referring directly to the interactions in question we can elicit a less abstract account than offline interviews often generate.

Digital interaction can in many cases be verified. After Olivia said she appreciated that a "cute" boy named Kevin said "Wassup?" on her wall rather than with a message, I looked up that interaction after the interview. I scrolled through her page until I found, from two months earlier, "OLIVIA WASS GOODIE"—the equivalent of "Wassup?" Then I looked for Olivia's other interactions with Kevin to see that they matched her account that she preferred to keep things on the wall. Jerolmack and Khan write that when ethnographers do interviews we have the benefit of situating subjects' verbal accounts "in relation to observed interactions that occur before and after the interview."[11] Digital urban ethnography goes beyond that standard by locating whenever possible the digital interactions we hear about. We can see for ourselves communication we missed the first time and look at this content both on our own and with our subjects who were there. Retrieving situated interactions to discuss with subjects also goes beyond digital research that "scrapes" social media data to evaluate on its face. Bringing the digital into studies in person and bringing people (back) into their digital data are simply good research practices.

I could go on with additional evidence of the online meeting norm, but I think I've made my point: Digital urban ethnography generates more opportunities to see and evaluate what our subjects say and do. By seeing the same thing from more vantages and in more types of data, we build confidence in our inferences. In the language Mario Small uses, we gain *complementarity*, as each kind of data collection compensates for the other, and we gain *confirmation* by finding the same phenomenon in different kinds of data.[12] But there's still another mode of digital knowing to discuss. On top of my neighborhood- and feed-level fieldwork, I also came to know my subjects through their networks.

In the Networks

I thought more about my location in the field after I attended a 2013 conference convened by Janet Vertesi at Princeton University on "The Ethnographer in the Network." The conference presenters discussed their research on distributed work teams, online communities, and the use of various digital platforms. To study these sites they imagined their field as a network in which they located themselves and their fieldwork.[13] Urban ethnographers sometimes relate to the people and neighborhoods they study in network terms also. Liebow gave a classic example in his conceptualization of *Tally's Corner* as the convergence of personal networks belonging to several men who gathered on a street corner in Washington, DC.[14] By shadowing his subjects, Liebow carried out an interconnecting series of egocentric network analyses. Each man was a node in a network in his study.

Digital urban ethnography utilizes the fact that social media and mobile devices render egocentric networks and network activity. As I got to know my subjects and moved about the neighborhood with them, I turned my attention to the phones they carried and their social media accounts. These technologies offered perspective on my subjects' networks beyond what could be verbalized or the people I happened to hear about or meet while we were together. Such consideration was also necessary, given that people typically use communication technologies in tandem with contact in person to maintain their networks and what Jeffrey Boase terms a "personal communication system."[15]

Borrowing from Heather Horst and Daniel Miller's study of cell phone networks, I asked Pastor if I could download the contacts and text messages on his BlackBerry.[16] Pastor's generosity with his phone allowed me to further see the social world he had opened and to articulate his position inside this world as a middleman between people and institutions. When I mapped his contacts I found that Pastor bridged the uptown setting of Harlem and the downtown of the courts and other government functions. I accessed also the lists to which Pastor sent his "blasts," revealing how he segmented and integrated the community in his outreach work. In his one-to-one text messages I saw backchannel communication that showed that some of the teens most involved in conflict were also Pastor's most helpful sources. This was information shared in bits and pieces in our conversations that became verifiable and more robust in phone data. Bringing the digital into my neighborhoods rounds with Pastor allowed me to see how he used a mobile infrastructure of communication to prioritize and direct his outreach efforts. I came to realize that Pastor had reinvented a traditional social role—the street pastor—in urban black neighborhoods for the contingencies of digital communication.

Digital networks open the door for urban ethnographers to reconsider traditional notions about social organization in neighborhoods based on analog studies. Returning to girls and boys, by studying their networks I realized that girls occupied a distinct network position that I would have missed had I focused exclusively on face-to-face street life, in which boys and young men were more visible and seemed dominant. Fixating here would have led to the flawed assumption that men hold the power in neighborhood space where, in reality, women are some of the most powerful and central components. It's only by looking at networks—which were of course always there but are now made visible by social media—that the centrality of girls became obvious in contrast to the centering of boys in the street-life literature. By examining not just the content but the network composition of subjects' social media accounts, I became more conscious of the authority and vulnerability of girls in contentious public spaces. For instance, when I sat with Rochelle to go through her emerging friends list on her new Facebook page, I found that her network connected at least twenty-four active cross-neighborhood rivalries. I was able to visualize and mark out her social location. Over and over again I learned that young women bridged otherwise estranged neighborhood networks in which boys were tightly bound by violence with limited outlets for peer communication apart from girls. Digital urban ethnography utilizes a network-level mode of knowing that may reveal the bias of traditional field methods and thinking about urban space.

I saw my fieldwork and myself in the networks as well. The time I spent with the people I studied was sometimes written about. I was tagged in photographs. I used this information as study feedback. For instance, one day when I sat on the library steps at Columbia University with Christian and JayVon I checked my feed and saw that Christian had posted a photograph of our view at the moment with the caption, "I could get use to this College Life =)." He tagged JayVon, who posted his own status update shortly after, "College life coming soon." I took their "college life" posts as a measure of reassurance that I hadn't alienated them by bringing them to an Ivy League school and that they related to this location positively. This was a check on the nature of my involvement.

I was also an entry in my subjects' phone contacts. In Christian's phone in Figure A.2, I was "White Jeff." Christian never called me "White Jeff" in person. I did not mind the name, which made me think of Carol Stack, a white researcher of a black community, for whom this open designation expressed endearment.[17] Christian simply said that there were two other Jeffs in his phone and I was the only white one. In comparison with my entry in JayVon's phone, I thought "White Jeff" signaled a different kind of relationship connection.

FIGURE A.2 Entry for author in Christian's contacts (left) and in JayVon's contacts (right).

JayVon entered my name in his contacts as "Mentor Jeff," which was consistent with how he introduced me to others. I played a more involved role in JayVon's life than in anyone else's in this research by offering regular advice, paying for groceries, MetroCards, and other basics, and helping to place JayVon at a residential services program. I took on a level of responsibility that did not apply to my relationship with Christian or others. Typically I volunteered to help subjects in small ways (with rides, advocating, dealing with bureaucracies, etc.). To dictate these relationship terms was a position of privilege. I was also in a position of privilege with JayVon, only JayVon asked for more of my help and assigned responsibilities to me for which I wasn't always prepared. I cared about JayVon and acted to be a positive mentor but I also felt overwhelmed by the relationship. To Christian, by contrast, I imagined that I was a white guy in the neighborhood who was studying his life and with whom he did not expect more than friendly rapport and my asking questions.

Challenges

I've described the major ethnographic gains associated with digital urban ethnography. Now I want to discuss the challenges of boundaries, privacy, and visibility. I felt most ethical about my fieldwork by developing relationships that started in person before they extended online and when I discussed the digital content I collected with its authors. When digital access outpaced my relationships in person I felt less comfortable. To bring the three modes of knowing into alignment not only generates better data quality but also mitigates lurking and exploiting blurred distinctions between public and private spaces online.[18] There's a level of transparency in consistently responding to content and asking about it, and I was expected to keep up. But such signaling shouldn't preclude explicitly asking for study permission and feedback on an ongoing basis. During my study I checked in to see what my subjects thought of having me around in the multiple ways I was there. "You're good," I was told by several people. It was possible those I asked didn't want to hurt my feelings, but I felt accepted and often embraced.

Where I felt more conflicted was around the access to people who didn't consent to my presence who were connected to those who did.[19] Urban ethnographers have always observed and heard about the relationships of their subjects. However, by taking screenshots I collected identifiable records of nonparticipants. I took for granted a level of access to my subjects' networks. Once I collected content that revealed persons attached to my subjects I had to decide whether to inform them and seek their permission to use or quote what was also their material. Whether I sought their permission—and their perspective on the interaction—was a decision I handled case by case. I felt most compelled to reach out about longer forms of communication and communication presumed private. In the girls and boys chapter, for instance, I discussed with Denelle that I wanted to use her Facebook conversation with JayVon and got her permission as I also checked my assumptions about their interaction. I felt no obligation, however, to contact the seven young men in Olivia's inbox to ask about their propositioning messages. That seemed awkward and unnecessary. In the case of Pastor's contact list, I took the liberty of referencing people by their roles rather than making each person aware of my intention, which might have created a conflict for the contact and for Pastor. Managing the privacy of my subjects and their networks was stressful. Anonymizing my field site might have eased concerns, but I wasn't prepared to do that. Irina Shklovski and Janet Vertesi define anonymization in terms of "un-Googling work" to scrub identifying details that might otherwise serve as search terms leading back to subjects and "the environments where ethnographic encounters happened."[20] These precautions include even obscuring the country of data collection. I felt strongly about presenting a narrative true to the time and place of Harlem as I understood this setting and its digitization. Meanwhile, concealing locations within Harlem became increasingly untenable once the gang indictments and their media coverage started. Publicly available legal documents and news stories about 129th Street and the other targeted areas shaped public knowledge of these localities, and when journalists asked my opinion I weighed in. As the visibility of my field site changed, my research evolved into a sociological response to these judicial and journalistic narratives.

In the end, I settled upon a series of trade-offs to manage the visibility of and around my subjects. I gave subjects pseudonyms. Pseudonyms provided a layer of privacy and plausible deniability. Yet, by referencing the names of locations, social media content, and public legal documents, people's identities were less protected than if I had systematically excluded this information. In the era of Google, Colin Jerolmack and Alexandra Murphy propose the opposite of Shklovski and Vertesi: unmasking subjects on both ethical and cumulative-science grounds.[21] I considered asking subjects to reconsent to the research under their real names. Only I decided that was extreme because it went both beyond name-disclosure norms in many cases and because Google Books exposes content beyond printed pages. Some subjects welcomed publicity or named themselves in news stories, but I did not want to *add* visibility by naming names. Ultimately, I talked with subjects about issues of visibility and took steps to protect their identities. I Googled content I wished to quote and made occasional minor changes to mask identifiable details. I excluded sensitive information and consulted a lawyer to read passages. I also felt more comfortable to publish this book given the length of time that had elapsed since I collected the data and that the evidence I discussed had already been brought in cases that were adjudicated.

From the beginning to the end of this study, managing its boundaries was an ongoing challenge for which I used my discretion. But I don't see any turning back to study contemporary social life.

The Technology of Shoe Leather

The style of digital urban ethnography developed here merges three ways of being and moving through the field. It integrates fieldwork on the ground and in the feeds and networks of a single set of subjects to see and compare more of what subjects say and do. By layering and contrasting these modes of field knowledge, we can elevate the quality and reliability of our data to reach stronger conclusions.

In this approach, digital ethnography is neither a substitute nor an add-on to the classic method of doing fieldwork in the neighborhood. Instead, neighborhood roles and relationships carry through the communication and technologies of our subjects to extend the limits of shoe-leather fieldwork. This represents a major shift from the way urban ethnographers usually employ technology. To use as an archetype Elijah Anderson's *Streetwise*, when Anderson wanted to understand how the gentrification of Philadelphia shaped public interaction he spent countless hours on the streets and in various neighborhood locales and "photographed the setting, videotaped street corner scenes, recorded interviews, and got to know all kinds of people, from small-time drug dealers to policemen, middle-class whites, and outspoken black community activists."[22] Anderson used recordings primarily to address the ephemerality of the fieldwork in person. I suggest we do fieldwork of our subjects' digital social life and that our fieldwork cross over between the neighborhood and the technology.[23] This way, tech serves not simply to record but to expand the field in order to collect posts, comments, ties, traces, and other aspects of online activity digital ethnographers examine. Digital ethnography already draws on the urban tradition as a primary model.[24] By rooting digital research in the rounds and routines of urban ethnography, we can leverage the combined value of shoe leather and digital ethnography.

In response to "Talk Is Cheap," Michèle Lamont and Ann Swidler contend that ethnography privileges immediate situations over other sociological explanations of behavior.[25] Being there doesn't mean ethnographers can just see why people do things. That's fair—it's a judgment call from up close. But putting these three modes of knowledge together gives us more of our subjects' social situations so that we're able to make our best calls. In other words, we're seeing more of what's right in front of us.

Notes

Preface

1 Elijah Anderson, *Code of the Street* (New York: Norton, 1999).

2 Robert Garot, *Who You Claim* (New York: New York University Press, 2010).

3 danah boyd uses the term "networked publics" in reference to teenagers' peer worlds embedded in social media: danah boyd, *It's Complicated: The Social Lives of Networked Teens* (New Haven, CT: Yale University Press, 2014). Kazys Varnelis and collaborators introduce the term more broadly, including urban spaces networked through the use of information and communication technologies: Kazys Varnelis, ed., *Networked Publics* (Cambridge, MA: MIT Press, 2008).

4 On neighborhood effects research, see Robert J. Sampson, *Great American City: Chicago and the Enduring Neighborhood Effect* (Chicago: University of Chicago Press, 2012).

5 On the exacerbation of aggression through increased risk exposure online, see Robin M. Kowalski and Susan P. Limber, "Electronic Bullying Among Middle School Students," *Journal of Adolescent Health* 41, no. 6, Supplement (2007): S22–S30. On the digital bystander effect, see Clyde Haberman, "What the Kitty Genovese Killing Can Teach Today's Digital Bystanders," *New York Times*, June 4, 2017. Video retrieved from: https://www.nytimes.com/2017/06/04/us/retro-report-bystander-effect.html; Kelly P. Dillon and Brad J. Bushman, "Unresponsive or Un-noticed?: Cyberbystander Intervention in an Experimental Cyberbullying Context," *Computers in Human Behavior* 45 (2015): 144–150. On the packaging of fight videos as racialized entertainment, see Brooklynn K. Hitchens, "Girl Fights and the

189

Online Media Construction of Black Female Violence and Sexuality," *Feminist Criminology* (2017): 1–25.

Chapter 1

1 Sampson, *Great American City*.

2 See, among other excellent recent works on neighborhood effects, David J. Harding, *Living the Drama* (Chicago: University of Chicago Press, 2010); Sampson, *Great American City*; Robert J. Sampson, Jeffrey D. Morenoff, and Thomas Gannon-Rowley, "Assessing 'Neighborhood Effects': Social Processes and New Directions in Research," *Annual Review of Sociology* 28 (2002): 443–478; Patrick Sharkey, *Stuck in Place: Urban Neighborhoods and the End of Progress Toward Racial Equality* (Chicago: University of Chicago Press, 2013).

3 Lee Rainie and Barry Wellman, *Networked: The New Social Operating System* (Cambridge, MA: MIT Press, 2012).

4 The study of urban community, communication, technology, and media were originally joined together in the Chicago School of Sociology. By the middle of the twentieth century, however, sociology and communication had decoupled: Vikki S. Katz and Keith N. Hampton, "Communication in City and Community: From the Chicago School to Digital Technology," *American Behavioral Scientist* 60, no. 1 (2016): 3–7. In recent decades, the communication perspective on urban life has been driven by Sandra Ball-Rokeach and the Metamorphosis Project at USC Annenberg School for Communication and Journalism: http://www.metamorph.org. The Urban Communication Foundation provides another hub of urban research in the communication discipline: https://urbancomm.org. Urban research also has a home in communication and media studies. Two recent works in this area that have influenced my thinking about the digital street include Myria Georgiou, *Media and the City: Cosmopolitanism and Difference* (Cambridge, MA: Polity, 2013); Andreas Hepp, Piet Simon, and Monika Sowinska, "Living Together in the Mediatized City: The Figurations of Young People's Urban Communities," in *Communicative Figurations: Transforming Communications in Times of Deep Mediatization*, ed. Andreas Hepp, Andreas Breiter, and Uwe Hasebrink (Cham, Switzerland: Palgrave Macmillan, 2018), 51–80.

5 W. E. B. DuBois, *The Philadelphia Negro* (Philadelphia: University of Pennsylvania Press, 1996, original work published 1899); Mitchell Duneier, Philip Kasinitz, and Alexandra Murphy, eds., *The Urban Ethnography Reader* (New York: Oxford University Press, 2014).

6 See Geoffrey Canada, *Fist Stick Knife Gun: A Personal History of Violence in America* (Boston: Beacon, 1995). The language in the mission statement appeared for a number of years on the HCZ website: https://hcz.org/about-us/.

7 Anderson, *Code of the Street*, 135. Anderson discusses the influence of commercial rappers on pages 36, 107, 151, 154–155, and 205.

8 Canada, *Fist Stick Knife Gun*; Geoffrey Canada, adapted by Jamar Nicholas, *Fist Stick Knife Gun: A Personal History of Violence in America: A True Story in Black and White* (Boston: Beacon, 2010).

9 Elijah Anderson, *Streetwise* (Chicago: University of Chicago Press, 1990); Anderson, *Code of the Street*; Elijah Anderson, "The Code of the Streets," *The Atlantic*, May 1994, 81–94.

10 Nikki Jones, *Between Good and Ghetto* (Piscataway, NJ: Rutgers University Press, 2010).

11 Anderson, *Code of the Street*, 50.

12 Ibid., 287. See also Harding, *Living the Drama*, 149.

13 Anderson, *Code of the Street*, 36. See also L. Janelle Dance, *Tough Fronts: The Impact of Street Culture on Schooling* (New York: Routledge, 2002), 52; Jones, *Between Good and Ghetto*, 10.

14 Dance, *Tough Fronts*.

15 Garot, *Who You Claim*.

16 Harding, *Living the Drama*.

17 Anderson, *Code of the Street*, 34.

18 In his chapter on Geoffrey Canada, Mitchell Duneier discusses this turning point in urban violence: Mitchell Duneier, *Ghetto: The Invention of a Place, the History of an Idea* (New York: Farrar, Straus and Giroux, 2016).

19 Alfred Blumstein and Richard Rosenfeld, "Factors Contributing to U.S. Crime Trends," in *Understanding Crime Trends: Workshop Report*, ed. Arthur S. Goldberger and Richard Rosenfeld (Washington, DC: National Academies Press, 2008), 13–44.

20 Jens Manuel Krogstad, "Gun Homicides Steady After Decline in '90s; Suicide Rate Edges Up," Pew Research Center, October 21, 2015, http://www.pewresearch.org/fact-tank/2015/10/21/gun-homicides-steady-after-decline-in-90s-suicide-rate-edges-up/.

21 Franklin E. Zimring, *The City That Became Safe: New York's Lessons for Urban Crime and Its Control* (New York: Oxford University Press, 2011).

22 Stephanie Ueberall and Ashley Cannon, "Assessing New York City's Youth Gun Violence Crisis: Crews—Volume 1: Defining the Problem," Citizens Crime Commission of New York City, May 2015, http://www.nycrimecommission.org/pdfs/CCC-Crews-Vol1-DefiningTheProblem.pdf.

23 Harding, *Living the Drama*, 33.

24 Calvin John Smiley, "From Silence to Propagation: Understanding the Relationship Between 'Stop Snitchin' and 'YOLO,'" *Deviant Behavior* 36, no. 1 (2015): 1–16.

25 Alice Goffman, *On the Run: Fugitive Life in an American City* (Chicago: University of Chicago Press, 2014); Victor Rios, *Punished: Policing the Lives of Black and Latino Boys* (New York: New York University Press, 2011); Kathleen Nolan, *Police in the Hallways: Discipline in an Urban High School* (Minneapolis: University of Minnesota Press, 2011); Carla Shedd, *Unequal City: Race, Schools, and Perceptions of Injustice* (New York: Russell Sage Foundation, 2015).

26 On the extent of crime control and surveillance measures, see Sarah Brayne, "Surveillance and System Avoidance: Criminal Justice Contact and Institutional Attachment," *American Sociological Review* 79, no. 3 (2014): 367–391.

27 Desmond U. Patton, Robert D. Eschmann, and Dirk A. Butler, "Internet Banging: New Trends in Social Media, Gang Violence, Masculinity and Hip Hop," *Computers in Human Behavior* 29, no. 5 (2013): A54–A59.

28 District Attorney, New York County, "District Attorney Vance and Police Commissioner Bratton Announce Largest Indicted Gang Case in NYC History," June 4, 2014 [press release].

29 Office of the Mayor, New York City, "Mayor Bloomberg, US Department of Housing and Urban Development Secretary Shaun Donovan, Goldman Sachs Group President and Chief Operating Officer Gary Cohn and New York City Housing Authority Chairman John Rhea Join the Harlem Children's Zone to Break Ground on the New Promise Academy Charter School Building and Community Center at the St. Nicholas Houses," April 6, 2011 [press release].

30 Matthew Bloch, Ford Fessenden, and Janet Roberts, "Stop, Question and Frisk in New York Neighborhoods," *New York Times*, July 11, 2010. Interactive map retrieved from http://www.nytimes.com/interactive/2010/07/11/nyregion/20100711-stop-and-frisk.html.

31 All teen interview subjects were paid $20 in cash. I also paid some teens $20 per hour for exercises to collect data, such as reviewing one's ties on social media to characterize these relationships. Over the course of fieldwork, I sometimes gave teens small amounts of cash (i.e., $5 or $10) for things like food or transportation. In the case of JayVon, I gave him small amounts of money more often because he frequently asked for such help during a time of hardship.

32 Sarah Pink, *Doing Sensory Ethnography* (London: Sage, 2009). For an outstanding overview of digital ethnographic methods, see Christine Hine, *Ethnography for the Internet* (London: Bloomsbury, 2015).

33 For a discussion of crossing racial and social orders in the context of street ethnography, see Philippe Bourgois, *In Search of Respect: Selling Crack in El Barrio* (Cambridge: Cambridge University Press, 1995).

34 danah boyd, "Friendship," in *Hanging Out, Messing Around, and Geeking Out: Kids Living and Learning with New Media,* ed. Mizuko Ito et al. (Cambridge, MA: MIT Press, 2010), 79–84.

35 Amy L. Gonzales, "Health Benefits and Barriers to Cell Phone Use in Low-Income U.S. Neighborhoods: Indications of Technology Maintenance," *Mobile Media & Communication* 2 (2014): 233–248.

Chapter 2

1 Aaron Smith and Monica Anderson, "5 Facts About Online Dating," Pew Research Center, February 29, 2016, http://www.pewresearch.org/fact-tank/2015/04/20/5-facts-about-online-dating/.

2 Brooklynn K. Hitchens and Yasser Arafat Payne, " 'Brenda's Got a Baby': Black Single Motherhood and Street Life as a Site of Resilience in Wilmington, Delaware," *Journal of Black Psychology* 43, no. 1 (2017): 50–76.

3 See Anderson, *Streetwise,* 114–115; Anderson, *Code of the Street,* 142–178.

4 Amy Best, *Fast Cars, Cool Rides: The Accelerating World of Youth and Their Cars* (New York: New York University Press, 2006), 63.

5 Jody Miller, *Getting Played: African American Girls, Urban Inequality, and Gendered Violence* (New York: New York University Press, 2008), 47–48.

6 For statistics on sexual health disparities, see "Youth Risk Behavior Surveillance System (YRBSS)," Centers for Disease Control and Prevention, http://www.cdc.gov/healthyyouth/data/yrbs/index.htm.

7 Joyce A. Ladner, *Tomorrow's Tomorrow: The Black Woman* (Garden City, NY: Doubleday, 1971); Jones, *Between Good and Ghetto*, 158.

8 I transcribed this inbox message as well as the next message I quote from an audio recording of my interview with Olivia. This is my written representation rather than how it was written online, which may have been different.

9 On the online management of intimacy by teenagers, see C. J. Pascoe, "Intimacy," in *Hanging Out, Messing Around, and Geeking Out: Kids Living and Learning with New Media*, ed. Mizuko Ito et al. (Cambridge, MA: MIT Press, 2010), 117–148.

10 Miller, *Getting Played*, 153.

11 Jones, *Between Good and Ghetto*, 153.

12 On Jane Jacobs's concept of "eyes on the street" applied to social media, see boyd, *It's Complicated*, 126–127.

13 Candace West and Don H. Zimmerman, "Doing Gender," *Gender & Society* 1 (1987), 125–151.

14 Robin Stevens et al., "The Digital Hood: Social Media Use Among Youth in Disadvantaged Neighborhoods," *New Media & Society* 19, no. 6 (2017): 950–967.

15 Frederick Willis, *101 Jubilee Road: A Book of London Yesterdays* (London: Phoenix House, 1948), 82–83.

16 Pascoe, "Intimacy." See also Howard Gardner and Katie Davis, *The App Generation: How Today's Youth Navigate Identity, Intimacy, and Imagination in a Digital World* (New Haven, CT: Yale University Press, 2013). On young people's "reading" each other digitally, see Naomi S. Baron, *Always On: Language in an Online and Mobile World* (Oxford: Oxford University Press, 2008); Jesse Fox and Katie M. Warber, "Social Networking Sites in Romantic Relationships: Attachment, Uncertainty, and Partner Surveillance on Facebook," *Cyberpsychology, Behavior, and Social Networking* 17, no. 1 (2014): 3–7.

17 On Victorian London see Judith R. Walkowitz, "Going Public: Shopping, Street Harassment, and Streetwalking in Late Victorian London," *Representations* 62 (1998): 1–30; Willis, *101 Jubilee Road*. On Edwardian London see Clarence Rook, *London Side-Lights* (London: E. Arnold, 1908). On Chicago, see Jane Addams, *The Spirit of Youth and the City Streets* (1909; reprint, Urbana, IL: University of Illinois Press, 1972).

18 Nationally representative data on thirteen- to seventeen-year-olds collected in 2014 and 2015 showed that 57 percent of teens have started at least one new friendship online; 24 percent of teens who say they are dating said they have dated or "hooked up" with someone they met online. See Amanda Lenhart, Aaron Smith, and Monica Anderson, "Teens, Technology and Romantic Relationships," Pew Research Center, October 1, 2015, http://www.pewinternet.org/2015/10/01/teens-technology-and-romantic-relationships/.

19 boyd, *It's Complicated*, 7.

20 danah boyd and Nicole Ellison, "Social Network Sites: Definition, History, and Scholarship," *Journal of Computer-Mediated Communication* 13, no. 1 (2007): 210–230.

21 Eszter Hargittai and Yu-li Patrick Hsieh, "Predictors and Consequences of Differentiated Practices on Social Network Sites," *Information, Communication & Society* 13, no. 4 (2010): 515–536.

22 See Pascoe, "Intimacy"; Fox and Warber, "Social Networking Sites in Romantic Relationships"; Shanyang Zhao, Sherri Grasmuck, and Jason Martin, "Identity Construction on Facebook: Digital Empowerment in Anchored Relationships," *Computers in Human Behavior* 24 (2008): 1816–1836; Adalbert Mayer and Steven L. Puller, "The Old Boy (and Girl) Network: Social Network Formation on University Campuses," *Journal of Public Economics* 92 (2008): 329–347.

23 Nicole B. Ellison, Charles Steinfield, and Cliff Lampe, "Connection Strategies: Social Capital Implications of Facebook-enabled Communication Practices," *New Media & Society* 13, no. 6 (2011): 873–892.

24 Keith Hampton et al., "Why Most Facebook Users Get More Than They Give: The Effect of Facebook 'Power Users' on Everybody Else," Pew Research Center, February 3, 2012, http://www.pewinternet.org/2012/02/03/why-most-facebook-users-get-more-than-they-give/.

25 This basic network analysis was completed in August and September 2011 with the help of a research assistant. To estimate gender breakdown, a research assistant went through the list of friends on each sampled individual's Facebook profile. The list loaded as a series of pages, each with sixty friends (fewer on the last page to load). Working through each page, the presumptive sex of the first two and last two friends on each page was coded. I claim no

statistical significance from this convenience sample. I selected accounts on the basis of teens I knew.

26 By the date of this data collection in November 2012, four of the thirty people sampled (two boys, two girls) had either deactivated their Facebook accounts or restricted the visibility of their network. These profiles were omitted from the calculations. Between September 2011 and November 2012, over roughly fourteen months, average network size increased by 819 friends.

27 The average acquisition of seven friends per month was reported in Hampton et al., "Why Most Facebook Users Get More Than They Give," which collected nationally representative data in November 2010.

28 Erving Goffman, *Relations in Public: Microstudies of the Public Order* (1971; reprint, New Brunswick, NJ: Transaction Publishers, 2010), 191.

29 On moral assessments based on people's appearances in public space, see Carol Brooks Gardner, *Passing By: Gender and Public Harassment* (Berkeley, CA: University of California, 1995); Lyn H. Lofland, *A World of Strangers: Order and Action in Urban Public Space* (New York: Basic Books, 1973); Goffman, *Relations in Public*. On the categorization of girls in inner-city Boston, see Harding, *Living the Drama*, 162–203.

30 Nicholas A. Christakis and James H. Fowler, *Connected: The Surprising Power of Our Social Networks and How They Shape Our Lives* (New York: Little, Brown, 2009).

31 Jones, *Between Good and Ghetto*.

32 This finding has been reported many times over, including by Gerald Suttles, *The Social Order of the Slum: Ethnicity and Territory in the Inner City* (Chicago: University of Chicago Press, 1968); Harding, *Living the Drama*.

33 Jones documented violence between girls in Philadelphia that did not entail gunplay. Jones also described relational and situational strategies to mitigate conflict: Jones, *Between Good and Ghetto*.

34 Anderson, *Code of the Street*, 77.

35 Of all Rochelle's connections, she said she had met about 55 percent (185) in person. Of these 185 face-to-face ties, roughly 32 percent (59) she knew through school. Rochelle was tied to young people in four of the five boroughs of New York City (excluding Staten Island); in Poughkeepsie, New York; Hackensack, New Jersey; Pennsylvania; "down south"; and places unknown. The vast majority of her network resided in Harlem. She was able to say with a level of confidence exactly where in Harlem 144 ties lived.

36 Sociologist David Finkelhor, Director of the Crimes Against Children Research Center, points out that when adults get paranoid about kids on the Internet they assume online space is more dangerous than the preexisting environment. If the offline comparison is boys and girls on the street, we see here how digitization can add control aspects. See David Finkelhor, "The Internet, Youth Safety and the Problem of 'Juvenoia,'" A Report of the Crimes Against Children Research Center (2011): 3.

37 Anderson, *Code of the Street*, 142–178. On the connection between the street code and relations between girls and boys, see also Miller, *Getting Played*, 5; Harding, *Living the Drama*, 199–200; for a broader discussion of the intersectionality of race, gender, and sexuality, Patricia Hill Collins, *Black Sexual Politics: African Americans, Gender, and the New Racism* (New York: Routledge, 2004).

38 Harding found that boys drew a similar distinction between "sisters" from their neighborhood and potential romantic and sexual partners from other neighborhoods: Harding, *Living the Drama*, 120–122. We find historical precedent in societies of all sorts for the notion that women fill the structural holes between groups vis-à-vis exogamy, the arrangement of marriage only outside of one's social group. See, for instance, Claude Lévi-Strauss, *The Elementary Structures of Kinship* (Boston: Beacon, 1949).

39 Jones, *Between Good and Ghetto*, 11.

Chapter 3

1 For a discussion of the origins of the term "context collapse" (first attributed to danah boyd) and the development of the research field, see Jenny L. Davis and Nathan Jurgenson, "Context Collapse: Theorizing Context Collusions and Collisions," *Information, Communication & Society* 17, no. 4 (2014): 476–485.

2 Goffman developed the audience segregation concept over decades, beginning with Erving Goffman, "Embarrassment and Social Organization," *American Journal of Sociology* 62, no. 3 (1956): 264–271, and expounding upon it until his final book: Erving Goffman, *Forms of Talk* (Philadelphia: University of Pennsylvania Press, 1981).

3 St. Clair Drake and Horace R. Cayton, *Black Metropolis: A Study of Negro Life in a Northern City* (New York: Harcourt, Brace, 1945).

4 Leo Kuper, ed., *Living in Towns* (London: Cresset Press, 1953).

5 Herbert Gans, *Urban Villagers* (New York: Free Press, 1962).

Notes

6 Terry Williams and William Kornblum, *Growing Up Poor* (Lexington, MA: Lexington Books, 1985).

7 Goffman elaborates on these aspects of audience segregation in the following works: Goffman, "Embarrassment and Social Organization," 267–268; Erving Goffman, *The Presentation of Self in Everyday Life* (New York: Doubleday, 1959), 49; Erving Goffman, *Asylums* (New York: Anchor, 1961), 90–91.

8 Joshua Meyrowitz, *No Sense of Place: The Impact of Electronic Media on Social Behavior* (New York: Oxford University Press, 1985).

9 Davis and Jurgenson, "Context Collapse." For a discussion of the "audience problem" in relation to context collapse, see Keith N. Hampton, "Persistent and Pervasive Community: New Communication Technologies and the Future of Community," *American Behavioral Scientist* 60, no. 1 (2016): 101–124.

10 danah boyd, "Social Network Sites as Networked Publics: Affordances, Dynamics, and Implications," in *A Networked Self: Identity, Community, and Culture on Social Network Sites*, ed. Zizi Papacharissi (New York: Routledge, 2010), 39–58.

11 Goffman, *Relations in Public*, 76.

12 Goffman, *Stigma* (New York: Simon & Schuster, 1963).

13 Davis and Jurgenson, "Context Collapse." An exception to typical studies of normative identities is Sun Sun Lim et al., "Facework on Facebook: The Online Publicness of Juvenile Delinquents and Youths-at-Risk," *Journal of Broadcasting & Electronic Media* 56 (2008): 346–361. Lim et al.'s study in Singapore provides a parallel case to Harlem.

14 Kimberlé W. Crenshaw, "Black Girls Matter: Pushed Out, Overpoliced and Underprotected," African American Policy Forum, 2015, https://static1.squarespace.com/static/53f20d90e4b0b80451158d8c/t/54dcc1ece4b001c03e323448/1423753708557/AAPF_BlackGirlsMatterReport.pdf.

15 Anderson, *Code of the Street*, 98–99. For an alternative account of the transition between "street" and "decent" selves, see Mary Pattillo-McCoy, *Black Picket Fences: Privilege and Peril Among the Black Middle Class* (Chicago: University of Chicago Press, 1999).

16 On the labeling and social role of "girl fighters," see Jones, *Between Good and Ghetto*.

17 Garot, *Who You Claim*. Garot found that teens labeled as fighters or gang members did the most code switching. Kids outside of gangs kept their heads

down and did not act tough in public spaces. I think Anderson and Garot were both right in their respective accounts. Although researchers refer to a singular street code, each study captures temporal and regional variation in the enactment and authority of the code. The case could also be made that researchers have actually described multiple street codes, a point suggested to me by Paul DiMaggio.

18 Twitter and then Facebook served as the primary social media of everyday interaction for the teens and the coordination hub for secondary, specialized media, such as YouTube and the video-chat platform Oovoo. Teens did not expect the adults to be competent with these specialized technologies. Teenagers without the burden of the street code use partitioning by social network sites to separate peers from the adults in their lives: Sarah Michele Ford, "Reconceptualizing the Public/Private Distinction in the Age of Information Technology," *Information, Communication & Society* 14, no. 4 (2011): 550–567. Office workers have also been found to partition personal and professional ties by social network sites: Jessica Vitak et al., "Why Won't You Be My Facebook Friend?: Strategies for Managing Context Collapse in the Workplace," *Proceedings of the 2012 iConference* (New York: Association for Computing Machinery, February 7–10, 2012), 555–557.

19 boyd, *It's Complicated.*

20 On the origins of Facebook and its associations with higher social status, see danah boyd, "White Flight in Networked Publics? How Race and Class Shaped American Teen Engagement with MySpace and Facebook," in *Race After the Internet*, ed. Lisa Nakamura and Peter Chow-White (New York: Routledge, 2011), 203–222.

21 In November 2009, "What's happening?" replaced "What are you doing?" as the prompt for tweets.

22 On self-censorship among young people online, see Alice E. Marwick and danah boyd, "I Tweet Honestly, I Tweet Passionately: Twitter Users, Context Collapse, and the Imagined Audience," *New Media & Society* 13 (2011): 114–133. Adults in the professional world tend to present a more cautious self on social network sites, according to Bernie Hogan, "The Presentation of Self in the Age of Social Media: Distinguishing Performances and Exhibitions Online," *Bulletin of Science, Technology & Society* 30, no. 6 (2010): 377–386.

23 According to Anderson, "street-oriented people can be said at times to mount a policing effort to keep their decent counterparts from "selling out" or "acting white"; that is, from leaving the community for one of higher socioeconomic

status. This retaliation, which can sometimes be violent, against the upwardly mobile points to the deep alienation present in parts of the inner-city community" (Anderson, *Code of the Street*, 65). See also Signithia Fordham and John Ogbu, "Black Students' School Success: Coping with the 'Burden of "Acting White,"'" *Urban Review* 18 (1986): 176–206.

24 John Devine, *Maximum Security: The Culture of Violence in Inner-City Schools* (Chicago: University of Chicago Press, 1996), 41; See also Pedro Mateu-Gelabert and Howard Lune, "School Violence: The Bidirectional Conflict Flow Between Neighborhood and School," *City & Community* 2, no. 4 (2003): 353–368.

25 Jennifer Weiss, "Under the Radar: School Surveillance and Youth Resistance" (PhD dissertation, City University of New York, 2008), 10; Devine, *Maximum Security*, 23.

26 According to a Brookings report, New York City's high school graduation rate increased by 18 percent between 2004 and 2005 and 2011 and 2012, as students graduated *less* prepared for college: Grover (Russ) Whitehurst with Sarah Whitfield, "School Choice and School Performance in the New York City Public Schools—Will the Past Be Prologue?" Washington, DC: The Brown Center on Education Policy at Brookings, October 2013, https://www.brookings.edu/wp-content/uploads/2016/06/School-Choice-and-School-Performance-in-NYC-Public-Schools.pdf. On the widespread lack of college readiness at New York City high schools see also Fernanda Santos, "College Readiness Lacking, Report Shows," *New York Times*, October 25, 2011, A25.

27 Jane Jacobs, *The Death and Life of Great American Cities* (New York: Random House, 1961); Mitchell Duneier, *Sidewalk* (New York: Farrar, Straus and Giroux, 1999).

28 Anderson, *Code of the Street*, 66–106.

29 Ibid., 68–72.

30 On Tuesday afternoon, Christian responded to Andre's provocations on Facebook. Christian posted in short succession on his wall: "LMS [Like my status] if you wanna Fight"; "Im Happy i dont live in The Projects Niggas is DustBuckets"; "Store run . . . i hope I run into someone special lol." Andre liked the first post without responding to the other two "subliminals." Christian and four others also went after Andre but did not catch him.

31 boyd, *It's Complicated*, 31.

32 Ibid., 40.

33 On partitioning strategies among professionals, see Vitak et al., "Why Won't You Be My Facebook Friend?"; On tempering strategies, see Hogan, "The Presentation of Self in the Age of Social Media."

34 Elijah Anderson, *A Place on the Corner* (Chicago: University of Chicago Press, 1978), 19.

35 As Robert Garot found in Los Angeles, I found that the street code endured in Harlem through a taken-for-granted authority as opposed to the sense of utter hopelessness. The moral bonds of fighting together and the emotionalism of seeing friends victimized also fueled neighborhood violence.

36 Goffman, *Stigma*, 7, 19.

Chapter 4

1 Paul Tough, *Whatever It Takes: Geoffrey Canada's Quest to Change Harlem and America* (Boston: Houghton Mifflin, 2008).

2 Service totals appeared on the HCZ's website, http://hcz.org/wp-content/uploads/2014/04/FY-2013-FactSheet.pdf.

3 See criticism by Diane Ravitch, "The Myth of Charter Schools," *New York Review of Books*, November 11, 2010, http://www.nybooks.com/articles/2010/11/11/myth-charter-schools/.

4 Anderson writes at length about old heads. See Anderson, *Code of the Street*, 102, 144–146, 185, 204, 206–207, 292–296, 310–311, 324; Anderson, *Streetwise*, 3–4, 69–76, 101, 103–105, 242–243.

5 See, for instance, Jacobs, *The Death and Life of Great American Cities*; Alford A. Young, "The Redeemed Old Head: Articulating a Sense of Public Self and Social Purpose," *Symbolic Interaction* 30, no. 3 (2007): 347–374.

6 Young, "The Redeemed Old Head"; Forrest Stuart and Reuben Jonathan Miller, "The Prisonized Old Head Intergenerational Socialization and the Fusion of Ghetto and Prison Culture," *Journal of Contemporary Ethnography* 46, no. 6 (2017): 673–698.

7 Omar McRoberts, *Streets of Glory: Church and Community in a Black Neighborhood* (Chicago: University of Chicago Press, 2003); Jenny Berrien, Omar McRoberts, and Christopher Winship, "Religion and the Boston Miracle: The Effect of Black Ministry on Youth Violence," in *Who Will Provide?: The Changing Role of Religion in American Social Welfare*, ed. Mary Jo

Bane, Brent Coffin, and Ronald Thiemann (Boulder, CO: Westview, 2000), 266–285.

8 Jacobs, *The Death and Life of Great American Cities*; Suttles, *The Social Order of the Slum*.

9 Jacobs, *The Death and Life of Great American Cities*, 68–69.

10 Suttles, *The Social Order of the Slum*, 61–93.

11 Rainie and Wellman, *Networked*.

12 Rainie and Wellman, *Networked*. See also Keith Hampton, "Internet Use and the Concentration of Disadvantage: Glocalization and the Urban Underclass," *American Behavioral Scientist* 53, no. 8 (2010): 1111–1132. Hampton found that the use of digital media by residents could enhance social cohesion and collective action in higher-poverty areas.

13 On status competition inside a high school see Murray Milner, Jr., *Freaks, Geeks, and Cool Kids: American Teenagers, Schools, and the Culture of Consumption* (New York: Routledge, 2004).

14 On school-based peer worlds embedded in social media see boyd, *It's Complicated*; boyd, "Friendship," 79–84.

15 This operating budget figure comes from Sharon Otterman, "Lauded Harlem Schools Have Their Own Problems," *New York Times*, October 12, 2010, https://www.nytimes.com/2010/10/13/education/13harlem.html.

16 On old heads and passive recruitment, see Stuart and Miller, "The Prisonized Old Head."

17 Berrien, McRoberts, and Winship, "Religion and the Boston Miracle."

18 Mary Pattillo, *Black on the Block: The Politics of Race and Class in the City* (Chicago: University of Chicago Press, 2007), 113.

19 African American clergy typically play an extra-religious role in the community. See, for instance, W. E. B. DuBois, *The Souls of Black Folk* (1903; reprint, New York: Cosimo Classics, 2007); Franklin E. Frazier, *The Negro Church in America* (Liverpool: Liverpool University Press, 1964); Pattillo-McCoy, *Black Picket Fences*. But few African American pastors venture onto the street to serve, according to research by Drake and Cayton, *Black Metropolis*, 618; McRoberts, *Streets of Glory*; Berrien, McRoberts, and Winship, "Religion and the Boston Miracle."

20 Venkatesh described work in this capacity by Pastor Jeremiah Wilkins, in Chicago: Sudhir Allah Venkatesh, *Off the Books: The Underground Economy*

of the Urban Poor (Cambridge, MA: Harvard University Press, 2006). For a broader discussion of the middleman in African American communities, see Pattillo, *Black on the Block.*

21 Max Weber, "The Three Types of Legitimate Rule," trans. by Hans Gerth, *Berkeley Publications in Society and Institutions* 4, no. 1 (Summer 1958), 1–11.

22 Berrien, McRoberts, and Winship discussed the moral authority of street pastors primarily in terms of these first two attributes: Berrien, McRoberts, and Winship, "Religion and the Boston Miracle." Jacobs emphasized the breadth of their network: Jacobs, *The Death and Life of Great American Cities.*

23 Venkatesh, *Off the Books,* 257, 266–272.

24 See "The Book Vendor" chapter on Hakim Hasan in Duneier, *Sidewalk,* 17–42.

25 Anderson, *Code of the Street,* 102, 204.

26 On Geoffrey Canada and the development of the HCZ see Tough, *Whatever It Takes;* See also Duneier, *Ghetto,* 185–216.

27 Much research finds, however, that any approach without the targeted action of law enforcement falls short in reducing neighborhood violence. See a metareview of 1,400 antiviolence efforts: Thomas Abt and Christopher Winship, *What Works in Reducing Community Violence: A Meta-Review and Field Study for the Northern Triangle* (Washington, DC: United States Agency for International Development, 2016).

28 Eric Gordon and Adriana de Souza e Silva, *Net Locality: Why Location Matters in a Networked World* (Malden, MA: Blackwell, 2011), 1.

Chapter 5

1 Anderson, *Code of the Street,* 30, 34, 47, 81, 127.

2 Rios, *Punished.*

3 Victor Rios, *Human Targets: Schools, Police, and the Criminalization of Latino Youth* (Chicago: University of Chicago, 2017).

4 William J. Chambliss, "The Saints and the Roughnecks," *Society* 11, no. 1 (1973): 24–31.

5 Rios, *Human Targets,* 66.

6 On the asymmetry, invisible action, and other aspects of social media policing see Daniel Trottier, "Policing Social Media," *Canadian Review of Sociology/ Revue Canadienne de Sociologie* 49, no. 4 (2012): 411–425; Christopher J.

Schneider, *Policing and Social Media: Social Control in an Era of New Media* (Lanham, MD: Lexington Books, 2016).

7 Helen Nissenbaum, *Privacy in Context: Technology, Politics, and the Integrity of Social Life* (Stanford, CA: Stanford Law Books, 2009).

8 For an overview of information visibility, including as a form of social control, see Brenda L. Berkelaar and Millie A. Harrison, "Information Visibility," *Oxford Research Encyclopedia of Communication*, July 2017, http://communication.oxfordre.com/view/10.1093/acrefore/9780190228613.001.0001/acrefore-9780190228613-e-126?result=3&rskey=cu9qX4; On framing, see Robert M. Entman, "Framing: Toward Clarification of a Fractured Paradigm," *Journal of Communication* 43, no. 4 (1993): 51–58; On editorial control, see David M. White, "The 'Gate Keeper': A Case Study in the Selection of News," *Journalism Quarterly* 27, no. 4 (1950): 383–390; Barbie Zelizer, *Taking Journalism Seriously: News and the Academy* (Thousand Oaks, CA: Sage, 2004).

9 On the notion that journalists respond to news materials rather than simply create news see Michael Schudson, "The Anarchy of Events and the Anxiety of Story Telling," *Political Communication* 24 (2007): 253–257. On the problems of constructing gangs offline see Scott Decker and Kimberly Kempf-Leonard, "Constructing Gangs: The Social Definition of Youth Activities," *Criminal Justice Policy Review* 5, no. 4 (1991): 271–291. On gang performances through social media, see David C. Pyrooz, Scott H. Decker, and Richard K. Moule, "Criminal and Routine Activities in Online Settings: Gangs, Offenders, and the Internet," *Justice Quarterly* 32, no. 3 (2015): 471–499; Timothy R. Lauger and James A. Densley, "Broadcasting Badness: Violence, Identity, and Performance in the Online Gang Rap Scene," *Justice Quarterly* (2017): 1–26. Available online at: https://www.tandfonline.com/doi/full/10.1080/07418825.2017.1341542.

10 Of the 509 law enforcement agencies across the country to respond to the question "When did your agency start using social media?" in a survey by the International Association of Chiefs of Police (IACP), only 34 agencies indicated "2006 or before": International Association of Chiefs of Police, *2015 IACP Social Media Survey*, http://www.iacpsocialmedia.org/wp-content/uploads/2017/01/FULL-2015-Social-Media-Survey-Results.compressed.pdf.

11 Patton et. al, "Internet Banging." Phillips (1999) and Ley and Cybriwsky (1974) document four classic types of gang graffiti that have since digitized: *hitting up* and *roll calls* (to affirm one's gang and gang membership), *crossing out* (to slander other gangs in the same gang system), and *RIPs* (to memorialize deceased members). Susan A. Phillips, *Wallbangin': Graffiti and Gangs in L.A.*

(Chicago: University of Chicago Press, 1999); David Ley and Roman Cybriwsky, "Urban Graffiti as Territorial Markers," *Annals of the Association of American Geographers* 64 (1974): 491–505.

12 danah boyd, "Friends, Friendsters, and MySpace Top 8: Writing Community Into Being on Social Network Sites," *First Monday* 11, no. 12 (2006), http://www.danah.org/papers/FriendsFriendsterTop8.pdf.

13 *New York Times* coverage of Cyrus Vance Jr. called attention to the drop in the murder rate under Morgenthau. See Chip Brown, "Cyrus Vance Jr.'s "Moneyball" Approach to Crime," *New York Times*, December 3, 2014, https://www.nytimes.com/2014/12/07/magazine/cyrus-vance-jrs-moneyball-approach-to-crime.html.

14 Ibid.

15 Elizabeth E. Joh, "The New Surveillance Discretion: Automated Suspicion, Big Data, and Policing," *Harvard Law & Policy Review* 10 (2016): 15–42.

16 On socially mediated visibility and association see Jeffrey W. Treem and Paul M. Leonardi, "Social Media Use in Organizations: Exploring the Affordances of Visibility, Editability, Persistence, and Association," *Annals of the International Communication Association* 36, no. 1 (2012): 143–189.

17 Markus D. Dubber and Tatjana Hörnle, *Criminal Law: A Comparative Approach* (Oxford: Oxford University Press, 2014), 371.

18 See Jens Meierhenrich, "Conspiracy in International Law," *Annual Review of Law and Social Science* 2, no. 1 (2006): 341–357.

19 Dubber and Hörnle, *Criminal Law.*

20 The local application and understanding of conspiracy law in gang cases comes from the federal Racketeer Influenced and Corrupt Organizations Act (RICO) of 1970, a version of which was later added to New York's Penal Law. RICO modified the traditional objective of a conspiracy from commission of a specific crime to promotion of a criminal enterprise, a group with a continuous criminal purpose and organization "beyond the scope of individual criminal incidents." See New York Penal Code Article 460, et seq., http://codes.findlaw.com/ny/penal-law/pen-sect-460-00.html.

21 This figure comes from data provided by the CalGang Executive Board that a journalist accessed through the California Public Records Act. See Ali Winston, "You May Be in California's Gang Database and Not Even Know It," *Reveal* from The Center for Investigative Reporting, March 23, 2016, https://www.revealnews.org/article/you-may-be-in-californias-gang-database-and-not-even-know-it/.

22 On issues of networked data and privacy, see Nissenbaum, *Privacy in Context*; danah boyd, "Networked Privacy," *Surveillance & Society* 10 (2012): 348–350; Davis and Jurgenson, "Context Collapse."

23 I excluded in this chronology types of activity on social media cited in fewer than five acts, as well as any acts on Facebook without specification of the type of activity (a message, status update, etc.).

24 Samuel Nunn, "'Wanna Still Nine Hard?': Exploring Mechanisms of Police Bias in the Translation and Interpretation of Wiretap Conversations," *Surveillance & Society* 8, no. 1 (2010): 28–42.

25 Desmond Patton et al., "I Know God's Got a Day 4 Me: Violence, Trauma, and Coping Among Gang-Involved Twitter Users," *Social Science Computer Review* 35, no. 2 (2017): 226–243; Desmond Patton et al., "'Police Took My Homie I Dedicate My Life 2 His Revenge': Twitter Tensions Between Gang-Involved Youth and Police in Chicago," *Journal of Human Behavior in the Social Environment* 26, no. 3-4 (2016): 310–324.

26 Legal scholars who study social media point to a number of admissibility issues. These largely pertain to First Amendment rights, which protect free speech, and Fourth Amendment rights, which protect against unreasonable search and seizure by the government. See Adrian Fontecilla, "The Ascendance of Social Media as Evidence," *Criminal Justice* 28, no. 1 (2013): 55–56; Althaf Marsoof, "Online Social Networking and the Right to Privacy: The Conflicting Rights of Privacy and Expression," *International Journal of Law and Information Technology* 19, no. 2 (2011): 110–132.

27 District Attorney, New York County, "DA Vance Announces Guilty Pleas of Final Defendants in Takedown of Three of Manhattan's Most Violent Gangs," April 24, 2014 [press release].

28 District Attorney, New York County, "DA Vance: '3 Staccs' Gang Member Taylonn Murphy Convicted at Trial of Murdering Walter Sumter, Conspiring To Commit Murder, and Related Charges," April 14, 2016 [press release].

29 "CUNY TV Presents ABNY: Cyrus R. Vance Jr., Manhattan District Attorney," YouTube video, 28:29, posted by CunyTV75, July 7, 2014, https://www.youtube.com/watch?v=yThVILMecSM.

30 Forrest Stuart, *Down, Out, and Under Arrest: Policing and Everyday Life in Skid Row* (Chicago: University of Chicago Press, 2016).

31 Rikers injury logs were obtained by *The New York World*, a publication of Columbia Journalism School: Beth Morrissey and Maura R. O'Connor, "Rough Numbers Open Window into Rikers Violence," *The New York World*, July 31, 2013, http://www.thenewyorkworld.com/2013/07/31/rikers-violence/.

32 Michelle Alexander, *The New Jim Crow: Mass Incarceration in the Age of Colorblindness* (New York: New Press, 2012); Devah Pager, *Marked: Race, Crime, and Finding Work in an Era of Mass Incarceration* (Chicago: University of Chicago Press, 2007).

33 Jeff Mays, "District Attorney Cast Too Wide a Net in Harlem Gang Crackdown, Critics Say," *DNAinfo New York*, October 6, 2014, https://www.dnainfo.com/new-york/20141006/west-harlem/vance-cast-too-wide-net-harlem-gang-crackdown-families-say.

34 New York Civil Liberties Union Stop-and-Frisk Data, http://www.nyclu.org/content/stop-and-frisk-data.

35 Joseph Goldstein and J. David Goodman, "Frisking Tactic Yields to a Focus on Youth Gangs," *New York Times*, September 18, 2013, https://www.nytimes.com/2013/09/19/nyregion/frisking-tactic-yields-to-a-focus-on-youth-gangs.html.

36 On aging out of violence, see Travis Hirschi and Michael Gottfredson, "Age and the Explanation of Crime," *American Journal of Sociology* 89, no. 3 (1983): 552–584. On aging out of gangs, see Robert J. Durán, *Gang Life in Two Cities: An Insider's Journey* (New York: Columbia University Press, 2013); Terence P. Thornberry et al., *Gangs and Delinquency in Developmental Perspective* (Cambridge: Cambridge University Press, 2003).

37 Harding, *Living the Drama*.

38 On third-party software marketed to law enforcement to scan the universe of social media, see Alexandra Mateescu et al., "Social Media Surveillance and Law Enforcement," Data & Society Research Institute, October 27, 2015, http://www.datacivilrights.org/pubs/2015-1027/Social_Media_Surveillance_and_Law_Enforcement.pdf.

Chapter 6

1 Rainie and Wellman, *Networked*, 13.

2 For another context in which local residents calibrate personal space through social media use see Daniel Miller, *Social Media in an English Village: Or How to Keep People at Just the Right Distance* (London: University College London Press, 2016).

3 Katz and Hampton, "Communication in City and Community."

4 Rios, *Human Targets*, 8.

5 Ibid., 10.

6 Yong-Chan Kim and Sandra J. Ball-Rokeach, "Civic Engagement From a Communication Infrastructure Perspective," *Communication Theory* 16 (2006): 173–197.

7 Stuart, *Down, Out, and Under Arrest*.

8 On the pursuit of a rap career in the context of gang violence, see Jooyoung Lee, *Blowin' Up: Rap Dreams in South Central* (Chicago: University of Chicago Press, 2016).

9 Amy Waldman, "Beneath New Surface, an Undertow," *New York Times*, February 19, 2001, https://www.nytimes.com/2001/02/19/nyregion/beneath-new-surface-an-undertow.html; Waldman, "In Harlem's Ravaged Heart, Revival," *New York Times*, February 18, 2001, https://www.nytimes.com/2001/02/18/nyregion/in-harlem-s-ravaged-heart-revival.html.

10 On "the 'fuck it!' mentality" see Duneier, *Sidewalk*, 60–80.

11 Malcolm Gladwell, "The Coolhunt," *New Yorker*, March 17, 1997, https://www.newyorker.com/magazine/1997/03/17/the-coolhunt; Robert L. Goldman and Stephen Papson, *Sign Wars: The Cluttered Landscape of Advertising* (New York: Guilford, 1996).

Appendix

1 This discussion of "shoe leather" builds on my earlier article: Jeffrey Lane, "The Digital Street: An Ethnographic Study of Networked Street Life in Harlem," *American Behavioral Scientist* 60, no. 1 (2016): 43–58. On the shoe leather of urban ethnography, see Mitchell Duneier, "Scrutinizing the Heat: On Ethnic Myths and the Importance of Shoe Leather," *Contemporary Sociology* 33 (2004): 139–150; Mitchell Duneier, "On the Legacy of Elliot Liebow and Carol Stack: Context-Driven Fieldwork and the Need for Continuous Ethnography," *Focus* 25 (2007): 33–38.

2 For a review of ethnographic work in the digital tradition see Hine, *Ethnography for the Internet*.

3 See Jeffrey Lane, "Review: *Ethnography for the Internet: Embedded, Embodied and Everyday*, by Christine Hine," *Contemporary Sociology* 45: 610–612.

4 Colin Jerolmack and Shamus Khan, "Talk Is Cheap: Ethnography and the Attitudinal Fallacy," *Sociological Methods & Research* 43, no. 2 (2014): 178–209.

5 Geertz's conceptualization of "being there" is widely employed as a premise of ethnographic practice and writing: Clifford Geertz, *Works and Lives: The Anthropologist as Author* (Stanford, CA: Stanford University Press, 1988). On being there in multisite ethnography see Ulf Hannerz, "Being there . . . and there . . . and there! Reflections on Multi-Site Ethnography," *Ethnography* 4, no. 2 (2003): 201–216. On being there in digital ethnography see Sarah Pink et al., *Digital Ethnography: Principles and Practice* (London: Sage, 2015).

6 See the section "Ethnographers and their Subjects" in Duneier, Kasinitz, and Murphy, *The Urban Ethnography Reader*.

7 Elliot Liebow, *Tally's Corner: A Study of Negro Streetcorner Men* (Boston: Little, Brown, 1967), 256.

8 If there's another unusual aspect of my urban fieldwork aside from concern with social media, it's that I studied girls and boys together rather than separately.

9 boyd, *It's Complicated*; Paul Hodkinson, "Bedrooms and Beyond: Youth, Identity and Privacy on Social Network Sites," *New Media & Society* 19, no. 2 (2017): 272–288.

10 On the notion that digital content provides an elicitation tool for researchers to discuss with subjects rather than a final or self-evident account see Pink, *Doing Sensory Ethnography*.

11 Jerolmack and Khan, "Talk Is Cheap," 184.

12 Mario Small, "How to Conduct a Mixed Methods Study: Recent Trends in a Rapidly Growing Literature," *Annual Review of Sociology* 37 (2011): 57–86.

13 Jenna Burrell provides an eloquent conceptualization of the field site as a network based on her study of Internet use in Accra, Ghana: Jenna Burrell, "The Field Site as a Network: A Strategy for Locating Ethnographic Research," *Field Methods* 21, no. 2 (2009): 181–199. See also Hine, *Ethnography for the Internet*, 61, 65–67.

14 See especially the chapter "Friends and Networks" in Liebow, *Tally's Corner*, 161–207.

15 Jeffrey Boase, "Personal Networks and The Personal Communication System: Using Multiple Media to Connect," *Information, Communication & Society* 11, no. 4 (2008): 490–508.

16 Heather A. Horst and Daniel Miller, *The Cell Phone: An Anthropology of Communication* (Oxford: Berg, 2004).

17 Carol Stack, *All Our Kin: Strategies for Survival in a Black Community* (New York: Basic Books, 1974).

18 On issues of ethnographic lurking see Alyssa Richman, "The Outsider Lurking Online: Adults Researching Youth Cybercultures," in *Representing Youth: Methodological Issues in Critical Youth Studies*, edited by Amy L. Best (New York: New York University Press, 2007), 182–202.

19 For a broader discussion of how ethnographers deal with privacy in digitally networked field sites, see Tom Boellstorff et al., *Ethnography and Virtual Worlds: A Handbook of Method* (Princeton, NJ: Princeton University Press, 2012); Hine, *Ethnography for the Internet*; Dhiraj Murthy, "Digital Ethnography: An Examination of the Use of New Technologies for Social Research," *Sociology* 42 (2008): 837–855. On the challenges of managing boundaries between ethnographer and subjects on social media, see Jennifer A. Reich, "Old Methods and New Technologies: Social Media and Shifts in Power in Qualitative Research," *Ethnography* 16, no. 4 (2015): 394–415.

20 Irina Shklovski and Janet Vertesi, "'Un-Googling' Publications: The Ethics and Problems of Anonymization," CHI EA 2013, Extended Abstracts on Human Factors in Computing Systems, Paris, France (2013): 2172.

21 Colin Jerolmack and Alexandra K. Murphy, "The Ethical Dilemmas and Social Scientific Trade-Offs of Masking in Ethnography," *Sociological Methods & Research* (2017): 1–27. Available online at: http://journals.sagepub.com/doi/abs/10.1177/0049124117701483.

22 Anderson, *Streetwise*, ix

23 In bridging urban with digital studies, I've drawn on a number of seminal texts on digital ethnography, particularly Boellstorff et al., *Ethnography and Virtual Worlds*; Hine, *Ethnography for the Internet*; Laura Robinson and Jeremy Schulz, "New Avenues for Sociological Inquiry: Evolving Forms of Ethnographic Practice," *Sociology* 43 (2009): 685–698.

24 See Chapter Two, "Three Brief Histories" in Boellstorff et al., *Ethnography and Virtual Worlds*.

25 Michèle Lamont and Ann Swidler, "Methodological Pluralism and the Possibilities and Limits of Interviewing," *Qualitative Sociology* 37, no. 2 (2014): 153–171.

References

Abt, Thomas and Christopher Winship, *What Works in Reducing Community Violence: A Meta-Review and Field Study for the Northern Triangle* (Washington, DC: United States Agency for International Development, 2016).

Addams, Jane, *The Spirit of Youth and the City Streets* (1909; reprint, Urbana, IL: University of Illinois Press, 1972).

Alexander, Michelle, *The New Jim Crow: Mass Incarceration in the Age of Colorblindness* (New York: New Press, 2012).

Anderson, Elijah, *Code of the Street* (New York: Norton, 1999).

Anderson, Elijah, "The Code of the Streets," *The Atlantic*, May 1994, 81–94.

Anderson, Elijah, *A Place on the Corner* (Chicago: University of Chicago Press, 1978).

Anderson, Elijah, *Streetwise* (Chicago: University of Chicago Press, 1990).

Baron, Naomi S., *Always On: Language in an Online and Mobile World* (Oxford: Oxford University Press, 2008).

Berkelaar, Brenda L. and Millie A. Harrison, "Information Visibility," *Oxford Research Encyclopedia of Communication*, July 2017. http://communication.oxfordre.com/view/10.1093/acrefore/9780190228613.001.0001/acrefore-9780190228613-e-126?result=3&rskey=cu9qX4.

Berrien, Jenny, Omar McRoberts, and Christopher Winship, "Religion and the Boston Miracle: The Effect of Black Ministry on Youth Violence," in *Who Will Provide?: The Changing Role of Religion in American Social Welfare*, ed. Mary Jo Bane, Brent Coffin, and Ronald Thiemann (Boulder, CO: Westview, 2000), 266–285.

Best, Amy, *Fast Cars, Cool Rides: The Accelerating World of Youth and Their Cars* (New York: New York University Press, 2006).

Bloch, Matthew, Ford Fessenden, and Janet Roberts, "Stop, Question and Frisk in New York Neighborhoods," *New York Times*, July 11, 2010. *New York Times* website, http://www.nytimes.com/interactive/2010/07/11/nyregion/20100711-stop-and-frisk.html.

Blumstein, Alfred and Richard Rosenfeld, "Factors Contributing to U.S. Crime Trends," in *Understanding Crime Trends: Workshop Report*, ed. Arthur S. Goldberger and Richard Rosenfeld (Washington, DC: National Academies Press, 2008), 13–44.

Boase, Jeffrey, "Personal Networks and The Personal Communication System: Using Multiple Media to Connect," *Information, Communication & Society* 11, no. 4 (2008): 490–508.

Boellstorff, Tom, Bonnie Nardi, Celia Pearce, and T. L. Taylor, *Ethnography and Virtual Worlds: A Handbook of Method* (Princeton, NJ: Princeton University Press, 2012).

Bourgois, Philippe, *In Search of Respect: Selling Crack in El Barrio* (Cambridge: Cambridge University Press, 1995).

boyd, danah, "Friends, Friendsters, and MySpace Top 8: Writing Community Into Being on Social Network Sites," *First Monday* 11, no. 12 (2006). http://www.danah.org/papers/FriendsFriendsterTop8.pdf.

boyd, danah, "Friendship," in *Hanging Out, Messing Around, and Geeking Out: Kids Living and Learning with New Media*, ed. Mizuko Ito et al. (Cambridge, MA: MIT Press, 2010).

boyd, danah, *It's Complicated: The Social Lives of Networked Teens* (New Haven, CT: Yale University Press, 2014).

boyd, danah, "Networked Privacy," *Surveillance & Society* 10 (2012): 348–350.

boyd, danah, "Social Network Sites as Networked Publics: Affordances, Dynamics, and Implications," in *A Networked Self: Identity, Community, and Culture on Social Network Sites*, ed. Zizi Papacharissi (New York: Routledge, 2010), 39–58.

boyd, danah, "White Flight in Networked Publics? How Race and Class Shaped American Teen Engagement with MySpace and Facebook," in *Race After the Internet*, ed. Lisa Nakamura and Peter Chow-White (New York: Routledge, 2011), 203–222.

boyd, danah and Nicole Ellison, "Social Network Sites: Definition, History, and Scholarship," *Journal of Computer-Mediated Communication* 13, no. 1 (2007): 210–230.

Brayne, Sarah, "Surveillance and System Avoidance: Criminal Justice Contact and Institutional Attachment," *American Sociological Review* 79, no. 3 (2014): 367–391.

Brown, Chip, "Cyrus Vance Jr.'s "Moneyball" Approach to Crime," *New York Times*, December 3, 2014. https://www.nytimes.com/2014/12/07/magazine/cyrus-vance-jrs-moneyball-approach-to-crime.html.

Burrell, Jenna, "The Field Site as a Network: A Strategy for Locating Ethnographic Research," *Field Methods* 21, no. 2 (2009): 181–199.

Canada, Geoffrey, *Fist Stick Knife Gun: A Personal History of Violence in America* (Boston: Beacon, 1995).

Canada, Geoffrey, adapted by Jamar Nicholas. *Fist Stick Knife Gun: A Personal History of Violence in America: A True Story in Black and White* (Boston: Beacon, 2010).

Chambliss, William J., "The Saints and the Roughnecks," *Society* 11, no. 1 (1973): 24–31.

Christakis, Nicholas A. and James H. Fowler, *Connected: The Surprising Power of Our Social Networks and How They Shape Our Lives* (New York: Little, Brown, 2009).

Collins, Patricia Hill, *Black Sexual Politics: African Americans, Gender, and the New Racism* (New York: Routledge, 2004).

Crenshaw, Kimberlé W., "Black Girls Matter: Pushed Out, Overpoliced and Underprotected," African American Policy Forum, 2015. African American Policy Forum website, https://static1.squarespace.com/static/53f20d90e4b0b80451158d8c/t/54dcc1ece4b001c03e323448/1423753708557/AAPF_BlackGirlsMatterReport.pdf.

Dance, L. Janelle, *Tough Fronts: The Impact of Street Culture on Schooling* (New York: Routledge, 2002).

Davis, Jenny L. and Nathan Jurgenson, "Context Collapse: Theorizing Context Collusions and Collisions," *Information, Communication & Society* 17, no. 4 (2014): 476–485.

Decker, Scott and Kimberly Kempf-Leonard, "Constructing Gangs: The Social Definition of Youth Activities," *Criminal Justice Policy Review* 5, no. 4 (1991): 271–291.

Devine, John, *Maximum Security: The Culture of Violence in Inner-City Schools* (Chicago: University of Chicago Press, 1996).

Dillon, Kelly P. and Brad J. Bushman, "Unresponsive or Un-noticed?: Cyberbystander Intervention in an Experimental Cyberbullying Context," *Computers in Human Behavior* 45 (2015): 144–150.

District Attorney, New York County, "District Attorney Vance and Police Commissioner Bratton Announce Largest Indicted Gang Case in NYC History," June 4, 2014 [press release].

District Attorney, New York County, "DA Vance: '3 Staccs' Gang Member Taylonn Murphy Convicted at Trial of Murdering Walter Sumter, Conspiring To Commit Murder, and Related Charges," April 14, 2016 [press release].

Drake, St. Clair and Horace R. Cayton, *Black Metropolis: A Study of Negro Life in a Northern City* (New York: Harcourt, Brace, 1945).

Dubber, Markus D. and Tatjana Hörnle, *Criminal Law: A Comparative Approach* (Oxford: Oxford University Press, 2014).

DuBois, W. E. B., *The Philadelphia Negro* (Philadelphia: University of Pennsylvania Press, 1996, original work published 1899).

DuBois, W. E. B., *The Souls of Black Folk* (New York: Cosimo Classics, 2007, original work published 1903).

Duneier, Mitchell, *Ghetto: The Invention of a Place, the History of an Idea* (New York: Farrar, Straus and Giroux, 2016).

Duneier, Mitchell, "On the Legacy of Elliot Liebow and Carol Stack: Context-Driven Fieldwork and the Need for Continuous Ethnography," *Focus* 25 (2007): 33–38.

Duneier, Mitchell, "Scrutinizing the Heat: On Ethnic Myths and the Importance of Shoe Leather," *Contemporary Sociology* 33 (2004): 139–150.

Duneier, Mitchell, *Sidewalk* (New York: Farrar, Straus and Giroux, 1999).

Duneier, Mitchell, Philip Kasinitz, and Alexandra Murphy, eds., *The Urban Ethnography Reader* (New York: Oxford University Press, 2014).

Durán, Robert J., *Gang Life in Two Cities: An Insider's Journey* (New York: Columbia University Press, 2013).

Ellison, Nicole B., Charles Steinfield, and Cliff Lampe, "Connection Strategies: Social Capital Implications of Facebook-enabled Communication Practices," *New Media & Society* 13, no. 6 (2011): 873–892.

Entman, Robert M., "Framing: Toward Clarification of a Fractured Paradigm," *Journal of Communication* 43, no. 4 (1993): 51–58.

Finkelhor, David, "The Internet, Youth Safety and the Problem of 'Juvenoia.'" A Report of the Crimes Against Children Research Center (2011). Crimes Against Children Research Center website, http://www.unh.edu/ccrc/pdf/Juvenoia%20paper.pdf.

Fontecilla, Adrian, "The Ascendance of Social Media as Evidence," *Criminal Justice* 28, no. 1 (2013): 55–56.

Ford, Sarah Michele, "Reconceptualizing the Public/Private Distinction in the Age of Information Technology," *Information, Communication & Society* 14, no. 4 (2011): 550–567.

Fordham, Signithia and John Ogbu, "Black Students' School Success: Coping with the 'Burden of "Acting White,"'" *Urban Review* 18 (1986): 176–206.

Fox, Jesse and Katie M. Warber, "Social Networking Sites in Romantic Relationships: Attachment, Uncertainty, and Partner Surveillance on Facebook," *Cyberpsychology, Behavior, and Social Networking* 17, no. 1 (2014): 3–7.

Frazier, Franklin E., *The Negro Church in America* (Liverpool: Liverpool University Press, 1964).

Gans, Herbert, *Urban Villagers* (New York: Free Press, 1962).

Gardner, Carol Brooks, *Passing By: Gender and Public Harassment* (Berkeley: University of California, 1995).

Gardner, Howard and Katie Davis, *The App Generation: How Today's Youth Navigate Identity, Intimacy, and Imagination in a Digital World* (New Haven, CT: Yale University Press, 2013).

Garot, Robert, *Who You Claim* (New York: New York University Press, 2010).

Geertz, Clifford, *Works and Lives: The Anthropologist as Author* (Stanford, CA: Stanford University Press, 1988).

Georgiou, Myria, *Media and the City: Cosmopolitanism and Difference* (Cambridge, MA: Polity, 2013).

Gladwell, Malcolm, "The Coolhunt," *New Yorker*, March 17, 1997. https://www.newyorker.com/magazine/1997/03/17/the-coolhunt.

Goffman, Alice, *On the Run: Fugitive Life in an American City* (Chicago: University of Chicago Press, 2014).

Goffman, Erving, *Asylums* (New York: Anchor, 1961).

Goffman, Erving, "Embarrassment and Social Organization," *American Journal of Sociology* 62, no. 3 (1956): 264–271.

Goffman, Erving, *Forms of Talk* (Philadelphia: University of Pennsylvania Press, 1981).

Goffman, Erving, *The Presentation of Self in Everyday Life* (New York: Doubleday, 1959).

Goffman, Erving, *Relations in Public: Microstudies of the Public Order* (1971; reprint, New Brunswick, NJ: Transaction Publishers, 2010).

Goffman, Erving, *Stigma* (New York: Simon & Schuster, 1963).

Goldman, Robert L. and Stephen Papson, *Sign Wars: The Cluttered Landscape of Advertising* (New York: Guilford, 1996).

Goldstein, Joseph and J. David Goodman, "Frisking Tactic Yields to a Focus on Youth Gangs," *New York Times*, September 18, 2013. https://www.nytimes.com/2013/09/19/nyregion/frisking-tactic-yields-to-a-focus-on-youth-gangs.html.

Gonzales, Amy L., "Health Benefits and Barriers to Cell Phone Use in Low-Income U.S. Neighborhoods: Indications of Technology Maintenance," *Mobile Media & Communication* 2 (2014): 233–248.

Gordon, Eric and Adriana de Souza e Silva, *Net Locality: Why Location Matters in a Networked World* (Malden, MA: Blackwell, 2011).

Haberman, Clyde, "What the Kitty Genovese Killing Can Teach Today's Digital Bystanders," *New York Times*, June 4, 2017. *New York Times* website, https://www.nytimes.com/2017/06/04/us/retro-report-bystander-effect.html.

Hampton, Keith, "Internet Use and the Concentration of Disadvantage: Glocalization and the Urban Underclass," *American Behavioral Scientist* 53, no. 8 (2010): 1111–1132.

Hampton, Keith, "Persistent and Pervasive Community: New Communication Technologies and the Future of Community," *American Behavioral Scientist* 60, no. 1 (2016).

Hampton, Keith, Lauren Sessions Goulet, Cameron Marlow, and Lee Rainie, "Why Most Facebook Users Get More Than They Give: The Effect of Facebook 'Power Users' on Everybody Else," Pew Research Center, February 3, 2012. Pew Research Center website, http://www.pewinternet.org/2012/02/03/why-most-facebook-users-get-more-than-they-give/.

Hannerz, Ulf, "Being There . . . and There . . . and There! Reflections on Multi-Site Ethnography," *Ethnography* 4, no. 2 (2003): 201–216.

Harding, David J., *Living the Drama* (Chicago: University of Chicago Press, 2010).

Hargittai, Eszter and Yu-li Patrick Hsieh, "Predictors and Consequences of Differentiated Practices on Social Network Sites," *Information, Communication & Society* 13, no. 4 (2010): 515–536.

Hepp, Andreas, Piet Simon, and Monika Sowinska, "Living Together in the Mediatized City: The Figurations of Young People's Urban Communities," in *Communicative Figurations: Transforming Communications in Times of Deep Mediatization*, ed. Andreas Hepp, Andreas Breiter, and Uwe Hasebrink (Cham, Switzerland: Palgrave Macmillan, 2018), 51–80.

Hine, Christine, *Ethnography for the Internet* (London: Bloomsbury, 2015).

Hirschi, Travis and Michael Gottfredson, "Age and the Explanation of Crime," *American Journal of Sociology* 89, no. 3 (1983): 552–584.

Hitchens, Brooklynn K. "Girl Fights and the Online Media Construction of Black Female Violence and Sexuality," *Feminist Criminology* (2017): 1–25.

Hitchens, Brooklynn K. and Yasser Arafat Payne, " 'Brenda's Got a Baby': Black Single Motherhood and Street Life as a Site of Resilience in Wilmington, Delaware," *Journal of Black Psychology* 43, no. 1 (2017): 50–76.

Hodkinson, Paul, "Bedrooms and Beyond: Youth, Identity and Privacy on Social Network Sites," *New Media & Society* 19, no. 2 (2017): 272–288.

Hogan, Bernie, "The Presentation of Self in the Age of Social Media: Distinguishing Performances and Exhibitions Online," *Bulletin of Science, Technology & Society* 30, no. 6 (2010): 377–386.

Horst, Heather A. and Daniel Miller, *The Cell Phone: An Anthropology of Communication* (Oxford: Berg, 2004).

Jacobs, Jane, *The Death and Life of Great American Cities* (New York: Random House, 1961).

Jerolmack, Colin and Shamus Khan, "Talk Is Cheap: Ethnography and the Attitudinal Fallacy," *Sociological Methods & Research* 43, no. 2 (2014): 178–209.

Jerolmack, Colin and Alexandra K. Murphy, "The Ethical Dilemmas and Social Scientific Trade-Offs of Masking in Ethnography," *Sociological Methods & Research* (2017): 1–27. Available online at: http://journals.sagepub.com/doi/abs/10.1177/0049124117701483.

Joh, Elizabeth E., "The New Surveillance Discretion: Automated Suspicion, Big Data, and Policing," *Harvard Law & Policy Review* 10 (2016): 15–42.

Jones, Nikki, *Between Good and Ghetto* (Piscataway, NJ: Rutgers University Press, 2010).

Katz, Vikki S. and Keith N. Hampton, "Communication in City and Community: From the Chicago School to Digital Technology," *American Behavioral Scientist* 60, no. 1 (2016): 3–7.

Kim, Yong-Chan and Sandra J. Ball-Rokeach, "Civic Engagement from a Communication Infrastructure Perspective," *Communication Theory* 16 (2006): 173–197.

Kowalski, Robin M. and Susan P. Limber, "Electronic Bullying Among Middle School Students," *Journal of Adolescent Health* 41, no. 6, Supplement (2007): S22–S30.

Krogstad, Jens Manuel. "Gun Homicides Steady After Decline in '90s; Suicide Rate Edges Up," Pew Research Center, October 21, 2015. Pew Research Center website, http://www.pewresearch.org/fact-tank/2015/10/21/gun-homicides-steady-after-decline-in-90s-suicide-rate-edges-up/.

Kuper, Leo, ed. *Living in Towns* (London: Cresset Press, 1953).

Ladner, Joyce A., *Tomorrow's Tomorrow: The Black Woman* (Garden City, NY: Doubleday, 1971).

Lamont, Michèle and Ann Swidler, "Methodological Pluralism and the Possibilities and Limits of Interviewing," *Qualitative Sociology* 37, no. 2 (2014): 153–171.

Lane, Jeffrey, "The Digital Street: An Ethnographic Study of Networked Street Life in Harlem," *American Behavioral Scientist* 60, no. 1 (2016): 43–58.

Lane, Jeffrey, "Review: *Ethnography for the Internet: Embedded, Embodied and Everyday*, by Christine Hine," *Contemporary Sociology* 45 (2016): 610–612.

Lauger, Timothy R. and James A. Densley, "Broadcasting Badness: Violence, Identity, and Performance in the Online Gang Rap Scene," *Justice Quarterly* (2017): 1–26. Available online at: https://www.tandfonline.com/doi/full/10.1080/07418825.2017.1341542.

Lee, Jooyoung, *Blowin' Up: Rap Dreams in South Central* (Chicago: University of Chicago Press, 2016).

Lenhart, Amanda, Aaron Smith, and Monica Anderson, "Teens, Technology and Romantic Relationships," Pew Research Center, October 1, 2015. Pew Research Center website, http://www.pewinternet.org/2015/10/01/teens-technology-and-romantic-relationships/.

Lévi-Strauss, Claude, *The Elementary Structures of Kinship* (Boston: Beacon, 1949).

Ley, David and Roman Cybriwsky, "Urban Graffiti as Territorial Markers," *Annals of the Association of American Geographers* 64 (1974): 491–505.

Liebow, Elliot, *Tally's Corner: A Study of Negro Streetcorner Men* (Boston: Little, Brown, 1967).

Lim, Sun Sun, Shobha Vadrevu, Yoke Hian Chan, and Iccha Basnyat, "Facework on Facebook: The Online Publicness of Juvenile Delinquents and Youths-at-Risk," *Journal of Broadcasting & Electronic Media* 56: 346–361.

Lofland, Lyn H., *A World of Strangers: Order and Action in Urban Public Space* (New York: Basic Books, 1973).

Marsoof, Althaf, "Online Social Networking and the Right to Privacy: The Conflicting Rights of Privacy and Expression," *International Journal of Law and Information Technology* 19, no. 2 (2011): 110–132.

Marwick, Alice E. and danah boyd, "I Tweet Honestly, I Tweet Passionately: Twitter Users, Context Collapse, and the Imagined Audience," *New Media & Society* 13 (2011): 114–133.

Mateescu, Alexandra, Douglas Brunton, Alex Rosenblat, Desmond Patton, Zachary Gold, and danah boyd, "Social Media Surveillance and Law Enforcement," Data & Society Research Institute, October 27, 2015. http://www.datacivilrights.org/pubs/2015-1027/Social_Media_ Surveillance_and_Law_Enforcement.pdf.

Mateu-Gelabert, Pedro and Howard Lune, "School Violence: The Bidirectional Conflict Flow Between Neighborhood and School," *City & Community* 2, no. 4 (2003): 353–368.

Mayer, Adalbert and Steven L. Puller, "The Old Boy (and Girl) Network: Social Network Formation on University Campuses," *Journal of Public Economics* 92 (2008): 329–347.

Mays, Jeff, "District Attorney Cast Too Wide a Net in Harlem Gang Crackdown, Critics Say," *DNAinfo New York*, October 6, 2014. https://www. dnainfo.com/new-york/20141006/west-harlem/vance-cast-too-wide-net-harlem-gang-crackdown-families-say.

McRoberts, Omar, *Streets of Glory: Church and Community in a Black Neighborhood* (Chicago: University of Chicago Press, 2003).

Meierhenrich, Jens, "Conspiracy in International Law," *Annual Review of Law and Social Science* 2, no. 1 (2006): 341–357.

Meyrowitz, Joshua, *No Sense of Place: The Impact of Electronic Media on Social Behavior* (New York: Oxford University Press, 1985).

Miller, Daniel, *Social Media in an English Village: Or How to Keep People at Just the Right Distance* (London: University College London Press, 2016).

Miller, Jody, *Getting Played: African American Girls, Urban Inequality, and Gendered Violence* (New York: New York University Press, 2008).

Milner, Jr., Murray, *Freaks, Geeks, and Cool Kids: American Teenagers, Schools, and the Culture of Consumption* (New York: Routledge, 2004).

Morrissey, Beth and Maura R. O'Connor, "Rough Numbers Open Window into Rikers Violence," *New York World*, July 31, 2013. http://www. thenewyorkworld.com/2013/07/31/rikers-violence/.

Murthy, Dhiraj, "Digital Ethnography: An Examination of the Use of New Technologies for Social Research," *Sociology* 42 (2008): 837–855.

Nissenbaum, Helen, *Privacy in Context: Technology, Politics, and the Integrity of Social Life* (Stanford, CA: Stanford Law Books, 2009).

Nolan, Kathleen, *Police in the Hallways: Discipline in an Urban High School* (Minneapolis: University of Minnesota Press, 2011).

Nunn, Samuel, "'Wanna Still Nine Hard?': Exploring Mechanisms of Police Bias in the Translation and Interpretation of Wiretap Conversations," *Surveillance & Society* 8, no. 1 (2010): 28–42.

Otterman, Sharon, "Lauded Harlem Schools Have Their Own Problems," *New York Times*, October 12, 2010. https://www.nytimes.com/2010/ 10/13/education/13harlem.html.

Pager, Devah, *Marked: Race, Crime, and Finding Work in an Era of Mass Incarceration* (Chicago: University of Chicago Press, 2007).

Pascoe, C. J., "Intimacy," in *Hanging Out, Messing Around, and Geeking Out: Kids Living and Learning With New Media*, ed. Mizuko Ito et al. (Cambridge, MA: MIT Press, 2010).

Pattillo, Mary, *Black on the Block: The Politics of Race and Class in the City* (Chicago: University of Chicago Press, 2007).

Pattillo-McCoy, Mary, *Black Picket Fences: Privilege and Peril Among the Black Middle Class* (Chicago: University of Chicago Press, 1999).

Patton, Desmond U., Robert D. Eschmann, and Dirk A. Butler, "Internet Banging: New Trends in Social Media, Gang Violence, Masculinity and Hip Hop," *Computers in Human Behavior* 29, no. 5 (2013): A54–A59.

Patton, Desmond U., Patrick Leonard, Loren Cahill, Jaime Macbeth, Shantel Crosby, and Douglas-Wade Brunton, "'Police Took My Homie I Dedicate My Life 2 His Revenge': Twitter Tensions Between Gang-Involved Youth and Police in Chicago," *Journal of Human Behavior in the Social Environment* 26, no. 3-4 (2016): 310–324.

Patton, Desmond U., Ninive Sanchez, Dale Fitch, Jaime Macbeth, and Patrick Leonard, "I Know God's Got a Day 4 Me: Violence, Trauma, and Coping Among Gang-Involved Twitter Users," *Social Science Computer Review* 35, no. 2 (2017): 226–243.

Phillips, Susan A., *Wallbangin': Graffiti and Gangs in L.A.* (Chicago: University of Chicago Press, 1999).

Pink, Sarah, *Doing Sensory Ethnography* (London: Sage, 2009).

Pink, Sarah, Heather Horst, John Postill, Larissa Hjorth, Tania Lewis, and Jo Tacchi, *Digital Ethnography: Principles and Practice* (London: Sage, 2015).

Pyrooz, David C., Scott H. Decker, and Richard K. Moule, "Criminal and Routine Activities in Online Settings: Gangs, Offenders, and the Internet," *Justice Quarterly* 32, no. 3 (2015): 471–499.

Rainie, Lee and Barry Wellman. *Networked: The New Social Operating System* (Cambridge, MA: MIT Press, 2012).

Ravitch, Diane, "The Myth of Charter Schools," *New York Review of Books*, November 11, 2010. *New York Review of Books* website, http://www. nybooks.com/articles/2010/11/11/myth-charter-schools/.

Reich, Jennifer A., "Old Methods and New Technologies: Social Media and Shifts in Power in Qualitative Research," *Ethnography* 16, no. 4 (2015): 394–415.

Richman, Alyssa, "The Outsider Lurking Online: Adults Researching Youth Cybercultures," in *Representing Youth: Methodological Issues in Critical Youth Studies*, ed. Amy L. Best (New York: New York University Press, 2007).

Rios, Victor, *Human Targets: Schools, Police, and the Criminalization of Latino Youth* (Chicago: University of Chicago Press, 2017).

Rios, Victor, *Punished: Policing the Lives of Black and Latino Boys* (New York: New York University Press, 2011).

Robinson, Laura and Jeremy Schulz, "New Avenues for Sociological Inquiry: Evolving Forms of Ethnographic Practice," *Sociology* 43 (2009): 685–698.

Rook, Clarence, *London Side-Lights* (London: E. Arnold, 1908).

Sampson, Robert J., *Great American City: Chicago and the Enduring Neighborhood Effect* (Chicago: University of Chicago Press, 2012).

Sampson, Robert J., Jeffrey D. Morenoff, and Thomas Gannon-Rowley, "Assessing 'Neighborhood Effects': Social Processes and New Directions in Research," *Annual Review of Sociology* 28 (2002): 443–478.

Santos, Fernanda, "College Readiness Lacking, Report Shows," *New York Times*, October 25, 2011, A25.

Schneider, Christopher J., *Policing and Social Media: Social Control in an Era of New Media* (Lanham, MD: Lexington Books, 2016).

Schudson, Michael, "The Anarchy of Events and the Anxiety of Story Telling," *Political Communication* 24 (2007): 253–257.

Sharkey, Patrick, *Stuck in Place: Urban Neighborhoods and the End of Progress Toward Racial Equality* (Chicago: University of Chicago Press, 2013).

Shedd, Carla, *Unequal City: Race, Schools, and Perceptions of Injustice* (New York: Russell Sage Foundation, 2015).

Shklovski, Irina and Janet Vertesi, "'Un-Googling' Publications: The Ethics and Problems of Anonymization," CHI EA 2013, Extended Abstracts on Human Factors in Computing Systems. Paris, France: 2013.

Small, Mario, "How to Conduct a Mixed Methods Study: Recent Trends in a Rapidly Growing Literature," *Annual Review of Sociology* 37 (2011): 57–86.

Smiley, Calvin John, "From Silence to Propagation: Understanding the Relationship Between 'Stop Snitchin' and 'YOLO,'" *Deviant Behavior* 36, no. 1 (2015): 1–16.

Smith, Aaron and Monica Anderson, "5 Facts About Online Dating," Pew Research Center, February 29, 2016. Pew Research Center website, http://www.pewresearch.org/fact-tank/2015/04/20/5-facts-about-online-dating/.

Stack, Carol, *All Our Kin: Strategies for Survival In a Black Community* (New York: Basic Books, 1974).

Stevens, Robin, Stacia Gilliard-Matthews, Jamie Dunaev, Marcus K. Woods, and Bridgette M. Brawner, "The Digital Hood: Social Media Use Among Youth in Disadvantaged Neighborhoods," *New Media & Society* 19, no. 6 (2017): 950–967.

Stuart, Forrest, *Down, Out, and Under Arrest: Policing and Everyday Life in Skid Row* (Chicago: University of Chicago Press, 2016).

Stuart, Forrest and Reuben Jonathan Miller, "The Prisonized Old Head Intergenerational Socialization and the Fusion of Ghetto and Prison Culture," *Journal of Contemporary Ethnography* 46, no. 6 (2017): 673–698.

Suttles, Gerald, *The Social Order of the Slum: Ethnicity and Territory in the Inner City* (Chicago: University of Chicago Press, 1968).

Thornberry, Terence P., Marvin D. Krohn, Alan J. Lizotte, Carolyn A. Smith, and Kimberly Tobin, *Gangs and Delinquency in Developmental Perspective* (Cambridge: Cambridge University Press, 2003).

Tough, Paul, *Whatever It Takes: Geoffrey Canada's Quest to Change Harlem and America* (Boston: Houghton Mifflin, 2008).

Treem, Jeffrey W. and Paul M. Leonardi, "Social Media Use in Organizations: Exploring the Affordances of Visibility, Editability,

Persistence, and Association," *Annals of the International Communication Association* 36, no. 1 (2013): 143–189.

Trottier, Daniel, "Policing Social Media," *Canadian Review of Sociology/Revue Canadienne de Sociologie* 49, no. 4 (2012): 411–425.

Ueberall, Stephanie and Ashley Cannon, "Assessing New York City's Youth Gun Violence Crisis: Crews—Volume 1: Defining the Problem," Citizens Crime Commission Of New York City, May 2015. Citizens Crime Commission Of New York City website, http://www.nycrimecommission.org/pdfs/ CCC-Crews-Vol1-DefiningTheProblem.pdf.

Varnelis, Kazys, ed. *Networked Publics* (Cambridge, MA: MIT Press, 2008).

Venkatesh, Sudhir Allah, *Off the Books: The Underground Economy of the Urban Poor* (Cambridge, MA: Harvard University Press, 2006).

Vitak, Jessica, Cliff Lampe, Rebecca Gray, and Nicole B. Ellison, "Why Won't You Be My Facebook Friend?: Strategies for Managing Context Collapse in the Workplace," *Proceedings of the 2012 iConference*, February 7–10 (New York: Association for Computing Machinery, 2012), 555–557.

Waldman, Amy, "Beneath New Surface, an Undertow," *New York Times*, February 19, 2001. https://www.nytimes.com/2001/02/19/nyregion/ beneath-new-surface-an-undertow.html.

Waldman, Amy, "In Harlem's Ravaged Heart, Revival," *New York Times*, February 18, 2001. https://www.nytimes.com/2001/02/18/nyregion/ in-harlem-s-ravaged-heart-revival.html.

Walkowitz, Judith R., "Going Public: Shopping, Street Harassment, and Streetwalking in Late Victorian London," *Representations* 62 (1998): 1–30.

Weber, Max, "The Three Types of Legitimate Rule," translated by Hans Gerth. *Berkeley Publications in Society and Institutions* 4, no. 1 (Summer 1958): 1–11.

Weiss, Jennifer, "Under the Radar: School Surveillance and Youth Resistance" (PhD dissertation, City University of New York, 2008).

West, Candace and Don H. Zimmerman, "Doing Gender," *Gender & Society* 1 (1987): 125–151.

White, David M., "'The Gate Keeper': A Case Study in the Selection of News," *Journalism Quarterly* 27, no. 4 (1950): 383–390.

Whitehurst, Grover (Russ), with Sarah Whitfield, "School Choice and School Performance in the New York City Public Schools—Will the Past Be Prologue?" Washington, DC: The Brown Center on Education Policy at Brookings, October 2013. https://www.brookings.edu/wp-content/

uploads/2016/06/School-Choice-and-School-Performance-in-NYC-Public-Schools.pdf.

Williams, Terry and William Kornblum, *Growing Up Poor* (Lexington, MA: Lexington Books, 1985).

Willis, Frederick, *101 Jubilee Road: A Book of London Yesterdays* (London: Phoenix House, 1948).

Winston, Ali, "You May Be in California's Gang Database and Not Even Know It," *Reveal* from The Center for Investigative Reporting, March 23, 2016. https://www.revealnews.org/article/you-may-be-in-californias-gang-database-and-not-even-know-it/.

Young, Alford A., "The Redeemed Old Head: Articulating a Sense of Public Self and Social Purpose," *Symbolic Interaction* 30, no. 3 (2007): 347–374.

Zelizer, Barbie, *Taking Journalism Seriously: News and the Academy* (Thousand Oaks, CA: Sage, 2004).

Zhao, Shanyang, Sherri Grasmuck, and Jason Martin, "Identity Construction on Facebook: Digital Empowerment in Anchored Relationships," *Computers in Human Behavior* 24 (2008): 1816–1836.

Zimring, Franklin E., *The City That Became Safe: New York's Lessons for Urban Crime and Its Control* (New York: Oxford University Press, 2011).

Index

accountability
  adults and, 89, 163
  identity and, 38
  justice system and, 121–122,
    153, 158
  social media and, vii–viii, 9, 13,
    28, 163
adults
  accountability and, 89, 163
  code switching and, 70–71, 77, 83
  competency of, 199n18
  drugs and, 11
  education and, 96
  fighting and, 83
  identity and, 70
  justice system and, 13, 96,
    136, 158
  reputation and, 10, 70
  social media and, ix, 11, 69, 73–74,
    80, 93–94, 118–119, 199
  street code and, 5, 80, 94
  violence and, xi, 1–3, 15, 24,
    91–96, 101, 113, 165–168

Akil, 121, 152–153, 156–157
alienation, 7, 9–10, 62, 182, 199n23
Anderson, Elijah
  on adults, 96
  on alienation, 9, 62
  on code switching, 24, 63, 69,
    198–199n17
  on ethnography, 186
  on gender, 59
  on hope, 10
  on institutions, 90
  on integration, 96
  on old heads, 94, 96, 115, 201n4
  on rap music, 5, 191n9
  on respect, 83, 90
  on selling out, 77, 199n23
  on street code, vii, 6, 8–10,
    12–13, 122
  on street pastors, 96
  on violence intervention, 5,
    10–11, 57, 78, 94, 96
Andre, 62, 81, 83–89, 154,
  173, 200n30

Tally's Corner (Liebow), 180
Tiana
  as brother's keeper, 58–60
  contact list of, 58
  dating by, 58
  fighting by, 81–83, 89, 100–101,
    175–176
  power over boys, 58
  rapping by, 167
  reputation of, 82
  retirement of, 81–83
  smartphone use by, 99–100
  social media use by, 58,
    72, 81–83, 89, 100–101,
    153, 176
  as source of information, 100
  on Twitter, 72
Tinder, 27
top-down approach to social control,
  24, 91, 94–96
toughness, 3, 8–9, 11,
  61, 65, 83
turf, 2, 12, 53–55, 54, 59, 103
"twerking," 37
Twitter
  adults and, 70, 72
  dating and, 42–43
  fighting and, 52–53, 71–72
  followers on, 112
  gangs and, 146–147
  guns and, 144
  inboxes on, 144
  justice system and, 144
  popularity of, 21, 70, 73,
    199n18
  privacy on, 70–71
  street code and, 72
  violence and, 15

urban ethnography, 4, 169–171,
  174–176, 180–181, 186
urban scholars, 3–4, 29, 62

Vance, Cyrus, Jr., 113, 128,
  151, 205n13
Varnelis, Kazys, 189n3
Venkatesh, Sudhir, 202n20
Vertesi, Janet, 180, 185
violence. *See also* fighting
  adults and, xi, 1–3, 15, 24, 91,
    93–96, 101, 113
  bystander effect and, x
  causes of, 94–95
  code switching and, 77
  dating and, 7, 29, 37
  decrease in, 11–12,
    155, 157
  drugs and, 10, 12
  gangs and, 155, 158
  gender and, 7, 16, 28, 37,
    55–56, 70, 76
  guns and, 1–2, 11, 55–56
  intervention on, 16–17, 25, 83,
    91, 93–96, 165, 176, 203n27
  justice system and, 12, 123, 130,
    134, 156, 159
  peer pressure and, 8
  prevalence of, 8, 62
  reputation and, 38
  respect and, 12, 56, 62, 83
  as socialization, 56
  social media and,
    x, 2–12, 28, 60, 74, 93–94,
    157, 165
  staging areas for, 57, 78
Violent Criminal Enterprises Unit
  (VCEU), 129